I0521506

STRONGER THAN THE STORM

ELIZABETH PIERCE

STRONGER THAN THE STORM

LESSONS LEARNED BY BETRAYAL

ELIZABETH PIERCE

Copyright @ 2025 Elizabeth Pierce

All rights reserved. No part of this publication may be reproduced, distributed, or transmitted in any form or by any means, including photocopying, recording, or other electronic or mechanical methods, without the prior written permission of the author or publisher, except in the case of brief quotations embodied in critical reviews and certain other noncommercial uses permitted by copyright law. The use of this work in AI learning or NFT is prohibited.

For permission requests, email the publisher, addressed Attention: Permissions Coordinator at admin@elizabethpiercebooks.com

ISBN: 979-8-9938179-0-3 (eBook)
ISBN: 979-8-9938179-1-0 (Paperback)

First printing edition, 2025

This work is a work of fiction inspired by true events. All characters, locations, incidents, and dialogue are products of the author's imagination or are used fictitiously. While the story draws upon historical contexts and certain real-world events, any resemblance to actual persons, living or dead, organizations, or occurrences is entirely coincidental and unintentional.

The content of this book is for narrative purposes only. It reflects the author's personal experience and research and is not intended to be a substitute for professional medical, psychological, legal, or financial advice, diagnosis, or treatment.

Always seek the advice of a qualified professional with any questions you may have regarding a medical condition, legal matter, or other personal circumstances. Neither the author nor the publisher shall be held liable or responsible for any misunderstandings or misuse of the information contained within this book.

If you are in crisis, please seek immediate help from a mental health professional or emergency services.

Dedication

This book is dedicated to my greatest blessings: To my sons, you are the heart, the fire, and the constant reminder of everything good. My love for you has always been, and will always be, unconditional—the simple truth and unshakeable anchor of my world. Please know that every difficult decision I made as your mother was solely driven by the fierce desire to give you the best of me and the best life has to offer. Thank you for your patience, for the deep comfort of your forgiveness, and for teaching me that the purest, most brilliant light always follows the darkest days. Watching you two become the men you are is my greatest reward; you are my true north and my beautiful certainty.

And to my husband, the unwavering love of my life and the truest definition of home. You are the steady anchor I never knew I needed. You came into a life that was complicated, messy, and utterly exhausted, yet you never once asked me to be less than myself. You didn't just love me; you taught me that love can be effortless, safe, and true. You built a safe harbor where fear cannot touch us, and you show me every single day what confidence and unwavering support truly feel like. Thanking you is not enough; committing my life to you is everything. You are my final, peaceful port and true home.

Finally, this is for every woman who currently feels she cannot weather the storm. To the one standing in the downpour, heavy with doubt, know this: The courage to weather this storm is not something you have to find; it is already within you. I wrote this book because I stood where you are now, and if I can find the sun again, I promise you can, too. Your courage will be your legacy.

Acknowledgment

This book is the truth of my survival, and that truth is: no storm is ever weathered alone. If my voice resonates in these pages, it is only because of the echoes of support, belief, and relentless grace from the people listed below.

To my inner circle, my anchors in the early downpour, and my first readers—you know who you are. The courage to share this story was forged in your living rooms and across those late-night phone calls. Thank you for offering comfort, perspective, and the unflinching, necessary truth at every stage of the writing.

I must also acknowledge the fierce professionals who were instrumental in securing my family's peace. To all the doctors, nurses, therapists, and at-home staff: You are literal lifesavers. You gave my son a future and, in doing so, gave me my independence. To the remarkable team at Minnetonka High School's Special Education Department: thank you for seeing my son's light, championing his potential, and creating a reciprocal community. Thank you all for your expertise, patience, and the quiet dignity with which you care for the most vulnerable among us.

And finally, to the foundation of my entire life: the love I dedicated this book to—my husband and my sons. Your unconditional love is the reason I learned to stand tall again. You are the constant source of my resilience, my peace, and my final, truest home. Without your light, this story would never have found its way out of the dark.

Preface

Life rarely unfolds as a straight path. It bends. It breaks. At times, it collides with the very essence meant to survive it. Stronger Than the Storm is more than a story of hardship. It is a story of endurance. Of resilience. Of the quiet power of hope when life seems determined to break a spirit.

At its heart, this book follows Kay, a young woman shows the true depth of human strength as she moves through grief, loss, and relentless trials. What begins as an ordinary life soon shifts into a powerful example of courage and endurance. Kay's narrative reflects the silent struggles that many people endure but that few publicly discuss through love, betrayal, hopelessness, and rebirth.

The darkness is welcomed by Elizabeth Pierce. She permits her main character to face them with sincerity and openness. Each chapter contains the sharpness of reality and the shine of potential. Within Kay's challenges, readers will discover reflections of their own difficulties. In her victories, they might find the reminder that recovery is not only achievable but also attainable.

This book is intended for individuals who have at any point felt unseen, shattered, or constrained by the burdens of their history. It serves as evidence that even in the deepest storms, a strength lies in wait to be revealed. A power that has consistently existed, prepared to emerge.

Contents

1

The Invisible Girl

Nestled in the serene landscape of central Florida's west coast, the quaint town of Belleview hummed with comforting predictability. Yet, one resident, Kay, defied the easy rhythm.

Unlike the vibrant flowerpots bursting from every windowsill in the town, Kay kept to herself, a wisp of a girl who seemed to melt into the background. Her dishwater blonde locks, always styled to perfection, enhanced her natural beauty. Her eyes held a depth rarely seen in such a young face, untouched by the need for glasses. She had an average look, a regular girl whose appearance was far from perfect. A quiet smile, hinting at an isolated world hidden beneath a surface of shyness, flickered occasionally, waiting to be discovered by those willing to look beyond the unassuming exterior. She was like a caterpillar in a cocoon, waiting to spread her wings and take flight.

Despite her reserved demeanor, Kay possessed a sharp intellect and a fierce independence that set her apart from her peers. She was a go-getter, always eager to explore new opportunities and chase after her dreams, often bringing laughter and joy to those around her. Though quiet, her mind was a three-ring circus, brimming with ideas and a thirst for adventure. Textbooks held little allure compared to the thrill of a whispered secret or socializing with her peers. School, with its rigid rows and droning lectures, felt like a cage for her boundless spirit.

One crisp autumn afternoon, as sunlight streamed through the classroom window, Ms. Charelston, Kay's history teacher with a perpetually pursed mouth, caught her doodling patterns on her notebook instead of taking notes.

"Kay!" Ms. Charelston's voice cracked like an overused record player, "Daydreaming again, are we?"

A blush crept up Kay's neck, staining her cheeks the color of a ripe tomato. Her brown eyes widened like a startled fawn's, and her doodle-filled notebook trembled in her hand. The whispered snickers of her classmates sent a wave of heat through her, making her want to shrink into her seat and disappear.

As time went by, Kay, with her quiet defiance, proved that intelligence could blossom in unexpected ways. Her ability to read people like open books and forge connections was a superpower in the bustling halls of Summerfield High. She effortlessly intertwined through social circles, a social butterfly flitting from conversation to conversation, leaving a trail of laughter and genuine connection in her wake.

Consequently, friendships blossomed organically around her. There was Michael, the shy boy in her class who had a passion for astronomy and found his courage ignited by Kay's infectious enthusiasm. And then there was Sarah, the class president with an ironclad exterior, who discovered a surprising vulnerability beneath Kay's easy smile. People were drawn to her magnetic charm, and she flourished in the spotlight, basking in the warmth of new friendships and connections.

Alongside Kay's ability to connect with others, she had a special knack for music. From a child, melodies surrounded Kay like fireflies on a summer night. They seemed like a language only she could understand.

Her room, a chaotic jumble of sheet music and instrument cases, cassettes, and CDs, painted a vivid picture of her exploration. Adding to the disorder, a landscape of clothes lay draped over the desk chair and pooled on the floor, a clear sign of a messy teenager whose priorities lay anywhere but in tidiness. Among this musical symphony, the flute stood out as her cherished companion. She poured her heart into mastering its melodies, finding solace and inspiration in its enchanting tunes. Though she studied music diligently, delving into the intricacies of singing, clarinet, and saxophone, it was the flute that held the most profound magic for her, adding layers of depth to her musical journey.

One rainy afternoon, Ms. Davis assigned a mountain of math homework, enough to bury even the most enthusiastic student. As the teacher droned on and the classroom filled with the scratching of pencils, a melody began to tug at Kay. It was a bright, cheerful tune and a sharp contrast to the gloomy day outside. Tapping her pencil against her desk in an unconscious rhythm, she began to hum softly.

The melody, barely a whisper at first, grew bolder, making its way through the scraping sounds. Soon, a curious silence fell over the class. Kay, oblivious, continued humming, her head swaying slightly to the internal beat. Then, a voice broke the silence.

"Wow, Kay," whispered Emily, the girl in the seat next to her, "that's beautiful! What is it?"

Kay's eyes flew open, and a blush flooded her cheeks. She hadn't realized how loud her humming had become.

"Oh, uh, I... I don't know," she stammered, suddenly self-conscious. "Just a silly tune that popped into my head."

A chorus of "Play it!" erupted from her classmates. Even the usually stoic Michael cracked a smile. Not encouraged by this unexpected support, Kay refused, her paralyzing shyness instantly overwhelming her.

As her love for music grew stronger, in middle school and high school, she was a familiar face in both marching bands and concert ensembles. The rhythm of the drums, the swell of the brass, and the harmony of the woodwinds became her companions as she poured her heart into each performance.

During her high school years, voice lessons became a cherished part of Kay's routine, a time dedicated to refining her skills and exploring the depths of her vocal range. While her peers focused on studying, Kay spent more time rehearsing for performances, approaching each session with eagerness. She understood that with every note practiced, she was one step closer to unlocking her full potential. Through it all, her love for music remained resolute. It was her haven, a place where she could lose herself in the melodies and find peace in the symphony of sounds. She was a musician through and through, with her soul tied to the very essence of music itself.

However, despite her deep connection to music and being labeled as a "Social Butterfly," Kay often felt like the black sheep of the family. Unlike Holly and Brandon, her siblings, she was fiercely more vocal, resourceful, and independent, unafraid to carve her own path in life.

Kay was a child of faith, raised on hymns and the warm glow of the church. From a young age, church was her second home, a place where laughter blended with whispered prayers and the strum of guitars during youth group meetings. More importantly, it was where her love for music found a public home; she played the flute in the church orchestra, finding a sense of belonging as her shyness melted away in the familiar companionship of fellow musicians and believers.

But while her family valued their faith, they also held strict standards of behavior, particularly the rigid notion of what it meant to be "ladylike." Kay's parents emphasized the importance of dressing modestly, behaving courteously, and presenting oneself in a prim and proper manner. For church and outings, beautiful dresses and polished footwear were her uniform, reflecting an expected elegance. However, the boundary between public and private life was erased by the family's in-home memory care business. Because patients and their families were frequently present, Kay knew she had to look nice and presentable even when she wasn't on an outing. She could never truly be laid back; even in casual moments, her hair was tidied and her makeup applied, a constant, visible indication of the necessity to always project a professional image to their clients.

This duality, faith, and societal expectations created a knot in Kay's heart. When it came to boys, the pressure intensified. Bringing a young man home felt like running an obstacle course blindfolded.

"What would Mom and Dad say?" she'd worry, picturing her parents' stern expressions and whispered disapproval.

Since her parents wouldn't approve, Kay's dates became secret adventures. She'd carefully plan where to meet, often choosing different locations across town to avoid suspicion. These places became hidden hideouts where she could meet her date, stealing shy smiles and nervous giggles under the pretense of being just another customer.

This constant interplay between her family's expectations and her own desires left Kay feeling perpetually judged. She couldn't deny the feeling that her friends were not considered polished enough or good enough in the eyes of her parents. It was a constant source of tension, a battle between her desire for acceptance and her longing to break free from the constraints of societal norms.

Strict as they may have been about proper manners, Kay's parents weren't all rules and regulations. They brought sunshine into their home, filling it with laughter that bounced off the walls. Dinnertime was at times a lively affair: Kay and her brother Brandon's witty table banter and running jokes regularly left everyone in stitches. Even her typically serious father couldn't resist their antics; they always found a way to make him laugh. Kay cherished these moments when the warmth of their family love wrapped around her heart like a comforting blanket.

Her parents' love story began in middle school, where they first met and forged a connection that would last what they thought would be a lifetime. Despite their youthful start, their love weathered the years, becoming the unshakeable core of the family and a constant source of hope and stability for Kay and her siblings.

They were more than just life partners; they were magnificent dance partners whose movements spoke a silent language of love. Dinner often marked the start of their evening routine. Some days, as the last bite disappeared from their plates, the perfect song would unexpectedly fill the air. Kay's parents would rise from the table, their faces lighting up with a special twinkle, embracing the spontaneous moment. Her dad would stretch out his hand to her mom, a silent invitation that spoke volumes. Her mom's smile, always warm and real, would widen even more.

One night, as the music churned around the room, Kay watched, completely captivated, from the doorway. Her dad, a playful glimmer in his eye, dipped his wife low as his laughter filled the room.

"See that, Kay?" he boomed, "That's the secret to a happy marriage – knowing when to lead and when to let your partner take the spotlight."

Kay's heart swelled with emotion. Watching their graceful movements, she recognized more than just a dance; she saw a silent, powerful love story, one that had defied the years and grown stronger with every shared turn.

Kay's mother, Jean, was a soft-spoken woman who, despite her passive demeanor, possessed a firm and strict will and a well-intended commitment to her children's moral compass.

In contrast, her father, Walter, was a more direct man of business and action whose drive for success set the tone for the household. Walter was relentlessly strict, and while he loved his children, he was simply not comfortable expressing emotion, a distance that often left his kids fearing him. He led the family with purpose, viewing his role as provider and authority figure with uncompromising diligence.

Kay's house wasn't your typical teenage warzone—a pristine orderliness permeated through every corner. The house remained spotless at all times, with zero mess ever tolerated. They were expected to keep their items in their rooms, contributing to the impeccably tidy atmosphere that pulsed through the very walls.

Instead of clocking in at typical nine-to-five jobs, her parents ran a specialized in-home memory care facility for elderly adults. This meant their house was perpetually dedicated to caring for patients grappling with dementia and other related conditions.

Her mother, a woman with a heart as boundless as the summer sky, treated each resident like family. Every morning, the aroma of freshly baked muffins would mingle with the gentle murmur of conversations as she helped them with their morning routines.

Mr. Johnson, a retired sailor with a mischievous gleam in his eye, was one of the residents at the memory care facility. He would often entertain Kay with tales of faraway lands over breakfast. Mrs. Ramirez, another resident and a former opera singer, would patiently teach Kay a few scales on the old piano in the corner. Kay would also attend lessons outside the home, as the house was primarily dedicated to business activities.

One particularly hectic afternoon, Kay burst through the door, backpack slung over one shoulder, ready to vent about a particularly dreadful math test. But the sight that greeted her stopped her short. Her mom, usually the picture of patience, was walking Mrs. Paul, a tiny woman with a crown of silver hair, around the living room.

Kay leaned against the doorframe as a smile tugged at her lips. This wasn't just a house; it was a hub of stories where each resident added their unique note to the beautiful chaos of their family. To their family, it was like living with lots of grandparents.

Unlike most teenagers who retreated to quiet bedrooms after school, Kay's home was a constant hum of life. Nurses in crisp uniforms flitted through the home, with their stethoscopes glinting in the afternoon light. Phone calls buzzed from various agencies coordinating care for their elderly residents. And family members streamed in and out for visits, with their hushed conversations disrupted by warm laughter or tearful goodbyes.

There was never a dull moment in the house as it presented a constant undercurrent of movement that vibrated through the very foundation of its walls.

Relaxation was a ghost in their busy house. While their parents offered a love that overflowed, they were relentlessly pulled away, their attention fractured. "Just a minute, honey," was the constant, echoing promise, a phrase that inevitably stalled precious conversations and snatched playtime away for a patient's needs or urgent business call. The children's lives were defined by waiting, as their world spun completely around the tireless needs of the residents.

One evening, Kay yearned for a movie marathon with Brandon, a simple pleasure that felt out of reach. As she slumped on the couch, a glint of silver caught her eye. Mrs. Ramirez sat across from her, a knowing smile playing on her lips.

"Feeling a little neglected, my dear?" she rasped, her voice a gentle melody.

Kay sighed, a small frown creasing her forehead. "I miss spending time with parents," she mumbled. "It feels like they're always busy."

Mrs. Ramirez patted her hand, her touch warm and comforting. "They have big hearts, Kay," she said. "They take care of so many, but that doesn't mean they don't love you too. Sometimes, the biggest act of love is making a sacrifice."

Kay pondered her words. Maybe Mrs. Ramirez was right. However, for the most part, despite being aware of her parents' love for her, she often felt like they were living under a microscope, with their every action scrutinized and judged by everyone.

As a result, it was difficult for Kay to have friends over. The nature of their family business, along with caring for the elderly, made it challenging to create a comfortable and welcoming environment for visitors.

Kay yearned for an ordinary life. Her house, brimming with the gentle hum of elderly care, felt a world away from the carefree laughter that echoed through her friends' homes.

Here, nestled among the constant bustle of nurses and family visits, the space for teenage normalcy seemed to shrink. She craved the freedom to sprawl on the living room floor with friends, giggling over silly movies and sharing secrets whispered in the dark.

This constant state of "on display" wore on her and her siblings. Kay longed to shed the invisible mask of perfect behavior, the one expected of her in a home that doubled as a professional setting. She yearned for a moment when her parents weren't the business owners, but simply relaxed, goofy humans at home. In a way, she wanted to discover who they truly were outside the roles they played so flawlessly every day.

Most of all, Kay ached for the simple freedom to be a kid. A kid who could invite friends over without worrying about disrupting the delicate order of their household. A kid who could blast music without wondering if it disturbed a resident's afternoon nap.

Amidst such hustle and bustle, Kay not only occasionally struggled with the dynamics at her home but also grappled with finding her place among her siblings. As the middle child, she often felt caught between the shadow of her older sister, Holly, and the adoration bestowed upon her little brother, Brandon.

Holly was a mystery wrapped in a teenager's scowl. Six years older, she moved through the house like a ghost, her headphones a constant barrier between her world and Kay's.

Kay craved a connection, a sisterhood built on whispered secrets and shared dreams. She desired Holly's acceptance and approval, that Kay wasn't just a pesky little shadow tagging along. But Holly remained distant, a solitary planet in their household's solar system.

Adding to Kay's sense of isolation was the feeling that Holly resented her and their brother, Brandon, believing they had been given an easier life. Holly's jealousy cast a shadow over their relationship, creating a barrier that seemed insurmountable.

The situation only worsened when Holly married at 18. The news hit Kay like a rogue wave. Holly was getting married. *Married? At eigh-*

teen? It felt like a scene straight out of a movie, a plot twist that left Kay confused. And then, the wedding photos, a flurry of white lace and awkward smiles, only solidified the distance growing between them.

Holly's new life became a world Kay could only glimpse through occasional visits. Conversations, once strained at best, became filled with talk of in-laws, new furniture, and the never-ending quest for the perfect shade of paint for her new home. Kay yearned to connect, to find a common thread within the domesticity that had swept Holly away.

As Holly built her own life, brick by brick, Kay felt a hollowness bloom in her chest. The sisterly bond she'd craved seemed to slip further and further out of reach. It wasn't just about missing Holly's presence; it was the absence of a female confidante, a built-in best friend Kay never truly had.

Growing up, Kay had watched movies and read books in which sisters were portrayed as partners in crime, fierce protectors, and keepers of each other's deepest secrets. She'd dreamt of sleepovers filled with giggles and whispered dreams of having someone who understood her teenage angst on a soul-deep level. But that attachment, the one she'd hoped to earn with Holly, never materialized; instead, when Holly had children, she only sought out Kay for babysitting, never prioritizing the opportunity to truly connect.

The impact was profound. Kay felt like she was navigating the stormy seas of adolescence alone, and worse, there was no lifeline. Her parents, bless them, weren't the kind to sit down for a serious talk; they dismissed her troubles as mere "teenage drama," making them a closed door for real conversation. Without a trusted hand to steady the boat, she had no one to share the thrill of a first crush, the sting of a schoolyard betrayal, or the quiet anxieties that loomed. She had friends, yes, but they couldn't provide the unique vulnerability and depth of understanding that only a sister could.

In the quiet moments, Kay couldn't help but wonder what it would have been like to have Holly in her corner, cheering her on and offering a shoulder to cry on. She often wondered why the sisterly bond she'd craved for so long, the one that felt like a birthright, was slipping through her fingers. Was it something she'd done? Some missteps that pushed Holly further away? The questions spun in her mind, with no clear answer in sight.

The loss felt like a physical weight on her chest, a constant ache that intensified with each unanswered phone call and distant greeting. Kay longed for a glimpse of the sister she thought Holly could be. But the distance only widened, making her feel that there was a missing piece in the puzzle of her life.

However, things were different with Brandon. Six years younger, he was the baby of the family and received abundant attention and affection. Despite the age gap, Kay and Brandon shared a mischievous streak that kept their household alive with laughter and excitement. They were partners in crime, always brainstorming new pranks and schemes to pull on unsuspecting victims.

For Kay, these moments of silliness were a welcome escape from the pressures of everyday life. Amidst the hustle and bustle of their parents' busy lives, she found comfort in the simple act of making her family smile, even if it meant resorting to slightly unconventional methods.

Yet, despite these playful moments and Kay's closeness to Brandon, there were moments when she couldn't help but feel a pang of annoyance, especially when her parents asked her to take Brandon with her everywhere. Kay couldn't shake the feeling that he was being used to spy and report back on her activities. It wasn't that she didn't love her brother, just that she cherished her independence and freedom, feeling stifled by the constant surveillance. Having Brandon tag along meant sacrificing her alone time and her moments of solitude where she could just be herself without any responsibilities or obligations.

But as much as Kay grumbled and complained about having her little brother in tow, later, she would come to cherish those moments, realizing that deep down, she wouldn't have it any other way. There was something special about their bond, something that transcended mere annoyance and frustration. It was a bond built on love, trust, and the shared joy of exploring the world together.

And so, from swimming and bike rides to games and movies, they were inseparable companions, exploring the ups and downs of a unique childhood together. Their weekends were often filled with camping trips, church events, and quality time spent with friends, creating memories that would last a lifetime.

Despite the challenges posed by her relationships with her siblings while growing up, Kay found strength and resilience within herself. She learned to steer her way through the complexities of family dynamics, finding reassurance in the love and support of her friends and the bond she shared with her brother.

Before the label of ADHD existed, Kay was simply defined as "not focused"—a teenager whose brilliant, restless mind flitted like a butterfly over everything but her textbooks. The abstract equations of Math and the tedious dates of History felt like mental wallpaper, holding no joy or gravity for her. Her academic life was an act of constant triage; grades hovered in a precarious C/D range, buoyed only by the genuine love she poured into tangible, hands-on classes like Band, Family Living, and Home Economics. There, she could physically channel her focus, finding satisfaction in hands-on assignments.

By her senior year, the weight of academic apathy finally reached a breaking point. Granted the coveted freedom of off-campus lunch, Kay found her true escape wasn't the crowded cafeteria, but the beach with her friends. The rhythmic, insistent call of the socializing easily drowned out the frantic, jarring clamor of the school bells. Class-skipping became a brazen habit, a neglect her preoccupied parents, consumed by the ceaseless demands of their own professional lives, never seemed to notice. She was drifting, an unmoored vessel, but the current felt undeniably sweet.

The only anchor in her sea of indifference was Senior Prom. Her date was David, the starting quarterback from the rival high school, and the consuming excitement of finally securing approval for an outside date was a drug. The day of the dance was a meticulous ritual of transformation: the hours-long session at the salon, the perfectly painted nails, the giddy anticipation that muffled all other anxieties.

She returned home to a profound, sickening silence. Her parents had already left. Their sudden absence was a silent, agonizing void where the congratulatory fuss and obligatory "before" pictures should have been. It was the deepest wound: a feeling of being missed, overlooked, a non-entity in her own life's milestone. Devastated but determined not to let their neglect ruin her night, Kay met David at his mother's house across town. David's mother, a woman who understood the silent language of parental oversight, became the unexpected surrogate. She took the obligatory photos, flashing a genuine smile before sending the happy couple off to their great night.

The evening was everything Kay had dreamed of—a bubble of flawless validation—until a sudden, tearing pain ripped through her stomach. It was sharp, terrifying, and demanded her full, immediate attention, extinguishing the magical glow of the night. Recognizing the severity, she had to break the spell. She asked David to take her home. He saw the genuine fear in her eyes and, despite the disappointing end to the night, knew something was profoundly wrong.

Kay crept into her house, the silk of her gown brushing the floor, and found her parents already in bed. When she told them she was unwell, her father's response was a chilling dismissal: without getting up, he simply told her to drive herself to the ER and take her younger brother, Brandon, so she wouldn't be alone. Kay felt a blinding surge of fury, but her anger was useless. She and Brandon drove themselves to the emergency room, where tests revealed an inflamed gallbladder requiring immediate surgery.

Her devastation was complete. Not only was she facing a major operation, but her already precarious, poor GPA meant missing the upcoming final exams would be disastrous. Released with a surgical consult, she saw the surgeon the very next day. The news was stark: the surgery couldn't wait. Kay was suddenly locked into a hospital bed, missing the last few critical weeks of school.

David, ever the sweetheart, visited every day, picking up her ordered copy of the yearbook. It was a sweet gesture; but the book was a blank slate, devoid of the signatures, inside jokes, and memories she was supposed to collect. Her senior year—the one meant to be the best—was spent lying in a hospital, then recovering at home, utterly separated from the outside world.

The cost of her illness was absolute. She missed every single final exam. With zeroes entered across the board for crucial, credit-bearing courses, her poor GPA was irrevocably sealed. The realization hit her with a sickening, physical force: all her careless skipping and last-minute efforts had finally caught up to her. She was going to fail, literally days before graduation. There would be no walking across the stage.

Her father made multiple calls to the school, pleading for leniency and a chance to retake the finals, but the answer was a cold, official "No." Kay's fate was sealed by policy and the numerical weight of her neglect. The school offered one single concession: she could return the following year for one semester to finish the missing credits.

Kay refused. The thought of watching her friends celebrate their escape while she returned to the empty, echoing halls as a fifth-year failure was an intolerable judgment. She had always managed to scrape by with a last-minute push or an appeal for extra credit—but this time, there was no charm, no special circumstance to get around the zeroes.

Her decision was met with immediate anger. Her parents called it selfish and stupid—it was only one semester, they argued. But for Kay, it was a moment of clarity and a visceral rejection of their neglect. College was never the defining conversation in their busy household;

life goals were a luxury her family never discussed. Kay had simply moved through high school, surviving each year, her passion reserved solely for her music.

Now, without a diploma, she was faced with the ultimate, terrifying question that had always been put off: What next? The chaotic flitting of the butterfly had crashed into a sudden, inescapable wall.

As soon as her surgical incision had healed, leaving only a pale, thin line as a permanent reminder of her failure, Kay put the diploma dilemma aside. The pressure to return to the school halls was gone, replaced by the immediate, practical need for independence. She took the terrifying leap into the adult job search, quickly securing employment in a busy retail environment where her hands-on energy and quick thinking were assets. The steady paycheck, a tangible reward for her effort, felt more validating than any abstract grade ever had. This new structure would serve as her temporary foundation, giving her the space and income she needed before she could tackle the daunting, but necessary, process of studying for the GED.

2

When the Sky Fell

The arrival of the festive season was heralded by the crisp December air, heavy with the scent of apples and cinnamon, making every breath feel celebratory. For Kay, Christmas was the grand, undisputed masterpiece of the year, her most cherished holiday. At their house, it wasn't just decoration; it was a full, two-week theatrical production, transforming their home into a flawless spread worthy of a Home and Gardens magazine cover.

Inside, the transformation was total, but the spectacle began outside. Her father, a meticulous perfectionist in this domain, treated the exterior like an artist's canvas. Every single bulb on the towering trees and along the eaves was perfectly spaced and precisely placed, resulting in a display that was stunningly elegant and classy, never gaudy. When the sun finally dipped below the horizon, the house ignited in a warm, sophisticated glow, a brilliant contrast to the cold, dark night.

Anticipation for this annual magic crackled like electricity in the air. Sunlight streamed through the windows, bathing the living room in a warm, inviting glow, momentarily highlighting the empty space before the meticulous, beloved chaos of decoration began. It was, unequivocally, the best time of the year.

One evening, Kay's parents ventured out to a Christmas program at a church a few hours away, leaving Kay and Brandon alone at home.

A close family friend was performing in the Christmas play, and Mr. and Mrs. Dillard they were eager to see their role in the production. On the other hand, Kay, ever the social butterfly, had fluttered off earlier that morning, promising an afternoon filled with laughter and friends. Her brother, Brandon, lingered behind, the echo of their playful bickering still clinging to the air.

"Clubs again, huh?" he'd grumbled, a hint of disappointment in his voice. Kay, already halfway out the door, had flashed him a cheeky grin.

"Sorry, little bro," she'd teased, "You're too young to go. Besides, Mom and Dad wouldn't be too thrilled about me sneaking you out."

Brandon resigned but understood and waved her off with a mumbled, "Have fun."

Now, in between the scattered remnants of his cleaning spree, a dull ache of loneliness settled in his stomach. Brandon's confinement to the house for the day, as a consequence of one of his usual pranks, heightened his sense of isolation. Kay's absence, usually a welcome break from her persistent teasing, felt strangely hollow today. With a sigh, Brandon walked over to the window, his gaze drawn to the sun-dappled street outside. It seemed the perfect kind of day for exploring, for adventures shared with a partner-in-crime. A pang of longing boomed in his heart. He missed having Kay by his side, even if their adventures often ended in playful arguments and gentle shoves.

Florida sunshine, a welcome divergence to the winter chill gripping most of the country, bathed the house in a warm glow. This kind of weather called for outdoor projects, and Brandon knew exactly where his day would be spent. Their sprawling backyard boasted a magnificent old oak tree, and its sturdy branches formed the perfect platform for his ultimate hangout: his treehouse.

Christmas lights, a box that he'd stolen from the garage with his usual mischievous grin, would be his afternoon project. He carefully strung them around the miniature wooden haven, with a sense of accomplishment blooming in his chest with each blinking bulb.

As the last string of lights twinkled into life, casting a festive glow on the treehouse, Brandon couldn't contain his pride. Before he finished, he ran inside to Sherry, one of the on-duty managers, eager to share his accomplishment. As busy as the staff was, he knew he should give her a heads-up to come look; he was nearly done. With a wide grin plastered on his face, he burst through the back door, excited to show off his handiwork. "Sherry! Sherry, come see what I did!" he hollered.

Sherry, one of the family's trusted caregiver managers, was a kind woman with a seemingly endless supply of patience for the resident patients and Brandon's occasional bursts of energy.

"Alright, alright. Give me a few minutes to finish my rounds," Sherry replied, and Brandon zipped off in a flurry to go and finish up the lights and complete his masterpiece before Sherry could see.

"Now, young man, what treasures have you unearthed this time?" Sherry chuckled as she made her way outside.

However, as she rounded the corner, her heart plummeted to the pit of her stomach, and a bloodcurdling scream tore through the peaceful afternoon. Sherry found Brandon lying on the ground, still and unmoving, at the foot of the tree. Her heart hammered against her ribs as her eyes raced towards the oak tree.

The twinkling lights dangling from the tree, a cruel mockery of the horrifying scene, seemed to taunt her from above. He must have fallen while making the final connection between the house and the tree.

At that moment, the world stopped. The air hung heavy with a sickening silence, broken only by Sherry's ragged gasps. Rushing to his side, she fell to her knees, her hands trembling as she searched for a pulse, a breath, anything.

But there was nothing—just a chilling emptiness.

Tears streamed down Sherry's face, blurring her vision. With a choked sob, she scrambled inside, reached for the phone, and dialed 911.

As she spoke to the receiver, relaying the horrifying news, a single thought echoed in her mind: this was the beginning of the end.

Desperate to inform the family, Sherry hurriedly flipped open the phone book she kept in the drawer. Realizing there was no way to contact Kay's parents, who were at the play, she recalled Holly's phone number. With a pounding heart, she dialed Holly, her voice trembling as she detailed the turn of events at home. Being just two blocks away, Holly dropped the phone, not wasting another breath. She was out the door and racing down the street, a single thought hammering in her head: get help.

This seemingly ordinary Sunday afternoon had shattered the family's world in an instant. The midday stillness, typically a gentle, predictable pause, was violently torn by a sound—a phone call, a knock, a distant siren—that rewrote their reality. The lingering warmth that once filled this house, a tangible residue of shared laughter and quiet comfort, was immediately shrouded in the chilling, suffocating darkness of grief. It felt as if the very air had become thick and cold, replacing the comfortable sunlight with a heavy, leaden atmosphere that promised no relief.

Kay, miles away amidst the flashing lights and throbbing music of a nightclub, felt a prickle of unease crawl up her spine. It was an unfamiliar sensation, a nagging feeling that whispered of something being wrong at home.

It was unusual for her to even consider calling home during an outing with friends, yet the feeling persisted, a fly buzzing persistently at the edge of her awareness. She brushed it aside, attributing it to the alcohol and loud music.

Throughout the evening, the distressing sensation wouldn't be silenced. It worried her, and she felt the feeling growing in her. Reluctantly, she pushed it down further, burying herself in the mindless partying.

Finally, as the night wore on and her friends began to tire, Kay found herself surprisingly eager to call it a night.

"Guys, how about we call a night?" she suggested.

Her friends, surprised by the sudden change, reluctantly agreed. Steadily, they piled into their cars and drove to Jim's condo, a usual routine they followed.

As they settled themselves in Jim's living space, Kay's resolve began to waver. Against her habits, she voiced a sudden desire to go home.

"You're gonna go home? Seriously? You just got here." Jim paused, a single eyebrow raised in suggestion and mild challenge. "Look, you can call home if you need permission or something."

Kay hesitated. The troublesome feeling had morphed into a powerful urge, an invisible hand pulling her toward home.

"Actually," she mumbled, "I think I just... I just need to go home tonight."

Jim furrowed his brow, his gaze sharpening with skepticism. "Are you absolutely sure about that? You've had quite a lot to drink tonight, Kay."

Kay waved his concern away with a dismissive flick of her wrist. "I'm fine, really," she insisted, her tone sharper than she intended. Jim's expression didn't change, so she rushed to appease him. "Just promise me you'll call me the minute you get home?" Kay flashed him a quick, fleeting smile, but the unsettling feeling of unease was growing stronger—a tight knot beneath her ribs that she couldn't ignore.

The drive home was shrouded in an unsettling silence. Kay gripped the steering wheel tightly, her eyes glued to the road ahead. The twenty-five-mile journey stretched on, with each passing mile amplifying the disquiet worry at her insides.

As she neared the familiar turnoff to her street, a wave of dread washed over her. The house, usually bathed in a warm evening glow, was ablaze with light. Several cars sat parked in the usually quiet driveway, and their presence presented a completely different setting to the peaceful Sunday evenings she was accustomed to.

Panic clawed at her throat. This wasn't right. Something was terribly wrong. Maybe her grandmother had passed away?

Parking haphazardly, she fumbled with her keys, her hands trembling uncontrollably.

As Kay opened the front door, a discord of hushed voices and muffled sobs greeted her. The sight that met her eyes was a display of raw grief.

In the living room, a group of people stood clustered around her parents. But it was her parents themselves who stole Kay's breath away.

Her mother sat crumpled in a wingback chair; her body wracked with sobs that echoed through the room. Her father knelt beside her, with his own face streaked with tears.

It was the most horrific scene Kay had ever witnessed.

The weight of the unknown pressed down on her, suffocating. Kay's eyes darted from one face to the next, searching for answers, for a shred of understanding amidst the overwhelming tide of grief.

"What's going on?" she stammered.

A tall woman, her eyes red-rimmed and swollen, stepped forward. It was Sherry, but she looked older somehow, her face ingrained with a weariness Kay had never seen before.

"Kay," Sherry choked out.

Kay's heart hammered against her ribs. "Sherry, what is it? What happened?"

A heavy silence descended upon the room, broken only by a single, heart-wrenching sob. Then, in a voice barely above a whisper, Kay's father uttered the words that would forever shatter Kay's world.

"He's gone."

Kay's mind spun with varying thoughts.

Her voice was shaky and paper-thin. "Who's gone?" she breathed, the whisper a plea rather than a question.

"Brandon," he breathed.

The world tilted on its axis. Kay's mind, already twirling from the night's events, struggled to comprehend her father's words.

Brandon? Gone? It was impossible.

Just that morning, she'd seen him, his face flushed with excitement as he'd insisted to come along with her. Everything had been normal. *Fine.*

But the raw grief on her parents' faces and the heartbroken sobs stemming from the living room painted a picture far bleaker than Kay's denial could manage.

A wave of nausea consumed her as the remnants of the night's partying turned sour in her stomach. The carefree laughter and music from the club seemed a lifetime ago, a cruel reminder of the normalcy she now desperately craved.

Denial, a flimsy shield against the onslaught of grief, crumbled instantly. Hysteria, a primal scream of disbelief and despair, tore from her throat.

"No! This can't be happening!" Kay shrieked.

Tears, hot and blinding, streamed down her face. Her breath hitched in her chest; each gasp a desperate attempt to pull in the air that felt thick and suffocating. Images of Brandon and his infectious laughter flooded her mind.

The weight of guilt, a crushing burden, settled on her shoulders. She should have called earlier and checked in at home. If she had been there, could she have prevented this somehow? The answer, a sickening certainty, echoed in the hollowness of her chest – no.

Kay crumpled to the floor. At that moment, a horrifying truth settled in Kay's heart: Brandon was gone, and a part of her would forever be lost with him.

Lost in the flurry of grief, Kay forgot the promise she'd made to Jim when she decided to drive back to her house.

Back at his place, an uneasiness grew on Jim. The night had taken an unsettling turn with Kay's sudden need to leave. He tried calling her house, but the line was perpetually engaged, indicating a hint of disorder unfolding there.

Fear, cold and sharp, twisted in Jim's gut. Images of Kay, alone and vulnerable on the road after a night of drinks, flickered through his mind. He couldn't let go of the feeling that something was terribly wrong. Still in his flannel pajamas, Jim jumped into his car without a second thought. The engine roared instantly to life, matching the frantic pulse in his ears, as he sped towards Kay's house.

Reaching the familiar street, a wave of anxiety washed over him. The house was bathed in an unsettling activity. Just then, he practically flew through the front door, with his heart hammering against his ribs.

The sight that greeted him mirrored the one Kay had stumbled upon moments earlier: a picture of raw anguish.

Kay was crumpled on the floor, with her cries echoing through the stunned silence of the room. Jim recognized Kay's grief instantly. He'd known Brandon well as a result of a bond forged over countless sleepovers and shared adventures. The house, usually filled with laughter, was now covered in a heavy cloak of sorrow. No one could quite believe the tragedy that had struck them so suddenly.

At that moment, Jim didn't hesitate to offer his support to his friend. He knelt beside her and scooped Kay in his arms.

In the following days, he became Kay's pillar of strength, a constant presence as she navigated the choppy waters of grief. The family doctor, overwhelmed by the sheer magnitude of the Dillard's family's loss, prescribed medications that would later leave fragmented memories of those initial, raw days.

But one thing remained crystal clear: Kay's life, and the lives of everyone who loved Brandon, had been irretrievably altered.

Days before Brandon's funeral, the house became the epicenter of a communal outpouring of grief. At Walter's insistent direction, Brandon was brought home, his casket placed right there in the living room. The private family space was instantaneously and jarringly transformed into a makeshift chapel. Hundreds of people—friends, family, distant acquaintances, news stations, teachers, and students from both schools, and members of their church community—poured in to pay their respects. The room overflowed with flowers and the constant, overwhelming murmur of shared memories and hushed condolences. Through all the chaos of the crowd, the immediate family remained anchored, a singular, sorrowful presence glued by Brandon's side.

Kay, absorbed in a sea of grief, moved through the days on autopilot. The sight of Brandon's casket, a stark, dark island highlighted by elegant gold trim amidst the towering floral arrangements, threatened to pull her under. At just thirteen years old and already standing at six feet tall, Brandon's sudden, quiet absence loomed even larger than his impressive stature.

The day of the funeral arrived, masked in a heavy, somber grey sky that perfectly mirrored the crushing weight in everyone's hearts. The sheer size of the crowd was staggering: hundreds of people filled every open space of the family home, spilling out onto the expansive lawn where they stood shoulder-to-shoulder, their silent presence a powerful testament to the vibrant life Brandon had touched. The eulogy, delivered through the strained, tear-filled voice of their pastor, beautifully painted a picture of a bright, good-natured, fun-loving boy with a perpetual, playful glint in his eye. As shared memories turned into collective sobs and tears flowed freely across the packed space, Kay felt a raw, exposed ache in her chest, a deepening hollowness that threatened to consume her entirely.

The final goodbye took place at the military cemetery, a place of quiet admiration where countless heroes lay to rest. Kay's father, an Air Force veteran, stood tall as Brandon was laid to rest.

As the days passed, the acute pain began to dull, replaced by a deep, lingering ache. The house, once filled with the sounds of Brandon's laughter, now held an unsettling, oppressive silence. This heavy quiet stood in stark contrast to Kay's mother, whose grief was not silent but fiercely active. She cried every single day, tears streaming down her face even as she pushed herself into nonstop labor—she was seen vacuuming with tears running down her cheeks, yet still maintaining the spotless order. Outside the home, she poured the same frantic energy into her professional life, diligently caring for her patients and tirelessly trying to maintain their family business, using routine and responsibility as a fragile shield against the heartbreak.

Kay clung to the memory of her brother as if it were a life raft. Yet, the weight of his absence pressed down on her as a constant reminder of his absence.

As time went by, the once vibrant home transitioned into a place of muted tones and tear-stained cheeks. Her parents, grieving in their own ways, seemed like strangers, and arguments, which seemed like a foreign sound in their household, erupted with a terrifying frequency.

As for her parents, they succumbed to varying coping mechanisms. Her mother retreated into a shell of despair, oblivious to the effect it'd have on Kay.

One horrifying night, Walter stumbled upon her slumped on the bathroom floor, an empty pill bottle beside her. The memory, relayed to Kay later, sent shivers down her spine. Imagining her mother in that state, a wave of helplessness and fear washed over her.

On the other hand, Kay's father sought comfort in the bottom of a bottle. The man who used to fix her scraped knees and teach her how to ride a bicycle now seemed lost, drowning his grief in alcohol, his sorrow morphing into anger.

That year, Christmas, a time usually filled with joyous anticipation, brought only a relentless surge of sorrow for the family. The house, once a fortress of holiday cheer, felt invaded by grief. The twinkling lights on the tree, typically a source of warmth, now seemed to mock the festive spirit with their relentless cheer, reminding them of Brandon's last project before he died. Most agonizing of all was the sight of Brandon's unopened, wrapped gifts still sitting beneath the tree, their bright paper and neat ribbons a jarring, heartbreaking monument to a future that wouldn't arrive. The empty chair at the table stood as a painful, inescapable notice of his absence, and each forced smile, each attempt at small talk, felt like a betrayal of the raw emotions existing and festering within them.

The picture-perfect family Kay once knew had shattered into a million pieces, leaving behind mere grief.

The realization struck Kay with the force of a tidal wave. Life, she understood with a painful, blinding clarity, was far too short—a fragile thing that could be stolen without warning. The carefree days of endless possibilities and living moment-to-moment were abruptly over. This trauma had yanked her out of her adolescent drift.

A demanding new question now echoed in the sudden silence of the house: What was she going to do with her life? Unlike her peers, she didn't have a plan for her education, no blueprint for a career, no roadmap for her adult life. The thought of simply existing in this grief-stricken vacuum, or returning to her former aimless habits, was intolerable; she couldn't live like this forever. The time had come to grow up, to seize control, and to figure out how to become an independent adult and start her own life, however intimidating that immense prospect seemed.

Being at home, surrounded by the ghosts of happy memories turned into painful reminders, was suffocating. Kay craved a change of scenery, a chance to escape the suffocating silence that pressed in on her from all sides. She wouldn't let Brandon's death define her. She would carry his memory with her, but she would also live for him and for herself.

But where to go? How do you move on from a loss that felt so all-encompassing?

A fragile spark of hope arrived a few weeks after the funeral in the form of an unexpected phone call. It was Stephanie, a high school acquaintance, reaching out to offer her condolences. Stephanie was never the closest of friends and was known more for her rowdiness than her social graces. The truth was, they had gone to school together since high school and shared a couple of classes, which was the extent of their bond. Occasionally, Stephanie would even ask Kay for a ride home. They were certainly not super close, but the call, however unexpected, was a break in the silence.

And so, Stephanie's call surprised Kay with her genuine concern.

Stephanie's voice, usually loud, was unusually hushed on the line. "Kay, I heard about Brandon," she began, the name catching slightly in her throat. "I honestly can't imagine what you're going through right now—the quiet must be impossible. But... look, I was thinking, I wanted to see if you'd be interested in... well, getting away for a bit? Just a change of scenery, you know? Get out of that house for a little while."

Kay raised an eyebrow. Stephanie and a weekend getaway were about as likely a pairing as sunshine and thunderstorms.

"Getting away?" Kay questioned, unsure where the conversation was headed.

"Yeah," Stephanie continued, her voice picking up its usual chipper tone. "I'm getting married in a few months, in Georgia. Preppy, right?" she chuckled. "Anyway, I was thinking maybe you'd like to come along? Help me with wedding plans."

Kay hesitated. The thought of being cooped up with Stephanie, infamous for her know-it-all personality, wasn't exactly appealing. But the alternative, staring at the walls of her childhood home, drowning in the silence, was even less appealing.

"Honestly," Kay admitted, "I don't know, Stephanie. It's a long drive."

"That's where the amazing part comes in!" Karen exclaimed. "You have that brand-new truck, right? It's perfect for a road trip!"

Kay sighed. Stephanie's motive was clear: transportation. Yet, the idea of a change of scenery, of escaping the suffocating atmosphere of her house, held a sliver of charm.

Upon hearing of the unexpected invitation, Kay's parents were cautiously optimistic. The idea of a break from the constant, suffocating cycle of grief felt like a necessary lifeline; perhaps some time away might actually do her some good. Her father, typically reserved with emotional gestures, quietly slipped her a wad of cash, a silent acknowledgment of the need for independence and a wish for things to feel normal again.

And so, with a hesitant nod and a tight knot of anxiety settling in her stomach, Kay found herself packing a bag. Beside her, Stephanie was already chattering excitedly, completely unaware of Kay's internal turmoil. With a final farewell, they pulled away, the open road stretching before them not just as pavement, but as a potential, necessary escape from the darkness that had suffocated her life for months.

"Maybe, just maybe," Kay thought to herself, watching the scenery blur, "this trip would be the first step—a tentative beginning on the long, intimidating road to healing." The thought solidified as the car sped toward North Georgia.

Kay adored driving, but the fact that she was traveling out of state alone (without parental supervision) felt like a monumental achievement and was pretty exciting. As they drove, Florida's flat, familiar landscape gradually surrendered to the rolling hills of Georgia, replaced by lush greenery and quaint farmhouses scattered across the countryside. The bustling coastal life she was used to faded into a distant memory. This striking shift in scenery was both immediate and soothing, providing a necessary and welcome contrast to the familiar chaos of her hometown and the grief she was leaving behind.

The journey into Georgia was a pleasant culture shock, a sudden, welcome departure from the mundane. Everything felt refreshingly different from the coastal familiarity of her hometown. The air even smelled distinct—less salt, more earth and pine. The thick, rolling Southern accents they encountered were a distinct dissimilarity to the clipped, quick tones of Central Florida, and the slow, musical cadence of the language tickled her ear. The small, often historic towns they passed through were charming and unhurried, with narrow main streets centered around courthouses or town squares. People seemed to have nowhere to be, waving from wide porches with smiles that felt genuinely unhurried—a stark, soothing contrast to the fast-paced, often impersonal environment she had left behind.

Upon arriving at their destination, Kay was immediately pulled into a bustling social circle. Stephanie introduced her to her fiancé and his parents—her soon-to-be in-laws—before turning to a lively group of friends who had gathered to welcome them. Kay was quickly immersed in the cheerful, loud dynamic of the new environment.

Kay, initially reserved, found herself warming up to the easy hospitality. Everyone seemed genuinely interested in getting to know her, and their questions mostly carried kindness that calmed the raw edges of her grief. For the first time in weeks, Kay found herself laughing easily.

The days on their Georgia adventure melted away, occupying the welcome pause between Christmas and New Year. The atmosphere was a fascinating mix, fueled by the happy chaos of wedding planning that provided a therapeutic distraction. Their schedule was packed: afternoons were devoted to everything from last-minute sightseeing and shopping for décor, and evenings were filled with lively family barbecues and informal planning sessions. Amidst this domesticity, Kay was also exposed to the stark realities of country living, including a night where she watched the men gut a deer right in the yard—a raw, visceral sight that highlighted the wild difference between this environment and her coastal home.

Kay, usually drawn to the hustle and bustle of city life, discovered a genuine appreciation for the simple, deliberate pleasures of small-town living. The community, radiating a deep sense of warmth, embraced Kay instantly. For a while at least, surrounded by the kindness of these new friends, the heavy burden of Kay's grief felt distinctly lighter.

The end of the year arrived, streaked with a bittersweetness Kay couldn't quite shake. While Christmas reminded Kay of the void in her life due to Brandon's absence, New Year's Eve held a different promise for her: a chance for a fresh start, a turning of the page.

Stephanie's future in-laws invited them to a New Year's Eve gathering at their home. The prospect of a large gathering filled Kay with a familiar shyness. Crowds, especially those filled with unfamiliar faces, tended to make her retreat into a quiet corner as a silent observer rather than an active participant.

"Don't worry, honey," Stephanie boomed, oblivious to Kay's unease. "Everyone's going to love you! My future mother-in-law, bless her heart, practically baked a pie in your honor."

Kay managed a weak smile. The thought of homemade pie held little charm compared to the prospect of strolling a room full of strangers.

As they walked to Mr. and Mrs. Miller's home—which was conveniently situated directly behind Stephanie's fiancé's house—the air was thick with the immediate, warm welcome of Mrs. Miller's famous Southern pecan pie and cookies. The house itself buzzed with festive chatter, the bright sound of laughter spilling out onto the porch. Kay, feeling the familiar, unwelcome wave of shyness wash over her, instinctively clung to Stephanie's side like a lifeline.

"Don't you just stand there, darlin'—come on in! Let's get you parked in the kitchen. We can talk a while, I finish up this pie."

It wasn't just the kitchen. The instant and genuine warmth of Mrs. Miller's disposition was the first thing that reached Kay, dissolving her anxiety. This sense of social comfort, blended with the physical heat of the oven and the sweet, comforting aroma of the baking pie, instantly put Kay at ease.

"So, Kay," Mrs. Miller began, placing a gentle hand on her arm, "during all our conversations since you arrived, I never got to talk to you about your brother. Tell me about him. It'd lighten your grief.

And Kay did. She spoke of Brandon's playful nature, his love for building elaborate model cars, and his infectious laugh. Mrs. Miller listened patiently as her eyes crinkled at the corners with each shared memory. For the first time that evening, Kay felt a lightness in her chest, a sense of connection that exceeded the barrier of their brief acquaintance.

Soon, guests were pouring in, and Kay was no longer a stranger, but simply one of the crowd. The spontaneous kindness of the Millers and their friends and family, the unexpected comfort of sharing stories, and the exhilarating promise of new beginnings were the defining gifts she received on that New Year's Eve, marking her passage out of grief.

Well, the most significant moment of the night was yet to reveal itself, and it arrived in the form of a friendly but slightly awkward proposition. A particularly warm smile caught Kay's eye across the room. And at that moment, a tall man with kind eyes and a welcoming aura was making his way towards her.

Richard stepped closer, offering a genuine, welcoming smile. "Hi there," he said, his voice easy and familiar. "I haven't seen your face around here before, and trust me, I see everyone. I'm Richard, by the way."

Kay smiled back, the shyness easing a little under his warm gaze. "Hi Richard, I'm Kay. I'm Stephanie's friend from Florida."

Richard chuckled and gave her a conspiratorial wink. "Well, welcome to the madhouse, Kay. Don't you worry. I promise not to hold it against you if you're friends with this one. You're just visiting to help her with wedding planning?"

Kay nodded. "Yes, just visiting for a bit, getting a much-needed change of scenery. Everyone's been so genuinely friendly; it's been a really nice change from back home."

"That's just how we do things, darlin'," Richard said, his smile widening. "We're a friendly bunch when we're not chasing deer. So, you're stuck here until after New Year's, then?"

"It looks that way," Kay confirmed, the thought now more exciting than intimidating. "I'm helping out with a few little things for the wedding, I guess."

"Well, you just enjoy it then," Richard said, giving her a friendly pat on the shoulder.

Richard's eyes sparkled with a sudden idea. I'm about to make a quick run up the mountain to my place. I need to fetch a couple of bottles of my homemade blackberry wine for the party—it's the good stuff, better than anything store-bought."

He paused, looking directly at Kay. "It's a heck of a view up there, not far at all. Why don't you come with me? Get away from this noise for a minute, and you can tell me what you think of the mountain air."

Kay hesitated. The invitation was friendly enough, but an instinctive hint of caution bubbled within her. She noticed Richard had spent most of the evening with a woman, laughing - presumably his wife. And so, the idea of getting in a car with a stranger, especially one seemingly attached, felt unwise.

"Thanks, Richard," she replied politely. "But I think I'll stick to the soda for now. I don't drink much anyway."

Richard seemed slightly taken aback, but he nodded in understanding. Kay, relieved to have politely declined, moved into the kitchen to join the ladies at the table.

While enjoying a generous slice of Mrs. Miller's famous pecan pie in the warm kitchen, Kay hesitantly recounted her recent encounter with Richard and his "wife." To her surprise, the entire group of women immediately burst into loud, shared laughter.

"Oh, honey, no!" one woman chuckled, wiping a tear from her eye. "That was Debbie! Lord, that's his *sister*, not his wife! They do favor each other quite a bit, though."

Kay's face instantly flushed crimson. Mortified by her blunder and the assumption she had made, she buried her face in her hands. Just then, Richard appeared in the doorway, drawn by the sudden, joyous sound of laughter.

"Well, speak of the devil," the woman who had corrected Kay announced with a knowing smile, her eyes sparkling. She gave Richard a firm nudge toward Kay. "Richard, you look like you've got something important to clear up right here and now with this poor girl."

Richard raised an eyebrow, genuinely confused. "Clear up what?"

The woman laughed again, pointing playfully at Kay. "She thought Debbie was your wife! And that's why she wouldn't take you up on that ride—she didn't want to go off with a married man!"

Richard's confusion immediately dissolved into a wide, disarming grin. He turned to Kay, shaking his head. "I promise you, I'm very much single. Debbie is my big sister. I guess I'd better make it up to you then, hadn't I? We still need that wine."

Kay, trapped in a web of well-meaning matchmaking, found herself with no graceful way out. Steeling her nerves, she forced a smile at Richard.

Kay conceded with a smile, a clear hint of a laugh in her voice. "Alright, alright, I'm in. Let's go get this famous wine."

With a deep, shaky breath, Kay climbed into the passenger seat of Richard's red Ford truck. Her heart was pounding fiercely—partially from excitement, but mostly from a raw, physical sense of nervous fear. She immediately noticed the official fire department plates and the array of specialized radios and comms equipment running both fire and EMS frequencies mounted inside the cabin. She instinctively scooted as close to the door as possible, pressing her back firmly against the vinyl seat, trying to occupy the smallest amount of space possible.

As they pulled away from the party, the specialized EMS scanner crackled suddenly to life in the background, filling the cab with a jarring, rapid-fire litany of emergency calls and coded chatter. Richard, completely unfazed by the sudden burst of noise and urgency, simply reached over and calmly turned the volume down until it became a low, familiar hum beneath their conversation.

Richard chuckled, catching her nervous glance toward the scanner. "Sorry about that," he said easily. "Just a work hazard of being me, I guess. I volunteer with the fire department and EMS. Keeps me busy, and definitely keeps me on my toes."

Kay nodded slowly, trying to process the danger he treated so lightly. "That sounds... intense."

The silence on the mountain road was broken only by the rhythmic hum of the engine and the occasional chirp of unseen crickets. Steadily, he launched into a story about a recent rescue mission. As Kay listened, her initial fear started to melt away, replaced by a grudging respect for the work he did.

The slow, winding drive up the mountain offered breathtaking glimpses of the valley, which was currently drenched in the deep, vivid colors of the sunset. Richard, relaxed behind the wheel, continued his easy chatter, speaking about his family, his love for the mountains, and his secret recipe for the famous blackberry wine.

"We're crossing the state line now," he announced, his voice tinged with excitement. "Welcome to Alabama!"

Kay managed to keep her voice even, though a cold dread was seizing her. She glanced at the sign marking the boundary. "Alabama? Wow, I didn't realize it was that close." Panic was a freezing wave inside her. She was in a strange man's truck, crossing state lines, and her parents had no idea she was out of Georgia. The terrifying, irrational thought screamed in her mind: What if this guy kills her? She fought to keep her expression blank, desperately trying to mask the fact that she was internally freaking out.

Richard grinned.

"This little stretch right here is what we call the tri-state corner," Richard said, tapping the steering wheel. "Georgia, Alabama, and Tennessee—they all meet up right here. It's a bit of a geographical oddity, and honestly, kind of neat, don't you think?"

Kay found herself nodding in agreement. The night, once filled with uncertainty, now held the promise of adventure. They arrived at a quaint home nestled amongst the trees, with its windows glowing with a warm, inviting light. Richard cut the engine and turned towards Kay, a question in his eyes.

"Would you like to come in for a minute?" he asked. "Perhaps properly taste the wine?"

Kay's heart hammered relentlessly against her ribs. The heavy, quiet atmosphere of the mountain and the isolation of the house amplified her fear. Stepping inside a complete stranger's house, especially at night and in such a remote, tri-state location, felt like a deliberate violation of every single safety rule her usually-absent parents had ever bothered to drill into her. This wasn't the spontaneous, harmless adventure she had agreed to anymore; it was rapidly transforming into a thoughtless diversion filled with real, tangible danger. The adrenaline was now laced with genuine terror.

"Thanks, Richard," she stammered. "But I think we should get back to the party. Stephanie will be wondering where we are."

Richard's smile faltered slightly, but he recovered quickly.

"Of course," he said. "No pressure at all. How about I just grab the wine and we head back?"

Relief washed over Kay in a tidal wave.

"That sounds perfect," she managed, forcing a smile.

A few minutes later, Richard emerged from the house, a few bottles cradled carefully in his arms. The gentle clinking of glass was audible, and the air was immediately filled with the sweet, rich scent of ripe berries.

The drive back down the mountain was filled with a comfortable silence. The earlier ease of conversation had been replaced by a thoughtful self-examination on Kay's part. She replayed the events of the evening in her mind, the initial fear, the unexpected adventure, and the unsettling realization of how easily she'd strayed from her comfort zone.

Back at the party, the festive atmosphere enveloped them once more. Kay and Richard, now sharing an easy rapport, quickly rejoined the social circle. The conversation flowed naturally within the lively group, but their focus remained connected. They spent the remaining hours talking and laughing, subtly learning more about each other's lives even amid the surrounding chatter.

The atmosphere in the living room was electric. Many of them were couples, pressed together, their eyes glued to the television screen as the final seconds of the year ticked away. The air was thick with shared anticipation. When the clock finally struck midnight, the room exploded in a rush of voices and congratulations. In that deafening chaos, Richard looked directly into Kay's eyes, then, without a word, he simply leaned down and kissed her for the very first time. The shock and sudden intimacy of the gesture stole her breath and silenced the world around them.

"Thank you," he said, his breath warm against her cheek. "For trusting me tonight."

Kay could only manage a shy smile in response. Her heart seemed to do a somersault against her ribs as a strange combination of nervousness and excitement bloomed within her.

The rest of the evening was a blur of laughter, stolen glances, and whispered conversations.

With Richard stepping easily into the role of her guide, the following days quickly unfolded into an unforgettable adventure. They explored the most scenic corners of North Georgia and Alabama, driving along breathtaking mountain roads that opened up to sweeping vistas. Their journeys led them through charming, sleepy towns nestled in the valleys, their main streets full of quaint shops and genuinely friendly faces. The simple rhythm of exploration became a soothing backdrop to the new, exhilarating connection forming between them.

Soon, Kay discovered that life in North Georgia was a far cry from the bustling pace of Florida. Here, time seemed to move a little slower, and the emphasis was more on community and connection rather than hurried commutes and impersonal interactions.

The beauty of the mountains and lush valleys offered a constant source of inspiration. Kay found herself drawn to this simpler way of life, a life that felt less dramatic, more grounded, and infinitely more appealing.

Every day, Richard was a constant presence. He would appear at Stephanie's house, his aunt and uncle's place, with suggestion for an adventure. His genuine smile put Kay at ease, and their connection deepened with each shared experience.

One evening, as they sat by a crackling bonfire, gazing up at a star-studded sky, Kay found herself opening up to Richard about Brandon. She spoke of their dreams and their goofy inside jokes.

Richard listened patiently, his hand resting gently on hers.

"He sounds like he was an amazing kid," Richard said softly when she finished. "And I know nothing can replace him, but I hope you know you don't have to walk this path alone."

Kay's throat tightened with warmth. She felt a vulnerability she hadn't dared to embrace in a long time. Looking into Richard's kind eyes, she felt a hint of hope revive within her.

Perhaps, she thought, with a cautious smile, a new chapter was waiting to be written, a chapter filled with new experiences, new connections, and maybe, just maybe, even new love.

3

The Empty Nest Syndrome

After spending an enriching time with Richard, Kay found herself drawn back to the familiar confines of her family home. The trip had been a much-needed respite, allowing her to explore and connect with a world so different from her own, filled with new landscapes and a slower pace of life that had begun to heal her bruised spirit. Yet, despite the peace she found in Georgia, there was an unavoidable pull to return, to face the realities of waiting at home, and to share her experiences with her family, who remained steeped in their own processes of grief.

The journey back was a quiet one, with Kay driving along the stretching highways that led from the serene valleys back to the bustling reality of her hometown. As she neared her family's house, the familiar sights brought a mix of comfort and a tightening in her chest. It wasn't just the place she had grown up in; it was also the place where she had last been whole before the tragedy that took Brandon had torn through their lives.

Upon entering her home, the shift in atmosphere was palpable. The vibrancy that once filled the air had diminished, replaced by a quiet so profound it felt like another presence in the room. Her parents, once the unbreakable pillars of strength and joy, now seemed like shadows of their former selves. Each moved through the day with a profound weariness that went beyond simple physical tiredness. Kay immediately sensed a growing, palpable distance between them—a cold void that suggested something bad was happening beneath the surface of their grief. It was into this deeply strained environment that Kay had to reintegrate herself, attempting to share stories of her adventures while desperately holding space for the sorrow that had never left.

The death of Brandon had hollowed out the once vibrant Dillard household, turning it into a mausoleum of memories where the shadow of his absence loomed large over every room. Kay, once brimming with youthful energy and laughter, now found herself drifting through the days, each moment steeped in a silence that was almost suffocating.

With the chill of winter giving way to the soft promise of spring, the stark branches of the trees outside seemed to soften, preparing to bud. Yet, this sign of renewal offered no comfort; it felt like a cruel reminder of the day Brandon had slipped, quite literally, from their lives. The house, once filled with the sound of Brandon's incessant chatter and the constant hustle of caring for the elderly residents, now seemed to echo only with the whispers of what-ifs and if-onlys.

Kay and Stephanie made several trips back to Georgia over the next few months, ostensibly for wedding planning, but secretly, Kay was driven by the desire to see Richard. Each taxing trip back and forth, however, seemed only to highlight the vast distance, not just geographically, but emotionally as well. By March 1996, a sense of quiet desperation hung over their phone calls. It was then that Richard, perhaps sensing this unspoken, exhausting strain, made a bold proposition: he asked Kay to move closer to him. This dramatic proposition, however, arrived at a time when Kay's own world felt increasingly fragile and unstable.

One particularly bleak evening, with the last light of a spring sunset fading, Kay found herself curled up in the living room. A book lay forgotten in her lap as she stared into the dark, still center of the room. Her mother, Jean, had taken to sitting in the dark these days, the light from the overhead lamp seemingly too harsh for her grief-stricken eyes. Her father, Walter, alternated between putting on a brave face and retreating into his study, where the persistent, quiet clink of ice in whiskey became his only conversation.

The silence was broken by Jean, her mother's voice, barely above a whisper, yet cutting through the quiet like a knife. "This house feels so empty without him," she murmured, her words heavy with sorrow.

Kay looked up, her eyes meeting her mother's grief-worn face. "It's like he's still here, somehow. I keep expecting him to burst through the door, all noise and energy."

Walter, overhearing the exchange from the doorway, added with a sad smile, "He had a way of filling up a room, didn't he?" "But we have to find a way to move forward, for his sake and ours."

The word 'forward' seemed utterly out of place in a home that felt permanently anchored in the past, forever tethered to the tragedy of Brandon's death. Kay felt a sharp pang of guilt for even considering her own future when the past still clung so tightly to her parents. Yet, deep down, she knew staying here was no longer sustainable; it was actively crippling her. She needed to be an adult, but living at home with her parents covering all her bills was getting her nowhere near independence. Her GED remained incomplete, and her life felt like a profound mess, consisting of little more than waking up and waiting for the next trip back to Georgia to see Richard. She wasn't going anywhere like this. She desperately needed to breathe, to find a space where every corner didn't echo with Brandon's memory.

Even though this might not be the right moment, with the raw grief still clinging to the air, Kay knew she had to speak her truth — something that had been on her mind ever since Richard's last visit.

"I... I've been thinking," she began hesitantly, her voice faltering as she noted the immediate tension in her parents' expressions. "Maybe it's time for a change. For me, at least. I need... I need to find a place where I can start fresh."

Her mother's eyes widened, hurt flashing across her features. "You want to leave? Now?" Her voice was a mix of disbelief and anger. "How can you even think about leaving us at a time like this?"

Kay leaned forward, her words tumbling out quickly. "It's not that I want to leave you, please understand. But I can't stay. I need to figure out how to be an adult. Living here, with you two doing everything and paying all my bills, is not going to help me grow up or become independent. I'm just treading water. And on top of that, everything here reminds me of him. I wake up, and for one brief moment, I forget he's gone. Then it all comes rushing back, and it's like losing him all over again."

Walter spoke quietly, trying to bridge the gap between his wife's anguish and Kay's desperate need for escape. "Maybe she has a point. It's not a bad idea. A new environment, a fresh start is probably what Kay needs to heal right now. We can't hold her here, tethered to our grief."

The idea of leaving felt like a sharp twist of betrayal and a profound sense of relief. Kay knew her parents were desperately struggling, but she was completely unaware of the extent of the damage to their marriage, only seeing the surface level of their shared sorrow. That heavy, suffocating weight of joint grief was simply too much for her to bear any longer. She needed to carve out a new path—one where she could finally step into the light without the enormous shadow of Brandon's absence darkening her every step.

As the conversation drew to a close with uneasy agreements and unspoken fears, Kay retreated to her room. She gazed out at the starless sky, her decision weighing heavily on her. Yet, amidst the turmoil, a faint spark of hope flickered. Perhaps a new beginning was possible, a chance to rediscover herself beyond the tragedy that had reshaped her world. The road ahead was uncertain and fraught with challenges, but it was a road she knew she needed to take, not just for her own sake, but perhaps, in some way, to honor the memory of the brother she loved and lost.

After the uneasy agreement that night, the atmosphere in the Dil-lard household grew even more strained. Each day that passed brought Kay closer to her decision, yet the thought of leaving seemed to drive a deeper wedge between her and Jean, her mother. Meanwhile, Walter tried to act as a mediator, a role that weighed heavily on him.

In a matter of days, the preparations for Kay's leaving were already underway. On one particular morning, Kay decided to busy herself in her room and pack some of her belongings. Sitting alone with her thoughts, the reality of the decision she had taken began to sink in. Then, there was a knock at her door before Jean her mother walked in, her face taut with unspoken words.

"Kay, are you really sure about this?" Her mother's voice cracked with raw emotion, betraying her fear. "You're throwing everything away and chasing a fantasy! You don't know the first thing about being on your own. You don't know what life is really like out there. It is not all sunshine and new beginnings, honey."

Kay stopped packing, her hands pausing over a folded sweater. She turned to face her mother, trying hard to mask her frustration with calm understanding. "Mom, I know this is hard for you, but staying here... it's actually harder for me. I feel like I'm suffocating." She took a deep breath. "I need a place where I can find out who I am now. A place where I have to figure out how to do things entirely on my own, without any safety net—not riding on your money or your help."

Jean sighed, a sound heavy with defeat and profound concern. "But why so far away? Why Georgia? It's not just an hour's drive, Kay. If anything goes wrong, we won't be able to get to you. We can't help you that far away."

Jean Kay gently placed the sweater in the box. "I need to feel alive again, Mom. And maybe... maybe a new place, new faces, will help me find pieces of myself that I lost."

The conflict in Jean's mother's eyes was evident. She didn't want to tie her daughter down, but she was scared of the world she was ven-turing out into.

"I just don't want you to regret this, to find yourself alone and wishing you'd never left."

"I know, Mom. And I love you for worrying about me. But I have to try this. For my own sake. I promise I'll visit, and we'll talk all the time."

The conversation lingered in the air long after Kay resumed her packing. Later that week, as the departure day arrived, the house felt even emptier, the walls echoing with the ghosts of past laughter and arguments alike.

Kay stood by the open door of the car, her bags packed in the trunk. Walter stood beside her, offering a brave smile as he helped her with the last of her luggage.

"Do you have your calling card?" he asked, his voice thick with worry. "Yes, Dad. I've got everything." Kay assured him, trying to infuse some cheer into her voice. "And I'll call as soon as I get there."

Jean's mother stood on the porch, her arms wrapped around herself as if holding on to the last vestiges of her family's togetherness. As Kay walked towards her for a final goodbye, her mother's resolve crumbled, and she pulled Kay into a tight embrace.

"Be safe, be smart, and remember, you can always come home," Jean whispered, her voice muffled by Kay's shoulder.

Kay hugged her mother tightly, her eyes wet with tears. "I will, Mom. Thank you."

Pulling away, Kay climbed into the car, turning to wave at her parents one last time. As the car pulled away, she didn't look back, not because she didn't care, but because she knew if she did, she might never leave. Part of her felt like she was abandoning her parents at the worst possible time, and the thought weighed heavily on her heart.

The open road stretched before her, an expanse of uncertainty and the promise of new adventures. As the last recognizable landmarks of her hometown disappeared in the rear-view mirror, Kay allowed herself to breathe deeply, feeling an enormous weight lift off her shoulders. She had made a clean, necessary break. She was on her own now, charting a course she alone had chosen. This journey wasn't just geographical; it was an emotional quest. And somewhere along this road, she intended to find a way to mend her broken heart and build a life that was finally her own.

As Kay drove through the rolling hills of Georgia, the sprawling landscapes replaced the familiar skyline of her hometown. The transition was stark. Every mile further north marked another step away from her past life and deeper into an uncharted future.

The scenic beauty of Georgia, with its lush greenery, expansive skies, and majestic mountain ranges, was both breathtaking and daunting.

She rented a small, single-wide trailer for a remarkable $135 per month and was absolutely bursting with pride for her independence, thrilled that this tiny space was entirely her own. Upon arriving at her new home, nestled right on the edge of a quiet, small town, Kay couldn't help but feel a raw mix of excitement and apprehension.

The reality of her new life struck her as she surveyed her surroundings—a far cry from the sleek urban environment she was accustomed to. Instead of the dull roar of traffic, her mornings were now greeted with the distant, gentle mooing of cows from the adjacent pasture. For Kay, who adored cows, this was a peculiar, unexpected form of charm. It certainly wasn't what most people, especially her family, would call comfortable; she could practically hear her mother's horrified gasp if she saw the place. But that didn't matter at all. This simple, inexpensive trailer was her own little haven, and she was fiercely proud of it.

During one of Richard's visits, as they sat on the rickety steps of her trailer, Kay shared her impressions. "Look at this place; I can hear myself think here, away from the city's constant roar."

Richard chuckled, handing her a steaming cup of coffee. "It's a different world, isn't it? Takes a bit of getting used to, but there's beauty in the quiet.

Kay nodded, her eyes scanning the horizon. "It's beautiful indeed. And so... open. It's just a lot to take in all at once."

Adjusting to rural life involved more than just appreciating the peaceful setting. Financial independence was a pressing challenge. Back home, Kay had never worried about money, sheltered by her parents' provisions. Here, she found herself juggling two jobs to make ends meet. Mornings were spent serving breakfast at a local diner in Alabama, just over the state line, and evenings were spent waiting tables at a pizza place back in Georgia.

The financial strain was palpable, and the reality of her new life began to set in. Kay's days became a blur of early commutes and late nights, her only solace being the brief interactions with locals who appreciated her warm smile and quick service. The tips were modest, often just enough to cover her monthly rent and utilities and leave a little left over for groceries.

Living conditions in the trailer were Spartan. The small space was heated by an old kerosene heater, which Kay only ran when she absolutely couldn't bear the chill any longer. Nights were spent curled under multiple blankets, sometimes still in her day clothes to keep warm.

"I never thought I'd find joy in thrift shopping, but here I am, picking out blankets and kitchen utensils from yard sales," she mused aloud one evening to Richard, who had stopped by after his volunteer EMS shift.

Richard, ever the pragmatist, smiled and gently took her hand, his thumb brushing her knuckles. "It's about making a home, Kay. It doesn't matter how small or how rustic it is. The important thing is, it's yours, and it's a start."

He squeezed her hand. "You're living on your own, and that's a huge step. You know, I'm older than you and still have to live at home with my mama and my siblings. She'd never, ever allow me to live with a girl before we were married. So trust me, this is a real accomplishment. It's independence."

Despite the hardships, life was simple in Georgia, and this appealed to Kay. The community was close-knit, and she gradually found herself forming friendships with neighbors and co-workers. The slower pace of life began to heal her in ways she hadn't anticipated.

The challenges of her new lifestyle were daunting, but Richard's presence brought a sense of comfort and belonging that eased her transition. Their relationship grew deeper with each passing day.

One brisk evening, while sharing a modest dinner at the local diner, Richard teased her with a warm chuckle, "You sure you're ready for this country life?" His eyes twinkled with amusement and affection.

Kay, stirring her coffee, smiled back at him, a genuine smile that reached her eyes. "I think I'm more than ready," she replied, her voice carrying a lightness that had been absent before her move. "I'm starting to love this life, the peace it brings, and having you here makes it all worthwhile."

Their evenings were often spent in conversation under the starlit sky, the quiet of the countryside enveloping them in an almost magical calm. During these talks, Richard would share stories of his childhood, of growing up in the area, horses, and the adventures he and his friends had embarked upon. Kay listened intently, her laughter mingling with the crickets' chirping, as she began to weave herself into the fabric of these tales.

One night, as they sat watching the stars from the back of Richard's pickup truck, he reached for her hand, his touch gentle. "You know, I never thought I'd meet someone who'd make me look at these old stars differently," he mused, his gaze fixed on the heavens.

Kay squeezed his hand, her heart full. "And I never thought I'd find so much happiness in such a quiet place," she confessed. The stars above seemed to nod in approval, their twinkling light reflecting the brightness growing inside her.

As summer's warmth gave way to the sharp, biting cold of winter, the challenges of Kay's new life did not wane. Financial strains continued, and the chill brought new difficulties to her modest living conditions. However, the hardship only served to draw Richard and Kay closer. He would often come over with hot leftovers from his mom or a thick blanket he had scrounged up, each caring gesture burrowing him deeper into her life.

During a particularly cold spell, when Kay's kerosene heater wouldn't light, Richard spent hours trying to fix it, his breath visible in the frigid air of her trailer. As he worked, Kay quickly made hot chocolate in the microwave. The simple warmth of the drink was a reflection of the deep gratitude she felt, which seemed to simmer just beneath the surface. When he finally got the heater running, his face lit up with triumph. "There we go, just a little southern engineering," he joked, wiping his hands on a rag.

"That's my hero," Kay laughed, handing him a mug of hot chocolate. Their eyes met, and in that simple exchange, there was an acknowledgment of something more profound than either had expected to find in the other.

"Kay, I know life here isn't easy, and I know it's a far cry from everything you've known. But I want you to know that as long as you want me here, I'm here for you. We're in this together."

"I wouldn't have it any other way," she affirmed, her voice steady and sure.

4

The Ring and the Reckoning

Kay was slowly but surely constructing a new life, a life that, despite its challenges, felt like exactly where she was meant to be. For the first time since the tragedy, she felt a genuine, quiet sense of hope for her own future.

That fragile sense of stability was shattered without warning. The devastating truth arrived in a phone call from her mother, whose voice was barely recognizable through the tears. The news was horrific: her father had recently been admitted to a mental hospital after attempting suicide. The immense and unaddressed grief and pain over Brandon's death, compounded by the crushing reality of Kay leaving home for her own life, brought their private struggles to a head. This emotional strain, combined with the profound loneliness and crippling financial burdens, had simply exposed the deep cracks of their underlying marital issues, proving to be too much for their foundation to bear. Kay's mother and her older sister were now frantic, her family was facing total collapse, and they needed Kay to come home immediately.

Evidently, Kay's parents had been grappling with deep issues that no one knew about, masters at hiding the cracks in their foundation from their children. Only a year prior, they had celebrated their thirtieth wedding anniversary, an outward display of commitment that masked their intense, private struggle to heal and save their marriage. Now, the sudden vacuum left by Brandon's death, compounded by Kay's departure for Georgia, proved catastrophic. The house was finally and completely empty of children—a threshold Walter could not cross. He had always vowed never to leave his wife as long as the children were home, and with that tether gone, the loss of control, amplified by unresolved grief and pain, sent him spiraling.

The decision was clear: Kay had to go home, but she couldn't face the crisis alone. She immediately requested that Richard go with her, reasoning that this devastating situation presented the only chance for her family to finally meet him. Though Kay was still uncertain of the full extent of the damage at home, she desperately wanted Richard by her side as a source of stability. By the time their long drive ended in Florida, the situation was already changing: Walter was out of the hospital but had separated from Kay's mother, signaling that the marital trauma was real and severe.

Upon their arrival, Kay's mother, Jean, poured out the events of the past agonizing months. She confessed to Kay that she had seen this coming—the signs of Walter's collapse, the cracks in the foundation—but felt powerless to stop it. With all the children gone, the house had become a cemetery: utterly quiet, empty of Brandon's noise and Kay's laughter. Her life had devolved into a grim, monotonous cycle: just the relentless demands of work, tending to her patients, and passing endless days that felt all the same, saturated only with sadness and the need to keep moving. The emotional vacuum created by the loss and the departure of her children was simply too profound to bear.

Since Walter's sudden departure, Holly had stepped up to shoulder the immense burden of the family business, running it in a desperate attempt to keep things afloat. Her devotion was immediate, but the sacrifice was enormous: Holly had a demanding family of her own, including a husband who worked over 60 hours a week and three young children, two of whom were twins. She was already stretched thin, and taking on the full weight of her parents' business meant pushing herself to a breaking point, prioritizing her family's survival over her own well-being.

Kay's mind immediately spiraled into a torment of guilt and suspicion. She questioned their motives: had they laid bare the full extent of their devastating crisis—the suicide attempt, the separation—simply as a desperate tactic to force her to come back home? The thought was painful, but she knew she couldn't go backwards. As much as she was struggling financially and still had mountains to climb in terms of independence, things were finally going well for her: she was enjoying the process of figuring out life, embracing the struggle, and building a new relationship. To return now, under the weight of their family's collapse, would be to undo all the vital progress she had fought so hard to make.

Kay and Richard were given the spare room, but the temporary accommodation did little to ease Richard's mounting anxiety. The house was huge and undeniably fancy—a museum of wealth worlds away from the small trailer and the familiar mountain homes he knew. The sheer scale and polished elegance of the environment made him instantly nervous and feel profoundly out of place. He was convinced her parents disliked him; he was a blue-collar guy, a volunteer EMT, not the "polished and educated" professional they had surely envisioned for their daughter. This tension wasn't lost on Kay, who worried that Richard was indeed too country for her sophisticated family, highlighting the vast cultural and social gap between their two worlds.

Later that evening, after being introduced to Walter and Jean, Richard pulled Kay aside, his voice low.

"This place is somethin' else, Kay," Richard muttered, glancing toward the sweeping staircase.

Kay squeezed his arm, trying to soothe his nerves. "It's just a house, Rich. Try not to worry."

"No, it ain't *just* a house. Look at me—I'm wearing my second-best button-down. Your mama probably thinks I track mud inside. I told you, I'm not who they expected."

"Don't be ridiculous. They're dealing with a lot right now. It has nothing to do with you," Kay insisted, though a knot of worry tightened in her own stomach.

Despite Richard's discomfort, Kay managed to steal time alone with her parents. To her surprise, they appeared outwardly "fine" and composed. They explained their separation as a necessary step, focused on therapy to heal the marriage, a measured response that made Kay wonder if the crisis call had been dramatically overblown. Had everyone made a bigger deal out of this than the reality warranted? Her father, Walter, even dismissed the devastating suicide attempt with shocking casualness.

"You don't need to worry, honey," Walter said, waving a hand dismissively. "I had a rough patch. Grief just took over, and I made a mistake. I didn't mean to try and kill myself; it was a lapse. I'm fine now. We're getting help. You should focus on your own life."

Kay frowned. "A lapse? Dad, Holly said you were—"

"I said I'm fine, Kay. We're fine. Now, tell me more about your new house. Is it really next to cows?"

This composed front, however, felt fragile and unconvincing; his quick dismissal of his own life-and-death trauma only made the air feel thinner. The simmering tension and forced normalcy exploded on the last night of their trip. Kay and Richard joined her parents for what was meant to be a nice, cordial farewell dinner at a quiet restaurant. The evening was going smoothly, the food was good, and the conversation was meticulously neutral. But the pretense of calm shattered as the waiter cleared their dessert plates.

Richard reached into his pocket, his movements slow and deliberate. He looked at Walter and Jean, then turned his focus entirely to Kay.

"Kay, look, I know this ain't the best time or the best place, and I'm about the furthest thing from the kind of man your folks probably dreamed of for you," he began, his voice surprisingly steady. He pulled out a small box, opening it to reveal a simple, delicate ring. "Kay," Richard began, his voice thick with emotion, "these past few months with you have been the happiest of my life. You make me laugh, you challenge me, and you make me want to be a better man."

He paused, then asked, simply: "Will you marry me?"

The sound of silverware dropping onto a plate echoed the sudden, heavy silence. Walter and Jean were visibly shocked, staring wide-eyed at the small diamond. The unexpected question annihilated any attempt at healing and control the family had managed to construct.

She looked at her father, then at her mother, seeing the fear in their eyes. She looked back at Richard, whose face was open, earnest, and completely terrified.

"Yes," Kay said, her voice shaking but firm. She smiled and reached for Richard's hand, the gesture a declaration of war against the family's expectations. "I will marry you."

Kay was caught between her love for Richard and her desire for her parents' approval, and she felt a knot of worry tighten in her stomach.

Her parents offered smiles that were strained and brittle. Kay, completely oblivious, saw only approval and basked in the warmth of the moment, missing the profound undercurrent of worry that swirled beneath their embrace.

Later that night, Kay, still buzzing from the whirlwind of Richard's proposal, sat curled up on the couch of their room with a mug of chamomile tea. The ring, a simple band with a sparkling diamond, felt impossibly heavy on her finger.

A soft knock at the door startled her. "Come in," she called, a smile playing on her lips.

The door creaked open, revealing Jean. Her eyes held a mix of worry and a forced smile. Walter lingered behind in the doorway. Jean closed the door gently and sat beside Kay on the couch.

"Honey," Jean began, her voice barely a whisper. "Can we talk?"

Kay sensed the shift in the atmosphere, the unspoken questions hanging heavy in the air. "Of course, Mom. What's wrong?"

Jean took a deep breath, her hands twisting in her lap. "Richard's proposal... it was wonderful seeing you so happy. But sweetheart, it all happened so fast." Tears welled up in her eyes, threatening to spill over. "Are you sure this is what you want? Are you sure about him? You are just 18." As she spoke, the weight of her young age added depth to her concerns.

Kay reached for her mother's hand, her own heart clenching. "Mom, I love him. I can't imagine my life without him."

Jean squeezed Kay's hand tightly, a single tear tracing a path down her cheek. "I know, honey. You're young, and love can be blinding sometimes. "But Richard... his lifestyle is so different from ours, Kay. You barely know him—you've been dating for less than six months! We just worry that you're throwing your life into this. You truly come from two very different worlds."

Kay listened, her smile fading. The weight of their concerns settled on her chest, a dark counterpoint to the joy of her engagement. "I understand," she said softly. "I really do. But you have to trust me. I know what I feel for Richard. It's real."

***

The news of their engagement brought a flood of congratulations, particularly from Kay's parents. The timing was bittersweet, as they had recently filed for divorce, but they were genuinely happy for Kay and Richard, viewing her happiness as a much-needed silver lining. However, the tone of the engagement quickly shifted as wedding planning commenced. Richard's mother, Mrs. James, immediately took the reins, insisting on a traditional church wedding where all decisions were tightly controlled to align with her strict Southern Baptist traditions.

Kay quickly learned that Mrs. James had very specific, unyielding ideas about how the wedding should be conducted. More than just vision, Mrs. James possessed the local authority to execute it, as she knew everyone in town and exactly who could do what, and for what cost. Making it instantly clear that the wedding was proceeding according to her plan and budget.

Kay, who was too soft-spoken to argue or plead her own wishes, felt a familiar wave of despair. She desperately wanted to be accepted by Richard's family. Kay often felt like a profound outsider, constantly aware of her status as the "city girl" who could observe their world but never fully belong to it.

Richard's mother was a strong Southern woman, deeply rooted in her Southern Baptist beliefs, dictating even how boys should behave with girls. Richard, the textbook definition of a "mama's boy," rarely opposed her. The planning of the wedding was no different—Mrs. Anderson picked the church, the dress, the food, and even the cake. Everything was aligned with her preferences, and Kay, eager to please and gain acceptance, complied with every choice.

As Mrs. Anderson orchestrated the details, Kay did her best to integrate herself into Richard's family. She attended church with Mrs. James, accompanied her to doctor's appointments, and invested herself in household duties—cooking, cleaning, and always ready to lend a hand. Her efforts, however, were met with a passive-aggressive demeanor from Richard's family. Richard revealed the unsettling truth to Kay that his family was just pleasant to her face, but their true feelings were often whispered behind closed doors.

The weeks rolled on, and Kay felt increasingly like an outsider slowly assimilated into a culture with unwritten rules that no one had explained to her. She struggled to voice her feelings to Richard, not wanting to deepen the rift that seemed to be growing between him and his mother.

Richard, however, quickly noticed Kay's growing quietness. One evening, he broached the subject. "You've been quiet lately. Is everything okay?"

Kay took a deep breath, the cool night air calming her nerves. "It's just... your mom has taken over the whole wedding planning. I appreciate her enthusiasm, but I sometimes feel like it's more about her than about us."

Richard listened, his face shadowed in the moonlight. " I got caught up trying to keep the peace and make Mama happy—since this is such a big deal for her.

Let's just go with the flow, smile, and nod our heads. After the wedding is over, we can do whatever we want afterwards. We'll be married, and we can build our life exactly the way we want it."

The process was not without its difficulties, but it taught Kay and Richard an invaluable lesson about balancing familial expectations with their own needs and desires, forging a partnership that was stronger for its trials.

As the February wedding date drew nearer, the starkly differing backgrounds of the two families became Kay's central source of anxiety. Kay was operating in a desperate balancing act from her small trailer, while Richard remained at home with his mother. Her family's arrival from Florida would force a collision of two entirely separate worlds. Richard's side was a large, stable community anchored by his mother, Mrs. James, who was happily running the entire show, supported by all his siblings and the watchful eyes of their local church congregation.

Kay's contingent, however, was a portrait of modern chaos: her newly divorced parents were coming, each bringing their new relationship partners. Adding to the drama was her sister, Holly, with her three small children.

The tension escalated immediately. Kay's mother, Jean, called with a rigid ultimatum that left Kay speechless.

"You tell your father this, Kay," Jean insisted, her voice tight with years of resentment. "I absolutely refuse to be in any of the pictures or attend the ceremony if that woman—his *date*—is there."

Before Kay could respond, her father, Walter, called with his own retaliatory demand. "If your mother brings her boyfriend, then I won't walk you down the aisle. I mean it, Kay. She has to choose: him or me."

This was Kay's worst nightmare: a spectacular, public display of dysfunction—a nightmare about to happen—right in front of the traditional, judgmental James family. The shame was crushing. The only frantic thought screaming in her head was, *How on earth could she possibly orchestrate this disaster and make her own family appear remotely sane to her almost new in-laws?*

Later, sitting on the porch of her trailer, Kay tried to relay the crisis to a sympathetic but pragmatic Richard.

"I don't know what to do," Kay whispered, burying her face in her hands. "They're going to ruin everything. Your family is going to think my family is completely insane."

Richard pulled her close. "Hey. Look at me. Your family *is* insane. Mine isn't far behind. Don't worry about what Mama thinks. She's busy making sure the preacher has enough hymn books."

He sighed, understanding the severity of the logistics. "We'll just have to deal with it. We'll keep them separated. We'll smile and nod, and remember: it's just a show. It's only one day, and then you're my wife. They can fight all they want back in Florida."

Despite the chaotic family dynamics and the cultural differences, the wedding day dawned clear and bright, a perfect reflection of the new beginning it symbolized for Kay. After much delicate negotiation, Kay and Richard had miraculously been able to talk both her parents into attending the ceremony with their significant others. The quaint church in the heart of the small Alabama town was adorned with homemade floral arrangements, a beautiful compromise between Richard's family tradition and a touch of Kay's personal style.

The church was filled with the soft murmurs of family and friends, a blend of Richard's local community and Kay's family who had traveled from afar, bringing together two distinctly different worlds in celebration of the couple's union. In a moment of moving, unified grace, Kay's father walked both her mother and her down the aisle before standing back to take his place. Richard stood at the altar, his eyes bright with anticipation as he watched Kay arrive.

As Kay approached Richard, her heart swelled with a mixture of nerves and joy, the weight of her past struggles blending into the excitement of stepping into a future she had chosen. Yet, in the back of her mind, a relentless and nagging question gnawed at her newfound certainty: Am I truly making the right decision? The fear was amplified by her parents' warnings: Are they right? Are Richard and I too different? The cultural chasm between the city life and his traditions felt enormous. Can I actually fit into this life with him, or am I just trading one kind of confinement for another? Are we going to make it, or am I setting us both up for failure? The weight of the diamond felt heavy, and the final, terrifying question eclipsed all others: Should I really get married right now, when my own life is still such a mess?

Standing before Richard, Kay took a deep breath as she prepared to recite her vows, her voice steady but filled with emotion. "I take you, Richard, to be my lawfully wedded husband," she declared, her eyes locking with Richard's. "I promise to be faithful to you, and to cherish you, from this day forward, for better, for worse, for richer, for poorer, in sickness and in health. I will love and honor you all the days of my life.

Richard took Kay's hands, his voice carrying the deep conviction of a man rooted in his promises. "I promise to be faithful to you, and to cherish you, from this day forward, for better, for worse, for richer, for poorer, in sickness and in health. I will love and honor you all the days of my life.

As they kissed and exchanged rings, the congregation erupted into soft applause, the air charged with a sense of communal joy and celebration. The reception that followed was a quiet, heartfelt gathering. Finger foods and a beautifully decorated cake graced the table, a small reception for the closest family and friends. Though there was no music or dancing within the church walls, a sense of joyful intimacy permeated the space. It was a short yet deeply meaningful celebration that left everyone with fond memories.

The cultural differences boiled over during the reception. Several of Richard's guests offered light-hearted but clearly pointed comments about Kay's mother, Jean, who wore a fur coat against the February chill. For the local crowd, who were dressed in their practical Sunday best, the coat was instantly read as an over-the-top, extravagant sign of big-city snobbery. The jokes and murmurs stung Kay deeply; she understood they weren't just laughing at the coat, but at their entire lifestyle it represented. She felt a profound wave of discomfort and shame as her mother became the object of their quiet amusement.

The wedding day concluded with a simple, relaxed spaghetti dinner hosted back at their new home. Kay and Richard were thrilled to move in together immediately after the ceremony, a dream made possible by Richard's quick thinking. He had managed to secure a land contract on a nearly-new double-wide trailer situated directly across the street from his mother's house. The trailer, though technically new, had suffered minor damage in a fire; after repairs, the owner was eager to sell, offering the favorable contract terms Richard accepted. This unassuming, fire-repaired double-wide was the simple, solid foundation for their new, independent life together.

As she cooked and mingled, Kay's thoughts drifted to the journey that had brought her here. The loss of Brandon, the painful departure from her parents, and the challenges of adapting to a new life all seemed both distant and intimately close in this moment of triumph. Each hardship had carved a part of her path, shaping her into the woman she now was.

As the evening wound down, Kay and Richard stole a moment for themselves outside under the starry sky. They sat close together on the makeshift stairs—a grouping of rough cinder blocks that served as a humble, temporary replacement for a front porch. The cool night air was a welcome breath of refreshment, a gentle pause in the whirl of wedding activities.

Look at us," Kay whispered, settling her head against Richard's shoulder. She let out a long, shaky breath of pure relief. "I honestly can't believe we made it through this month. My parents didn't kill each other; no one died or got hurt. It's amazing that we're sitting here right now."

Richard laughed, giving her a gentle shove back toward her side of the cinder blocks. "Life is unpredictable."

The wedding day finally concluded with laughter, warm wishes, and heartfelt goodbyes as both families departed, leaving a profound quiet behind. Kay and Richard were finally alone to prepare for their new life together. As Kay lay beside Richard in their modest, fire-repaired home, her mind teemed with vivid, hopeful dreams of the future. Yet, beneath the calm, the anxiety still pulsed: she couldn't shake the persistent worry that she had made the wrong choice. It felt as though every path she chose, every step toward happiness, only caused chaos to erupt elsewhere, and she remained completely unaware of the next wave of unraveling that lay ahead.

5

The Weight of Two Lives

The first golden light of a late spring morning was filtering through the curtains of the bedroom window, yet Kay was already dressed, a textbook balanced on her knee while the coffee machine sputtered its wake-up call in the kitchen. She looked from the neatly highlighted page on math to the crumpled pile of Richard's work clothes on the floor beside the bed. Just three months married, and already she felt the heavy, complex weight of a life being built—or perhaps, *forced*—together.

The knot in her stomach tightened. Two jobs, a newly shared life, and the ever-present, grinding knowledge that she was still missing her high school diploma. It was a phantom limb of inadequacy she couldn't ignore. *Two jobs for this?* she'd asked herself a thousand times, scrubbing a grease stain she knew Richard wouldn't even see. *I have to do better.*

"The application says classes run four hours a day, Monday through Friday," she announced over a dinner of her mother-in-law's famous, labor-intensive Smothered Fried Pork Chops and Gravy—a recipe she'd finally, after several failed attempts, managed to replicate to Richard's exacting standards.

Richard grunted, "For what? You gonna be a teacher now?"

Kay set her fork down, the clatter sharp in the quiet kitchen. "It's for the GED program, Rich. If I pass, I can get a better job. I can quit the diner and just work the retail gig until I figure out the next step. One job, Rich. Think about that."

His eyes narrowed. "You think some diploma is gonna magically land you a corner office? Look, you're a smart girl. But we're fine. I'm working overtime at the foundry. Plenty of money coming in."

She pressed her lips together, swallowing the bitter taste of his indifference. *We're not fine,* she wanted to shout, gesturing vaguely at the socks migrating from the hamper to the rug and the toothpaste crusting the bathroom sink. *I need to be more than just a wife waiting for you to get home.*

Despite the friction, Kay enrolled. For one solid, determined month, she disappeared into her books and the small, brightly lit classroom. When she finally walked out of the testing center, the results slip clutched tight in her sweaty hand, a wave of pure, triumphant relief washed over her.

She waited until Richard was home, until he'd had time to relax after a long shift. "I passed," she said, her voice trembling slightly with suppressed excitement. "The GED. I did it, Rich!"

He was already changing his clothes to head out to the firehall, lacing up his boots. "That's good, Kay. Didn't doubt you for a second," he said, without looking up. "The siren just went off, I gotta run. Dinner was good, though." And he was gone, the door slapping shut behind him, leaving Kay standing alone in the hallway, the feeling of pride evaporating like steam.

A few weeks later, Kay was on the road, commuting an hour to Northeast Alabama Community College in Scottsboro. She'd found a cost-effective program: Business Administration. It felt like a fresh start, a real pathway.

The classes were challenging, but Kay was a natural. The professors saw it immediately. She was meticulous, driven, and she absorbed concepts like a sponge. Her first semester was a blur of late nights and early mornings, culminating in a gleaming 4.0 GPA with Honors.

"My professor asked me to mentor three other students for the final project, Rich," she beamed one evening, peeling off her sweater after a particularly productive day. "He said my work on the market analysis was 'exemplary.' He actually used that word! *Exemplary.*"

Richard was slumped on the couch, flipping channels. He didn't look away from the TV. "Yeah, well, it's just a community college, Kay. I bet all those kids are just goofing off. Nothing hard about it, really."

The backhanded compliment stung more than outright criticism. His words were a cool, damp cloth pressed against her enthusiasm. Why couldn't he just be happy for her? Why did her success seem to shrink him?

Meanwhile, the dynamic at home was a constant tug-of-war. Kay's need for order clashed daily with Richard's ingrained messiness. She was constantly picking up after him, feeling less like a wife and more like a live-in maid.

The arrival of Richard's mother didn't help. She was a woman who arrived unannounced, assessing the state of the home with a sharp, critical eye.

"Kay, dear, you're not using Tide again, are you?" his mother asked, her voice dripping with disappointed concern, holding up one of Richard's t-shirts. "Richard's skin is sensitive. It's the only acceptable soap, you know. I can just take his things home with me. I don't mind. I'll drop them back tomorrow."

Kay, exhausted from studying and her evening job, simply nodded, too tired to argue that the store-brand detergent was all they could afford right now. The invasion of her domestic space, the subtle implication that she was failing as a caregiver, was demoralizing.

And then there was dinner. Kay, following the example of her own mother, who had lovingly *served* her father, tried to embody the ideal wife. This meant sacrificing sleep. At 1:00 a.m., her alarm would jolt her awake, and she would drag herself out of bed to stand at the stove.

Richard refused to eat "out of a box"—everything had to be fresh, hot, and cooked from scratch, a perfect replica of his mother's cooking. She was creating a demanding expectation, a self-imposed prison of service in the hopes of earning his love and praise.

One rainy Saturday, the tension that had been building like a slow pressure cooker finally blew.

Kay was meticulously organizing her closet, sorting through the shoes she had collected over the years. They weren't designer, but they were *hers*. Each pair—the brightly colored pumps, the delicate sandals, and yes, the many pairs of high-heeled shoes—represented a small, personal joy.

Richard stormed into the room, tossing a magazine onto the bed. "What is all this *crap*?" he demanded, kicking a shoe rack. "Look at all this stuff! The makeup, the lotions, these goddamn shoes!" He snatched a black stiletto and tossed it across the room. "We live in the country, Kay! Who are you dressing up for? You don't need all this. Get rid of it."

Kay's jaw tightened. "They are *my* things, Richard. I don't go through your hunting gear or your fire uniforms and tell you what to keep. I like looking nice. It makes me feel good."

"You want to look nice for someone else, huh?" he sneered, stepping closer, his face inches from hers. "You think you're too good for me and this house now that you're going to that little school?"

The argument escalated quickly, fueled by weeks of unspoken resentment and stress. Richard, his face red with anger, grabbed her arm. "I said, throw the damn shoes away! You have no use for them!"

When she instinctively pulled back, he shoved her. Hard.

Kay stumbled backward over the edge of the rug and crashed down onto the wooden floor of the bedroom.

She looked up at him, stunned, the air knocked out of her lungs. He was towering over her, his breathing ragged, his face a mask of rage and cold fury. It wasn't the force of the fall, but the sudden, horrifying *realization* of what had just happened that made her gasp.

Tears sprang to her eyes, blurring the outlines of the room. She scrambled to her feet, heart hammering against her ribs, a primal fear seizing her.

"I'm leaving," she choked out, grabbing a worn suitcase from the top shelf of the closet. "I'm not doing this. This is bullshit." She shoved clothes and papers into the bag haphazardly, her hands shaking violently.

She wrestled the overstuffed suitcase out the front door, her feet thudding down the long, dirt driveway. She didn't stop until she reached the asphalt county road.

She stood there, small and alone in the encompassing, suffocating country darkness. The nearest gas station was less than a mile, a tiny beacon of light in the distance, but the road was a pitch-black ribbon, silent and menacing. *What if I walk there? What if I call someone?*

What would I even say?

He shoved me over a pair of shoes.

A cold wave of paralyzing shame washed over her. *Am I a baby? Was I being unreasonable? Is this my fault?* The questions echoed, hollow and accusatory, in her mind.

After several agonizing minutes, shivering in the cool night air, she turned. The path back to the house, to the cold, quiet anger waiting inside, felt infinitely less terrifying than the dark, unknown road ahead.

When she walked back in, Richard was already retreating, his initial rage replaced by a hollow exhaustion. "I'm sorry, Kay," he mumbled, refusing to meet her eyes. "I'm just working long hours. So tired. I didn't mean to push you."

The apology felt like another insult. He seemed perpetually stressed, short-tempered, and distant.

Kay went to the bathroom, splashed cold water on her face, and looked at her reflection. She wanted, more than anything, a reason to be happy again. They had talked about children when they were dating; they had been trying for months. Now, more than ever, she felt a profound, aching loneliness. She wanted a baby. A piece of herself, a small, innocent life to focus on. Anything to fill the cavernous space where she thought her marriage should be.

She never told anyone. Not her mother. When she called home, she kept her voice light, talking about her 4.0 and her plans for a career. The only truth she allowed herself was the terrifying, sinking realization: *Did I make a massive mistake getting married?*

6

A Visitor's Gaze

It wasn't more than a few months after Richard and Kay's sharp, brutal fight—the one where the air finally curdled between them—that she was pregnant.

Kay had been ecstatic, dizzy with it. She clung to the hope like a life raft, certain that a baby would conjure the old Richard back into existence, the one who was present, who *saw* her. Surely, a child would melt the ice around the man who was now just a hollow, distant, cold stranger haunting their home. She couldn't wait to tell everyone, to dive into baby shopping, planning the nursery, and imagining the future, a future she was determined to make warm.

The initial shared joy from both families was a brief, welcome balm, and Kay took meticulous care of herself and the little life growing inside. But the distance was already setting in. Her bulging belly was a constant reminder of the changes she was facing almost alone. Richard's work schedule was the convenient, always-ready excuse for her solo trips to the OBGYN. And the baby shower? That was firmly in the hands of Richard's mother, who, with her typical flair for command, once again ran the show like she had with the wedding.

Then there was the name. Lucas. Kay had a softer, more classic name in mind, something that felt like a quiet blessing, but Richard demanded the name Lucas. He insisted. She gave in. She was already so utterly in love with this baby—her son, Lucas—before she'd even met him, and that love was her sole source of strength.

The financial collapse happened mid-pregnancy. They lost the double-wide, the home that was meant to be their beginning, because they couldn't meet the land contract payments Richard had secured. Now, they were crammed into a rented single-wide trailer a few miles down the road. The move was humiliating, a physical manifestation of the failure that Kay feared Richard laid entirely at her feet. She could feel his resentment: she was finishing her Business Administration program and wasn't pulling in a second income.

"I know, Richard, I know," she'd pleaded, her hands resting protectively on her stomach. "I'm almost done. Just six more weeks. I'm pregnant, yes, but I'll finish and I'll keep working, I promise."

And she did. She took classes, held down her job, reorganized their meager belongings in the small trailer, cooked fresh meals for him late at night, and set up a small nursery in the back bedroom. She even ran errands for his mother, taking her to appointments without a word of complaint. Every night, after the chores were done and the small trailer was finally silent, she studied by the dim light of a kitchen lamp. Money was impossibly tight—no cable TV, no home telephone. Her twice-monthly call to her own family was a logistical effort, a prepaid calling card held close to her ear in the humid air of a pay phone.

The stress was a physical weight. Richard's overtime had dried up, which only tightened the financial noose and ratcheted up the tension. Every small request from Kay—mow the lawn, fix the loose porch stair, take out the overflowing trash—was met with a sneer or a passive refusal. The less he worked, the more time he spent at the firehall, retreating from the burdens of home.

Kay was six months pregnant when the news arrived: her older sister, Holly, and her husband were driving up from Florida for a visit.

A wave of intense, desperate insecurity washed over her. She suddenly saw the rented trailer through her sister's eyes: the chipped linoleum, the cramped rooms, the raw, uncut weeds in the yard. The loss of the double-wide was a ghost she couldn't stand to have her family witness. She needed the trailer to look immaculate, to project an image of control and normalcy she no longer felt.

On Thursday night, as Richard sat slouched on the couch, flipping through a fire magazine, she tried to use her softest, most appealing voice.

"Honey? Holly and Frank will be here late tomorrow afternoon," Kay began, rubbing the small of her back. "Could you please, please, mow the yard tomorrow? I really want the place to look nice for them."

Richard sighed loudly and didn't look up. "It's fine. It's barely grown out. Stop worrying about it."

"It's not barely grown out, Richard, it's looking rough out there. And the ditch by the road is a jungle. Please. I've been studying all day, and I have a shift in the morning."

He finally tossed the magazine onto the worn carpet. He didn't just look at her—he measured her. His eyes were flat, dull.

"You know what your problem is, Kay?" His voice was low and clipped. "You're always trying to impress people. You care more about what your fancy sister thinks than you do about me."

"That is not fair," she whispered, stung. "I just want them to feel comfortable."

"The hell you do. I'll do it when I have time. Now I'm going to the firehall, I have a meeting. The grass can wait." He grabbed his keys and wallet from the counter.

"Richard, you have plenty of time. It takes an hour. Please. They're coming tomorrow, it needs to be done!"

He walked out and slammed the metal trailer door behind him. Kay flinched, feeling the vibrations travel up her feet.

She woke up on Friday morning to an empty house. Her sister would be here later in the day. Richard was still gone. Kay fought back the tide of tears—she wouldn't cry, she wouldn't give in.

She pulled on a pair of oversized shorts and an old t-shirt. She went to the small storage shed, dragged out the heavy, balky push mower, and pulled the stubborn starter cord until her shoulder screamed.

Kay, heavy with pregnancy, started pushing. The yard wasn't large, but it was uneven, and every push was a struggle that taxed her aching hips and strained her lungs. Then she got to the ditch. It was a steep, grassy bank that sloped down to the front yard. She had to brace her hip against the slope to keep the balky machine from rolling back, her breath coming in shallow, desperate gasps. Her shoulder screamed with every pull. The roar of the mower was a desperate soundtrack to her misery.

She was out there for nearly two hours, pushing, pulling, wiping sweat and tears, determined to finish what she had begged him to do. The roar of the mower was a desperate soundtrack to her misery.

Around three o'clock, the sound of a large engine made her look up. Her neighbor, an older man named Ted, was driving his riding mower out of his garage. He slowed down, killed the engine, and stared at her.

He swung off the seat and walked over. "Kay, honey, what are you doing?"

She stood stock-still, mortified, hot tears finally spilling over. "The... the grass," she managed, waving a shaky hand at the steep ditch. "I can't get this part."

"You're pregnant," Ted stated, his voice devoid of judgment, heavy with concern. "You shouldn't be out here. You'll hurt yourself and the baby." He paused, looking down the road toward Richard's truck, which was nowhere in sight. "Go inside. I'll bring the tractor over and knock this ditch out for you. No charge."

Kay could only nod, a hiccup catching in her throat as she gave him a weak, grateful smile. "Thank you, Ted. I... I can't tell you how much I appreciate that."

She stumbled back inside the trailer, exhausted, in pain, and utterly defeated. She scrubbed the grass clippings from her face and ran a hot shower.

Richard strolled in around six o'clock, just as Kay was finishing her makeup in the bathroom mirror, trying to erase the stress from her face.

He didn't notice the neat lines of the cut grass, the swept porch, or the way she was holding herself, stiff with fatigue. He didn't even say hello.

"Ted did a nice job on that ditch," he said, heading straight for the fridge.

Kay turned to face him, wiping the mascara from the corner of her eye. "I did the yard, Richard. Ted did the ditch because he saw me struggling and took pity on me. I was out there for three hours."

He pulled out a beer and twisted off the cap, completely unbothered. He didn't look at her.

"You didn't have to do that," he scoffed, taking a long drink. "This wasn't about the house, Kay. It was about Holly. You're always trying to impress people. The yard didn't need to be mowed that badly. It could've waited till next week."

His words, simple and cruel, hit her like a physical blow. Her shoulders slumped.

It didn't matter what she did. He found fault, or he minimized it, downplayed it. It was like nothing she did was right, or worse, she did things for the wrong reason. She was constantly striving, constantly trying to please a man who gave her nothing in return, trying to earn a love he never offered.

"Go take a shower, Richard," she said, her voice completely flat. "Holly and Frank will be here any minute."

Richard paused, turning his empty gaze on her, and gave a careless shrug. "Fine. But don't ask me to do anything else tonight. I'm tired."

Kay closed her eyes, fighting a desperate, silent battle with herself. He may never say it, but I am stronger than the storm, she thought, pressing her hand over the quickening heartbeat of her son. The vow was silent, final. I am stronger than the storm.

The sound of a car crunching on the gravel outside pulled her out of the darkness. Kay smoothed down her shirt, took a breath, and tried to summon the light she needed for her sister.

7

A Growing Threat

With the dawn of each new day, Kay's hope was rekindled by the presence of her baby boy, Lucas. He was more than just her son; as the first male grandchild, he was a beacon of immense pride for the family. In a sea of girls, Lucas's birth was a monumental event, celebrated with fervor by the family and the community alike. To share in this joyous occasion, Kay's sister traveled from Florida to be there for the birth. The little boy, seen as the carrier of the family name, was showered with love and attention from all sides. His arrival was heralded as a new beginning, a promise of continuity and strength that resonated deeply with everyone around him.

Kay's heart overflowed with joy and devotion. Every moment spent with her baby, Lucas, was a balm to her weary soul. She reveled in the simple pleasures of motherhood—rocking him gently, bathing him with tender care, dressing him in the cutest little outfits she could find. Each coo and gurgle Lucas brought light to Kay's eyes, a stark contrast to the darkness she often whispered into at night.

Yet, a shadow remained over this joy. During the birth, Kay's mother, who had always been a source of support, was not there. The requirements of her business kept her away, causing a gap in Kay's heart due to the lack of support during a crucial time. Her mother's words had left her with a blend of comprehension and sadness.

"I'm so sorry, darling," her mother said over the phone, her voice thick with regret. "I desperately wish I could be there, but I simply can't leave. My patients need me right now. I can, however, send you the money so you can come home."

Kay's grip tightened on the phone, her eyes welling up with tears. "I understand, Mom. It's just... I wish you could see him. Lucas is perfect. He has your eyes."

There was a pause on the other end, a moment where the weight of her mother's absence felt even more pronounced. "We'll come as soon as we can, Kay. I promise. I'm proud of you. You're going to be a wonderful mother."

Kay's voice trembled as she responded, "I miss you, Mom. I miss having you here."

"I miss you too, sweetheart. It breaks my heart not to be there with you. But you're strong, and I know you can do this. You have a beautiful son, and he's lucky to have you."

"I hope so," Kay whispered, her heart heavy with the distance between them.

This absence was a silent ache, a bittersweet note in the symphony of her new life. Despite this, Kay's joy remained undiminished. She clung to the moments with her baby, finding solace and strength in his innocence. He was her anchor, her reason to persevere amidst the growing storm. Kay vowed to safeguard Lucas's promising future and to nurture him with all the love and care she could muster, even as Richard's neglect and abuse began to loom large in their lives.

It started off in a subtle but profoundly disturbing manner. From the first night they brought Lucas home, Richard was adamant that the baby should sleep in his crib, separate from their bedroom. Kay felt great emotional pain thinking about being apart from her baby, but Richard was firm in his decision.

"He needs to learn to sleep on his own," Richard stated firmly, dismissing Kay's tears and pleas.

"But he's just a newborn, Richard," Kay pleaded, her voice trembling. "He needs to feel secure and close to us. I need to be able to hear him, to tend to him if he wakes up."

Richard's expression hardened, a flicker of impatience crossing his face. "Kay, you're being overly dramatic. Babies need to learn independence from the start. He's not going to become a healthy, well-adjusted kid if you're coddling him all the time."

Kay's eyes filled with tears as she tried to reason with him. "It's not coddling. It's just... he's so little, Richard. I want to be there for him."

Richard's tone grew sharper, the patience in his voice waning. "You need to stop being so emotional about everything. It's what's best for him. Besides, I need my sleep. I can't be kept up all night by a crying baby."

Kay's heart ached at his words, the dismissive tone stinging more than she expected. "But what about me?" she asked softly. "I'll get up with him. I'll make sure he doesn't disturb you. I just need him close."

Richard shook his head, the finality in his gesture leaving no room for further discussion. "No, Kay. This is how it's going to be. He stays in the crib. End of discussion."

That night, while Kay was unable to sleep, she listened carefully for any sound coming from the nursery, feeling a deep sense of isolation. The crib, originally intended as a secure space for their child, now represented the widening chasm between Kay and Richard. The suffocating silence of the room was a stark contrast to the storm inside her head. Tears soaked her pillow as she lay awake, caught between worry for her baby and the growing tension in her marriage. The only reprieve came when she quietly sneaked into Lucas's room. He had, miraculously, slept all through his first night home, offering her a few hours of grace. Finding solace in his peaceful, rhythmic breathing, she briefly escaped her own turmoil.

The next week, Richard's company went on strike, leaving him without work and throwing the house into significant tension and chaos. As the days dragged on, his true priorities became painfully evident. His commitment to volunteering with the Fire/EMS department took precedence over his duties as a father and a husband.

The incessant noise of the scanners constantly blared in the background, a jarring soundtrack to their crumbling peace and a continual indication of Richard's genuine interest. The static and sudden shouts disrupted Kay, often startling the baby, but Richard seemed oblivious. His focus remained solely on the next call, the next emergency, utterly deaf to the chaos he was creating at home.

One evening, as the scanner blared yet another alert, Kay felt her patience snap. She walked into the living room where Richard sat, eyes glued to the blinking lights and crackling voices. "Can you please turn that thing off for a little while?" Kay asked one evening, her voice strained with fatigue and frustration.

Richard barely looked up. "It's important, Kay. People rely on me."

"But we rely on you too," she whispered, feeling the weight of her words settle into the silence that followed. "Lucas needs you. I need you. You're never here, and when you are, it's like we don't exist."

Richard's eyes flickered with irritation. "Kay, you're being dramatic. This is important to me. You knew this when we got married."

Tears welled up in Kay's eyes, but she fought to keep her voice steady. "I thought I married someone who cared about his family, who would be there for us. But all I see is you running off to every emergency while ignoring the ones right here at home."

Richard sighed, leaning back in his chair. "You don't understand, Kay. This is about helping people."

"And what about helping us?" Kay shot back, her voice breaking. "What about helping our family? You think this is just about a noisy scanner? It's about you being absent, emotionally and physically. Lucas barely knows you, and I feel like a single parent."

Richard's patience was utterly spent, his face growing hard and cold. He took a half-step back, creating distance between them. "Go away, Kay," he ground out, the tone a low, dangerous warning, the word "spat" suggesting the sound was wet and contemptuous. He didn't need to say more; the hostility in his stance filled the rest of the silent room.

Kay's heart ached at his dismissive tone, the gulf between them feeling insurmountable. "I'm not asking for all your time, Richard. I'm asking for some. I'm asking for you to be present to show that you care about us as much as you care about everyone else."

Richard turned his back, the sudden movement a clear dismissal. He gave no sign that he had heard a single word she said.

Later that night, Lucas began gagging and vomiting violently, Kay was immediately alarmed. Richard, for once, met her concern, and they rushed the baby to the ER. Lucas was admitted and quickly diagnosed with Gastroesophageal Reflux Disease (GERD). The diagnosis instantly halted her breastfeeding, which left Kay devastated. Lucas had to be switched immediately to a special hypoallergenic Alimentum formula.

Richard's dedication to his volunteer work negatively impacted their family. Though Kay balanced caring for a newborn and managing the household, Richard was frequently missing, with his thoughts and emotions focused elsewhere. He overlooked important achievements, neglected duties, and abandoned Kay to deal with the difficulties of raising a child by herself. Richard seemed to consider Lucas as an afterthought, despite the immense joy he brought to Kay. His neglect extended beyond just not being physically present to also include an emotional emptiness and a lack of bonding that caused Kay to feel even more alone.

Kay began to cherish the hours Richard was away. When he left, the suffocating tension in the air vanished, replaced by a profound and much-needed peace. In the silence, the house became Kay's sanctuary, allowing her to devote herself completely to Lucas without agitation. She would fill the quiet with music—turning on soft melodies, singing gently to her baby, or taking out her flute. As the clear, melodic notes filled the room, Lucas would often reward her with a bright smile and an irresistible, bubbling laugh.

Richard maintained the facade of being the ideal father. He was always quick to lend a hand, his uniform a symbol of dedication and service. Others would often see him doting on Lucas, cooing and cradling him with what appeared to be genuine affection. It was not uncommon for them to be out in the yard when a neighbor would stop by.

"Richard's such a good dad," Mrs. Olive from next door would comment, watching Richard bounce Lucas gently in his arms.

Richard would smile modestly, glancing down at Lucas with a look of adoration. "Thanks, Mrs. Olive. Lucas is such a joy. I just want to make sure he's happy and well cared for."

Meanwhile, Kay stood nearby, a smile plastered on her face, but inside, she felt a pang of frustration. She knew that this doting father act was for show. She watched as Richard continued his performance, making small talk with the neighbors, basking in their admiration.

"Richard, you're so hands-on. I wish my husband had been like that when our kids were little," Mrs. Olive continued, unaware of the tension simmering beneath the surface.

"Oh, it's nothing," Richard replied, brushing off the compliment with a chuckle. "Lucas is such an easy baby. He makes it all worthwhile."

"He hardly ever cries, and he sleeps through the night." Richard continued. *God forbid he ever give me any compliments on being a good mother,* Kay couldn't help but think with a tinge of bitterness.

The adoration from Richard's family for Lucas was palpable, reinforcing the perfect image Richard so carefully curated. Kay, however, knew the reality behind closed doors. The image of the devoted father was a far cry from the truth. People saw a happy, well-adjusted family, while Kay saw a man who was more concerned with his own image than his family's well-being.

As they walked back into the house, Kay couldn't help but feel the sting of resentment. "It's funny how you always seem to be the perfect dad when someone is watching," she muttered under her breath as Richard closed the door.

"What was that?" Richard asked, his tone suddenly sharp.

"Nothing," Kay replied quickly, knowing better than to provoke him further.

Kay bit her tongue, her heart heavy with the weight of unspoken words. The perfect image Richard presented to the world was nothing more than a carefully constructed facade, hiding the turmoil and distress that plagued their home. The neighbors might see Richard as a devoted father, but Kay knew the truth all too well.

8

The Cold Barrel

Inside, the house felt colder, the walls closing in as the reality of their situation settled over her once more. Richard's behavior was far from perfect when no one was watching. He regularly grumbled about finances, resenting every cent used for Lucas's necessities. "Do you know how much diapers cost?" he would grumble, his frustration spilling over into every conversation.

"Richard, we need to buy diapers. It's not like we have a choice," Kay would reply, trying to keep her voice steady.

"We should be saving money, not wasting it," Richard would snap. "Maybe you should look for cheaper options or try to make them last longer. Do you have any idea how much we're spending on these?"

"I'll see what I can do," Kay would say softly, even though she knew she was already doing everything she could.

Kay was under increased pressure due to Richard's capricious directives as she tried to handle his numerous demands. "Don't rock the baby. He'll get used to it," Richard insisted one night, his voice sharp.

"But he's just a baby, Richard. Sometimes, he needs to be comforted," Kay argued gently, holding Lucas close.

"You're going to spoil him," Richard retorted. "He needs to learn to fall asleep on his own. You're not helping by giving in every time he cries."

Kay's heart sank at his words, but she nodded, feeling trapped between her instincts and Richard's harsh rules.

Richard's grievances extended beyond just financial matters. His stringent, sometimes unreasonable regulations applied to all areas of their lives. He controlled when and how Kay could take care of the baby, criticizing her techniques and eroding her self-assurance. "You're bathing him too often," he snapped one evening as Kay prepared the bath.

"But he enjoys his bath time, and it's good for him," Kay responded, trying to explain.

"He doesn't need a bath every day," Richard countered. "You're wasting water and time. Just because you enjoy it doesn't mean it's necessary."

Kay constantly received criticisms which made her feel inadequate; every attempt she made to take care of their child was closely examined and made to seem unimportant. The palpable distress between them grew, the tension thickening the air in their home. Each of Richard's remarks chipped away at Kay's confidence, leaving her feeling more isolated and overwhelmed with each passing day.

Richard's true self surfaced in the absence of any other individuals. The affectionate father figure vanished, substituted by a man consumed by his own desires and irritations. His once public display of warmth transitioned into a cold demeanor, with affection giving way to indifference and irritation. The contrast in Richard's behavior in public and private settings caused Kay to feel afraid and unsure. She was never sure which side of Richard she would encounter: the affectionate dad, the judgmental, inattentive spouse, or the angry man.

Richard's abusive behavior was subtle but troubling. It began with mild neglect and then escalated to physical violence. Kay had to get a job to support their struggling finances, leaving Lucas in Richard's care. He would leave Lucas unattended for extended periods, prioritizing his own comfort over the child's needs.

With Richard's company on strike, he had been watching Lucas while Kay worked at her new job in Chattanooga. The moment she stepped inside, her eyes locked on the shocking sight of Lucas's swollen, bruised eye.

Kay approached slowly, her heart pounding. "Tell me exactly what happened, Richard."

Richard's response was clipped, laced with impatience. "He fell. We were dozing in the chair, and he slipped. An accident. That's all."

"An *accident*?" she repeated, the word tasting like ash. "He has a black eye. That doesn't happen from a slip, Richard."

He rose suddenly, towering over her. "You know what? I'm sick of this. I was doing you a favor, but now you're going to cross-examine me? You're unbelievable. Stop questioning everything that happens while you're gone."

It was exactly what Kay suspected: he was deliberately trying to start a fight. A manufactured argument gave him the perfect excuse to walk out the door and head straight to the firehall, escaping the tension he created at home for the chaos he craved elsewhere. So many of their arguments now started from nothing, simply to give him that reason to leave.

Richard's neglect of the baby's needs became more blatant. He would fall asleep, leaving Lucas crying in his crib for hours. The neighbor would occasionally stop by, alerted by the persistent cries, only to find the house silent and unresponsive. Kay would come home from work to find Lucas in dirty clothes, a painful rash spreading from prolonged exposure to soiled diapers. The sight broke her heart, each rash and tear a testament to Richard's negligence.

The breaking point came after another violent altercation. It was a cold winter night, and the power had been cut off due to a past-due bill that Richard assured her he would take care of. Kay had wrapped Lucas in layers of blankets to keep him warm, but the cold still seeped into their bones. Richard returned home late, reeking of alcohol and frustration. The argument started over something trivial but quickly escalated. Richard's anger erupted, and he lashed out, knocking over a lamp and sending shards of glass across the floor.

In a fit of rage, he grabbed Lucas from Kay's arms, shaking him roughly. Kay's heart pounded in her chest as she pleaded with him to stop, tears streaming down her face. Richard, his face twisted with anger, accused her of being the reason for all their problems. He hurled Lucas into the crib, and the impact made the baby cry out in pain. Kay rushed to the crib, her hands trembling as she checked for injuries. The sight of her baby's tear-streaked face and the bruise forming on his tiny arm was the final straw.

Richard, not done with his tirade, grabbed Kay by the hair and threw her against the wall. The room spun, and pain shot through her body. As she tried to get up, Richard pulled out a gun and pointed it at her head.

"You're the one ruining everything," he snarled. The cold barrel pressed against her temple, and at that moment, Kay's life flashed before her eyes. She thought of Lucas lying helpless in the crib, and a surge of protective fury gave her the strength to act.

With a burst of adrenaline, she shoved Richard away, causing him to stumble and drop the gun. She grabbed Lucas and ran to the bedroom, locking the door behind her. Her heart raced as she whispered soothing words to calm the baby's cries, her mind already racing to find a way out of this nightmare. She knew she had to escape.

That night, Kay lay awake, formulating a plan. She decided that as soon as Richard left for the Fire Hall, she would take action.

The instant Richard was gone, Kay felt the knot of fear in her chest begin to loosen. She took a deep, shuddering breath of relief and walked quickly to a neighbor's house to use their phone. With trembling hands, she called her mother, finally sharing the terrifying full extent of the abuse and fear she had been secretly enduring. Unable to leave her business, Kay's mother immediately called her father, desperately hoping he could drop everything and travel to Alabama to help.

He didn't hesitate; he cleared his schedule of all commitments and immediately set out. His drive to Alabama was fueled by a fierce, urgent determination to reach his daughter and grandson as quickly as possible.

As Kay quietly packed Lucas's things, the truth of her actions became crystal clear: she was escaping. This was her one, critical opportunity to break free from the nightmare of her marriage. Every memory of a harsh word, every glance at Lucas's bruise, and the relentless pattern of Richard's erratic behavior coalesced into a single, unassailable truth: she had to leave.

As Kay started gathering her baby's belongings, the reality of her situation hit her hard. This was her only chance to escape the nightmare her life had become. Each bruise, each moment of neglect, and every instance of Richard's erratic behavior etched the threat deeper into her consciousness.

Richard was home when Kay's father arrived, and the fury in Richard's eyes was unmistakable. "What the hell do you think you're doing here?" Richard spat, his voice trembling with anger.

"I'm here to take my daughter and my grandson to home," Kay's father replied, his tone steady and resolute.

"You have no right!" Richard shouted, his face red with rage. "This is my family, my home!"

"And you've done nothing but terrorize them," Kay's father shot back. "I won't let you hurt them any longer."

Richard took a step forward, trying to intimidate Kay's father. "You think you can just walk in here and take them from me?"

Kay's father didn't flinch. "Yes, I do. You've crossed the line too many times, Richard. This ends now."

The standoff grew more heated, with Richard's anger boiling over. "Get out of my house!" he screamed, lunging forward. Kay's father stood his ground, his presence unwavering. "You don't scare me, Richard. I've seen men like you before—bullies who think they can control others through fear. Not today."

The baby whimpered softly, sensing the tension in the room. She tried to move quickly, her hands shaking..

"You're not taking my son," Richard growled, trying to push past Kay's father.

"Back off," Kay's father warned, his voice low and dangerous. "Or you'll regret it."

For a moment, it seemed like Richard might escalate further, but then he saw the determination in Kay's father's eyes. Fear flickered across Richard's face as he realized he was outmatched. He stepped back, his rage now mingled with uncertainty.

Kay, cradling the baby in her arms, finally made her way to the door. Her father shielded her from Richard, keeping a watchful eye on his every move.

"We're leaving, Richard," Kay said, her voice shaking but resolute. "And we're not coming back."

Richard glared at her, but he knew he had lost. "You'll regret this," he hissed, but the threat fell flat in the face of Kay's newfound strength.

As they neared the Florida state line, a sense of relief washed over Kay, but it was tinged with an underlying dread. The warmth of her father's protection and Lucas's peaceful slumber offered a fleeting comfort, yet Kay couldn't shake the fear that Richard's fury would not be left behind so easily. The journey to safety was just the beginning; the real battle lay ahead.

Kay's resolve hardened as she whispered to her sleeping child, "We are safe for now. He won't give up easily." The road ahead was uncertain, but Kay was determined to face whatever came next, her strength now fueled by the fierce love for her baby and the newfound courage to protect their future. Despite this determination, she felt a deep sense of failure—failure in her marriage and as a mother. She knew she would be stuck with Richard, and this was certainly not the end.

9

The Impossible Choice

Less than 24 hours after Kay left, Richard materialized on her parents' Florida doorstep. His sudden appearance caught everyone off guard, his desperation palpable as he pleaded to be let in. Determined to get her back by any means necessary, he'd showed up unannounced, his face a mix of desperation and determination.

Richard dropped to his knees, tears streaming down his face as he clutched her hands. "Kay, I was breaking! I know that doesn't excuse anything, but the financial pressure from this strike... it's been crushing me. The lack of work, the uncertainty of how we'll pay the bills—it all got to me." His voice cracked with guilt. "I know I've made terrible mistakes, but please, I'm begging you. I promise I'll be better. I will do better for you and Lucas."

Richard made promises that tugged at Kay's heartstrings. "I'll find a job. I'll be the husband and father you both deserve. I will change. I need you both in my life."

Kay stood there, holding Lucas close, her heart torn. She saw the pain in Richard's eyes, a sharp contrast to the anger and control she had grown accustomed to. The sincerity in his voice made her hesitate. She was young and didn't know any better; her hope for a better future clashed with the fear of making another mistake.

On one hand, she was deeply skeptical of his promises, aware that his behavior might not change. On the other hand, she clung to the hope that they could rebuild their marriage and create a stable home for Lucas. Her fear of failure loomed large, the desire to maintain a strong, healthy marriage like her parents, constantly battling with her doubts.

"I want to believe you, Richard," Kay said softly, tears in her eyes. "But things have to change. I can't go back to Alabama. I need to be near my family. I need their support."

Richard nodded eagerly, grasping her hands. "Anything, Kay. I'll do anything. We can stay here with your family. We'll make it work, I promise."

Her mother, though skeptical, allowed them to live in the guest house temporarily. She was a devout Christians who believed in the sanctity of marriage and hoped that with the right support, Kay and Richard could work things out. Kay's parents, while wanting to see her happy, also recognized the complexities of her situation and the genuine fear she had of raising Lucas alone.

For a brief period, it seemed like things might improve. Richard was on his best behavior, making an effort to integrate into the family. He volunteered to help around the house, fixing small things that had been neglected.

"I can handle that leaky faucet for you," he would say, grabbing his tools and setting to work. He even took the initiative to mow the lawn and assist with other household chores, actions that earned him nods of approval from Kay's mother.

At family dinners, he would engage in conversations, asking Kay's mom about her day and showing interest in her stories.

However, three weeks later, the strike ended, and Richard was called back to work. Instead of seizing the opportunity, he blew off the company and was fired for not showing up. Once again, he was out of work, and the pressure on Kay to provide for the family increased.

Richard struggled with his new surroundings. He felt out of place and resented the close-knit bond Kay shared with her family. His jealousy often surfaced in subtle, cutting remarks. "Your family seems to have a lot of opinions about our life," he would say, his tone laced with bitterness.

Kay tried to reassure him, "They're just trying to help, Richard. They want what's best for us."

He shook his head, his eyes narrowing. "It feels like they're judging me, constantly watching every move I make. Do they think I'm not good enough for you?"

"It's not like that," Kay replied softly, reaching out to touch his arm. "They're just worried because of everything we've been through."

Richard pulled away, his expression hardening. "Worried or not, I don't need their meddling. I'm your husband, and we should be able to handle our problems without their interference."

Kay's heart sank at his words, knowing that the peace they had briefly experienced was already crumbling. She could see the tension in his eyes, the insecurity that festered beneath his words, and it made her fear what lay ahead.

Despite his promises, Richard's dissatisfaction quickly became apparent. He was out of work, and his pride was wounded. Kay noticed how he would avoid her parents, retreating into himself or disappearing for hours at a time. The weight of his judgment hung over her, making her constantly question her decisions. She felt the strain on her mental health, the pressure to keep everyone happy wearing her down.

Determined to support her family, Kay threw herself into job hunting. She scoured local ads, filled out countless applications, and went on numerous interviews. Her efforts finally paid off when she landed a manager job at a local tobacco store. It wasn't her dream job, but it was a start, a way to bring in some money and regain a sense of independence.

Working long hours while caring for Lucas and managing the household took a toll on Kay. She found herself juggling multiple roles, often feeling overwhelmed and exhausted. Kay knew her mother was exhausted from working all day, constantly tied up taking care of her patients, and simply didn't have the capacity to babysit. The heavy weight of responsibility fell squarely on Kay's shoulders. She felt an immense pressure to succeed, driven by a fierce need to prove to herself—and to the world—that she could successfully provide for her family and that she was not a failure.

Richard was a constant source of friction. His simmering dissatisfaction with their financial reality was impossible to ignore, and he grew to resent Kay's job as a painful reflection of his failure. "I should be the one providing for us," he'd insist, his voice heavy with frustrated pride, "you shouldn't have to work like this." But this conviction was baseless. Richard was remaining unemployed by choice, rejecting any job offer that failed to meet his exact, high-end salary expectations. His rigid demands ensured he made little effort to find viable work, while his suppressed anger built, threatening to erupt at any moment.

Kay's mental health began to deteriorate. The constant stress and the emotional rollercoaster left her feeling drained. She experienced moments of intense anxiety, her thoughts racing as she tried to figure out how to keep everything together. The fear of failure gnawed at her, and the pressure to maintain a strong front became almost unbearable.

The impact on her relationship with Richard was significant. The once hopeful vision of rebuilding their marriage began to fade as reality set in. Kay realized that being near her family provided a sense of protection, but it also highlighted the growing rift between her and Richard. His jealousy and dissatisfaction created a toxic environment, making it difficult for her to focus on their future together.

Richard's resentment extended to Kay's relationship with her family. He viewed their support as interference, feeling judged and belittled. This only added to the tension, making Kay feel caught between her loyalty to her family and her commitment to her marriage. The emotional and psychological impact was profound, leaving her feeling trapped and unsure of how to navigate the complexities of her situation.

As the days turned into weeks, the initial relief Kay felt began to wane. The challenges of their new life in Florida, coupled with Richard's unpredictable behavior, took a heavy toll. Kay's mother was skeptical about Richard's return from the start. She had welcomed him into their home, hoping to provide a stable environment for Kay and Lucas, but her doubts lingered just below the surface. She watched Richard closely, noting his behavior and the impact it had on their daughter. The concern in her eyes was unmistakable.

"You can't have it both ways, Kay," her mother said. "You either commit to making this work with Richard, or you move on and focus on building a life for you and Lucas. But you need to decide."

Her belief in the sanctity of marriage conflicted with her desire to protect her daughter, creating a complex web of emotions and expectations. Kay felt trapped, caught between hopes for reconciliation and the harsh truth of her daily life with Richard.

However, despite the support from her parents, Kay still felt profoundly alone. Her mother was running the business alone and was often busy dealing with a house full of patients, leaving her to manage many challenges on her own. The fear of their situation becoming public added to her isolation. She knew that any slip would not only affect her but could also impact her mother's reputation and her business. This pressure made her hesitant to seek help beyond her immediate family.

Kay often found herself battling with the complexities of her emotions, feeling torn between her need for support and her fear of judgment. She longed for a sense of normalcy, but the reality of her situation was far from it. Despite having a couple of close girlfriends she could confide in, Kay hesitated to burden them with her troubles, not wanting to expose the full extent of her struggles.

One afternoon, her friend Emma called, her voice filled with concern. "Kay, how are you holding up? I've been thinking about you a lot lately."

Kay forced a smile, though Emma couldn't see it. "I'm managing, Emma. It's just... taking some time to adjust."

Emma's voice softened. "You know I'm here for you, right? If you need to talk or need any help, don't hesitate to reach out."

Kay felt a pang of gratitude mixed with guilt. "Thank you, Emma. I really appreciate it. I'll let you know if I need anything."

This brief conversation reminded Kay that she wasn't entirely alone, but it also highlighted the delicate balance she had to maintain between seeking support and protecting her family's privacy. This left Kay feeling isolated and overwhelmed by the weight of her responsibilities.

Her mother did what she could, covering unexpected expenses and providing a safety net when possible. "We'll help you get back on your feet," her mother would say, slipping her a few dollars when she could.

Yet, her ability to provide practical support was limited.

"Kay, I'm so sorry I can't help more," her mother would say, a hint of guilt in her voice. "Since the divorce, I've been financially devastated. Every month is a desperate struggle just to keep my head barely above water. Kay would nod, understanding the pressure she was under. "I know, Mom. It's okay. I appreciate everything you're already doing."

Her mother, despite her busy schedule, would try to offer support when she could. "Go take a rest, dear," she'd say, cradling Lucas in her arms whenever she could spare a moment. "I'll watch him for a while."

These acts of kindness gave Kay the strength to keep going.

As the reality of their situation settled in, Kay realized that the complexities of her marriage and the influence of her family were inescapable. The journey ahead was uncertain, but Kay knew she had to navigate it carefully, balancing her love for Richard with the need to protect herself and Lucas.

The tension in the household inevitably affected Lucas, even at his young age. The once peaceful environment Kay had hoped to create for her baby was now fraught with underlying stress and unease. Lucas, sensitive to the emotional climate around him, often responded with bouts of crying and restlessness, mirroring the turmoil in his parents' relationship.

One devastating incident shattered Kay's carefully constructed confidence regarding Richard's care. She had taken the job at the local tobacco store, relying on her family's presence to form a safety net around her son, Lucas. That fragile trust instantly collapsed when she came home to find Lucas, not safe, but with a shocking, undeniable black eye.

Kay's heart dropped as she rushed to her son, her hands trembling. "What happened?" she demanded, her voice shaking as she examined the bruise on Lucas's delicate face.

Richard, slouched on the couch with a beer in hand, barely bothered to look up. "It was an accident, Kay," he said, his tone utterly dismissive. "That plastic toy—the one hooked right onto the side rail of the crib—it just fell off and hit him. Kids get hurt all the time."

Kay held Lucas close, her mind racing. The explanation felt hollow, and the bruise on her baby's face told a different story. Fear gripped her as she considered taking Lucas to the doctor. What if they assumed she was responsible for the injury? What if they took him away from her? The thought was unbearable.

So, instead of seeking medical help, she decided to keep Lucas at home, hiding away until the bruise healed. She couldn't risk losing her baby. "I just want to make sure he's okay," she said, her voice shaking.

Richard scoffed. "Fine, do whatever you need to do. But don't make a big deal out of nothing," he said and left the house, slamming the door behind him —a loud, angry punctuation mark to the lie.

Kay waited only a moment before slipping across the hall with Lucas tucked against her chest, into the cool, quiet safety of her mother's room.

Her mother gently took the whimpering baby. Her soft voice was a hushed contrast to Richard's recent outburst. "Oh, sweet boy. What did he do?" she murmured, tracing the edge of the dark bruise.

"He said the crib toy did it," Kay whispered, her own voice brittle with exhaustion.

"That's ridiculous, honey. That toy has been secured to the side rail for a month. It doesn't just 'fall.' Her quiet gaze locked onto Kay. "He's lying, Kay. He laid a hand on this baby. He did something to this baby, I know it. You're not going to convince me otherwise, and you shouldn't be trying to convince yourself."

Kay swallowed hard, the denial dissolving into a knot of sickening dread. She didn't meet her mother's eyes, staring instead at the dark bruise on Lucas's face.

"I know, Mom. I know. When I saw it... I knew that crib toy couldn't do that. I just kept hoping that if I said the word 'accident' enough times, it would be true." Her voice cracked on the last word.

The incident deepened Kay's resolve to protect Lucas at all costs. She knew the road ahead would be fraught with challenges, but the safety and well-being of her son were paramount. Each day, she remained vigilant, determined to shield Lucas from any harm and to navigate the complexities of her troubled marriage.

Despite Richard's rehearsed and ultimately worthless promises to change, his behavior only spiraled into a deeper malignancy. The intimacy of their home was poisoned. Behind closed doors, Richard's temper didn't just flare; it became a weapon, wielded with growing frequency and precision. His verbal assaults were not just cutting, but relentless, designed to strip away Kay's self-worth until she felt utterly exposed and hollow. And when the physical abuse did occur, even its infrequency was a torment. Each occasional act now held a chilling, sinister undertone of control and domination, a clear message that his power over her body and her life was absolute, calculated to keep her in a constant state of anticipatory dread.

Kay's initial hope that moving to Florida would provide a fresh start began to fade. She had envisioned showing Richard a different life, filled with possibilities beyond the rural constraints they had known. Big cities, better jobs, fishing, beaches, and travel were dreams she clung to, hoping to inspire a change in him. However, the reality was far from her dreams.

Kay's resolve wavered, a fragile thing buckling under the enormous weight of her situation. The thought of finally leaving Richard felt like a necessary liberation, yet simultaneously, an insurmountable, terrifying challenge. She was haunted by the paralyzing fear of raising Lucas alone, constantly battling doubts about her own capacity to provide for him without Richard's unpredictable, but still present, financial support.

The vibrant dream of a better life in Florida—a world she had envisioned as a clean slate filled with opportunity—now violently clashed with the harsh, undeniable reality of their daily struggles and escalating abuse. While her head recognized the immediate danger, her heart stubbornly yearned to look backward: she longed to rewind, to find the man she once loved, and to finally show Richard the beauty of a new life away from the stifling, oppressive constraints of their past. She was trapped between the person he was and the threat he had become.

Kay's internal conflict deepened. She wanted to believe in the possibility of change, clinging to the hope that Richard could transform into the loving partner and father she had once envisioned. Despite the escalating abuse, her fear of failure and longing for a stable family kept her tethered to the marriage.

One evening, as Kay got Lucas ready for bed, she found herself staring out the window, her mind a chaos of emotional static. The necessary decision didn't just loom; it blocked out the light, rising before her like a dark, stormy horizon. The known dangers of staying were concrete, but the terror of the unknown—the impossible logistical puzzle of single motherhood—paralyzed her resolve. Richard's smooth, lying promises clashed violently with the fresh, brutal memory of his last outburst. The entire weight of her choice—a responsibility both suffocating and cruelly unavoidable—pressed down on her until she could barely breathe.

As the day's last glow dissolved into shadow, Kay committed to a choice born of paralyzing dread—she resolved to stay married to Richard.

This was a decision driven by deep, compounding fears: the terrifying specter of single motherhood and the claustrophobic trap of endless dependence on her mother's hospitality. Rather than seeing Richard's escalating violence as the enemy, Kay desperately convinced herself that the true source of their tension was the crowded house itself.

She fiercely hoped that if they could find a place of their own, Richard would finally feel less stress and the freedom he needed to settle down and find a good job. Her love and determination now hinged on this new plan, using it as a shield against the truth. Yet, beneath this frantic rationalization, a cold, undeniable seed of doubt had already taken root, whispering that the perilous road ahead wasn't about location, but about the man beside her.

In the stillness of the night, Kay whispered to herself, "This isn't over. I have to believe he can change. For Lucas, and for us." Little did she know that the hardest part of her journey was yet to come.

The known dangers of staying were concrete, but the terror of the unknown—the impossible logistical puzzle of single motherhood—paralyzed her resolve.

10

The Lost Embrace

The uncertainty of the future loomed like an impending storm. Just as she braced herself for the challenges ahead, life threw another unexpected twist her way—she discovered she was pregnant again.

The news was unexpected and brought a mix of emotions. On the one hand, there was a flicker of joy and the faint hope that a new life might bring about the change she so desperately needed. On the other hand, the reality of her situation cast a dark shadow over this hope. The struggles with Richard, the strain of living with her mother, and the demands of caring for Lucas made the prospect of another child overwhelming.

From the earliest weeks, Kay sensed a profound difference in this pregnancy compared to her first with Lucas. She vividly recalled the joyous, almost frantic activity of Lucas, his small body a constant, demanding reassurance punctuated by powerful kicks and vigorous rolls. This time, however, the life inside her felt unnervingly subdued. The baby was quieter, their movements sparse and almost tentative. Kay fought to rationalize the stillness, repeating the mantra that every pregnancy is unique, yet a cold, persistent knot of worry tightened in the back of her mind, refusing to be dismissed. It wasn't just different; it felt ominous.

As the weeks crawled by, Kay's premonition solidified into a persistent dread. By the sixth month of the pregnancy, the baby's unsettling quietness left her convinced that something was amiss. When her scheduled, routine check-up finally arrived, Kay didn't wait; she immediately voiced her specific concerns to the doctor, detailing the profound lack of movement compared to Lucas. The doctor, sensing the sincerity in Kay's worry, listened intently. To move beyond mere hope or fear, the doctor promptly ordered an immediate ultrasound to obtain a clearer, definitive picture.

Kay found herself at the local imaging center, the very one where her sister, Holly, worked. As Kay lay on the table, watching the monitor for any sign of movement, the ultrasound technician's movements grew hesitant, her brow deeply furrowed. The tech then abruptly excused herself and slipped out, leaving Kay alone with a mounting, cold anxiety.

The door soon opened again. It was Holly and the technician together. Holly's face was grave, confirming Kay's worst fears. "Kay," Holly whispered, her voice tight with professional risk, "We can't tell you the details. There are complications—things that need immediate attention. The doctor has to deliver the full, official review." Ignoring strict protocol, the technician quickly printed a small, silvery-white photo—a clear, unauthorized image of the tiny, threatened life—and pressed it into Kay's hand. Kay clutched the picture, knowing she was now tasked with the agonizing journey back to the physician for the definitive, frightening diagnosis.

Kay returned to the doctor's office in a state of brittle, agonizing anticipation, the unauthorized ultrasound image burning in her mind. The air in the consultation room felt heavy and cold as the doctor, his voice carefully measured, delivered the crushing news. The baby, a girl, had what appeared to be Turner Syndrome, though further testing would be necessary for absolute certainty. Far more immediate was the discovery of a massive, alarming growth on her neck—a grim visual confirmation of the high-risk complications Holly had hinted at.

The diagnosis instantly shattered Kay's remaining defenses. The doctor then outlined the impossible path ahead, placing the monumental decision squarely in her hands: she had to choose between continuing the high-risk pregnancy and facing a potentially grim outcome, or terminating the life she carried. Kay listened, every word a physical blow, until the room began to spin. She was utterly overwhelmed, suffocated by the moral weight of a choice that no parent should ever face. The fear she felt for her daughter's future was immense, yet the thought of choosing to end the pregnancy was a cold horror that paralyzed her heart.

Kay left the doctor's office in a daze, her mind reeling. She couldn't fathom the idea of abortion, yet the thought of carrying a baby that might not survive was equally unbearable.

When she arrived home, she sat on the couch, clutching her ultrasound photos, waiting for Richard to come back. The silence in the house was oppressive. Finally, the door opened, and Richard walked in, looking tired and irritable.

"Richard, can we talk?" Kay began, her voice trembling. She explained what the doctor had said, her eyes searching his face for any sign of empathy or support.

Richard listened, his expression unreadable. When she finished, he shrugged. "So, what are you going to do?" he asked, his tone flat.

"I don't know," Kay replied, tears welling up in her eyes. "The doctor said we have until our next appointment on Monday to decide whether to continue the pregnancy or terminate it."

Richard let out a heavy, impatient sigh and rubbed his forehead. He didn't look at Kay, only past her. "Honestly, Kay, I don't see what the big deal is. If the baby isn't developing normally, maybe it's actually a blessing in disguise. We certainly can't afford another kid—we're already crammed into your mother's guest room. This whole situation is just going to put more stress on me." His tone wasn't mournful, just utterly practical and cold.

"Richard, this is our child! How can you be so utterly cold and in-different?" Kay pleaded, her voice cracking with disbelief.

"I am not indifferent," he snapped, dragging the word out with heavy annoyance. "I'm being realistic, something you seem incapable of doing right now. We are barely scraping by with Lucas's daycare costs, and we're still crammed in your mom's house. Another baby would only compound the disaster."

Kay gripped the edge of the chair, tears starting to blur her vision. "But this is our baby girl! She's alive. I can't just... give up on her life."

Richard leaned in, his voice hardening into a cruel certainty. "You are being ridiculous and overly emotional. We need to think about what's best for Lucas and for us, Kay. This child, in her current state, would be a burden we absolutely cannot **afford** to take on."

Kay felt a devastating, cold emptiness settle in her core. "I just wanted you to be my husband," she whispered, her gaze heavy with disappointment. "To help me navigate this impossible choice. I feel completely abandoned and alone in this."

"I'm not abandoning you," Richard snapped, his defensiveness im-mediate. "I'm right here." He quickly retreated behind a wall of false practicality. "Just make the decision, Kay. It's your body, your call. I told you what I think. I'm not going to wear the guilt for you."

The entire weekend vanished in a suffocating blur of confusion and ceaseless tears. Kay remained utterly paralyzed, unable to bring herself to make a decision. Her deep-seated faith rigidly opposed the idea of abortion, making the thought of deliberately ending her baby's life feel like an unbearable transgression. This moral horror was com-pounded by the gnawing uncertainty—they didn't even have a defini-tive diagnosis.

The crisis fractured her only source of strength: her family. Instead of unified counsel, Kay received divided opinions and hesitant advice, leaving her more isolated than before. Feeling utterly incapable of making such a monumental, soul-crushing choice, she finally relinquished control. She decided to leave the fate of her baby in God's hands, an act born of spiritual exhaustion, not serenity.

The thought of losing her baby girl, the frightening uncertainty of their future, and the crushing weight of Richard's cold abandonment left Kay feeling profoundly, irrevocably lost. Her only anchor in this terrifying storm was Lucas. She clung to his small, innocent presence with a desperate, white-knuckled grip, drawing silent, fragile solace from his warmth even as the emotional tempest raged, threatening to consume her entirely.

Monday morning arrived like a cruel, unyielding deadline. Kay walked into the OBGYN office, feeling as hollowed-out and indecisive as she had been all weekend. The appointment began routinely enough, but as the doctor performed his examination, Kay sensed a terrifying, abrupt shift. He took much longer than usual, his movements becoming slow and deliberate, his brow deeply furrowed in concentration. The silence stretched, cold and absolute, before he finally set down his instruments. He didn't offer a word of explanation, only an urgent, quiet request: Kay needed to go back to imaging immediately for another ultrasound. He couldn't find the baby's heartbeat.

Kay lay rigid on the examination table, the deafening silence of the room a mockery of the heartbeat that should have been. The technician's grave, unmoving expression delivered the final, crushing verdict: the life was gone. Kay's heart simply ceased to function in her chest as the reality set in. A raw, wrenching grief clawed its way up her throat, manifesting as a torrent of uncontrollable tears. Every single hope, every desperate dream she had woven for her baby girl—even the desperate decision she had just deferred—vanished instantly into a terrifying void. The weight of her profound loss was a tangible, suffocating force, leaving her utterly empty and alone on the cold table.

Kay was told she needed to be admitted immediately for a birth induction, an immediate and brutal transition from pregnancy to the excruciating process of delivering a stillborn baby. The reality of the ordeal ahead was too raw to bear immediately. She requested a brief reprieve: a moment to go home, gather her personal things, and mentally brace herself before returning for the induced labor.

As Kay prepared to face this agonizing process, her only source of consistent female support, her mother, was once again tied down by the demands of the family business, unable to step away to be by her side. This left Kay reliant on the two men. Despite the emotional chasm that existed between them, Richard—the man who had coldly urged termination—and her father were both present, offering a strained, silent guard as she prepared for the most profound loss of her life. Kay knew that while their bodies were there, the emotional burden of the coming ordeal rested entirely on her.

The hours that followed became the most agonizing ordeal of Kay's life. Despite Richard and her father being present, the loneliness was a vast, overwhelming presence in the room. She moved through the motions of labor in a terrible solitude, each contraction a sharp, meaningless betrayal. They were the physical embodiment of the birth process, yet each wave of pain was nothing more than a cruel, searing reminder of the life that was already gone and the future that would never arrive.

When the baby was finally born, the silence was a horrifying vacuum in the room, thick and absolute. There was no first, triumphant cry, no sound of life—only the quiet movements of the medical staff. The nurses, their faces etched with sympathy, gently lowered the tiny, uncannily still form of her baby girl onto Kay's chest.

Kay's heart didn't just shatter; it felt as if it had dissolved entirely, leaving a gaping, physical ache. As she cradled her daughter, the weight of her profound grief was almost unbearable, a heavy shroud settling over her. Tears streamed down her face, uncontrolled and hot, as she whispered the only words that mattered: "I'm so sorry. I love you so much."

The nurses moved with a quiet reverence, taking tiny footprints and handprints, pressing the ink onto paper to preserve these fragile, permanent mementos of a life that never had the chance to utter a single sound. Kay held onto her baby girl with a fierce, possessive grip, her eyes desperately memorizing every perfect detail: the curve of her tiny cheek, the delicate fan of her eyelashes, the creases on her minute hands.

Finally, after an eternity that lasted only moments, the nurses gently, inevitably, whisked her away, leaving Kay with nothing but the haunting warmth, the fresh scent of her child, and the fleeting, heart-wrenching memory of holding her precious daughter.

In her grief-stricken, deeply dissociated state, Kay lacked the mental capacity to form questions; she didn't think to ask about final arrangements or her options for burial or cremation. She was too utterly consumed by the immediate, searing pain, both physical and emotional, to register the clinical details of what was happening around her. The world had shrunk to the cold emptiness in her arms, leaving her unable to process the critical next steps of her profound loss.

The next stage of her trauma was the D&C procedure, a final, cruel irony as it was the same medical process she had refused for her living child. It was invasive, cold, and excruciatingly painful, both physically and emotionally. Kay lay on the sterile, unforgiving table, a profound sense of violation washing over her as she felt every deliberate, metallic tug and scrape of the instruments. The harsh, clinical efficiency of the medical team and the dreadful sound of the instruments contrasted savagely with the profound, silent scream of her loss.

She could barely comprehend that this impersonal procedure was the final, devastating chapter in her baby's brief life. The decision to perform the D&C was made quickly by the staff, and Kay, paralyzed by grief and shock, felt utterly powerless to object or even inquire.

11

The Concrete Vow

In the weeks that followed, this lack of agency solidified into a terrible truth: she had never been given the opportunity to bury her daughter, to give her a proper farewell. That oversight became a gaping, unhealing wound in Kay's heart, a haunting, permanent legacy of her loss, poisoning her grief with a profound, irreversible lack of closure.

As time crawled forward, Kay's initial raw sorrow did not heal; it simply morphed into a lingering, corrosive pain rooted in unanswered questions—questions that sharpened into accusation. The central anguish was the theft of a final goodbye: Why had no one informed her of burial or cremation options? Had Richard told the staff she didn't want them? Could something so profound and final have been decided without her consent, while she lay helpless in shock?

These gnawing regrets became a cruel, additional layer of anguish, burdening a soul already crushed by loss. She desperately wanted to honor her baby girl's short, silent life, to have a sacred plot of ground where she could visit and mourn her daughter. Instead, she was left with a hollow, aching void—an empty-handed sorrow that words could never adequately fill, and a corrosive suspicion that Richard was responsible for her missing closure.

The emotional impact of not having closure was profound. Kay found herself trapped in a cycle of grief and regret, unable to move forward. The pain of her loss, coupled with the unresolved feelings about her daughter's unburied body, weighed heavily on her. It was a constant reminder of the life she had lost and the love she had never been able to fully express.

In the wake of the stillbirth, Richard's behavior shifted dramatically. Rather than offering comfort, he became emotionally distant and detached. The loss of their child, which had left Kay devastated, seemed to barely affect him. His focus was on practical concerns and the financial strain of having another child they "couldn't afford." To him, the baby was already a non-issue, and he dismissed Kay's profound grief as her being overly emotional.

Richard's increasing control over Kay began to manifest in more overt ways. He dismissed her feelings, minimized her pain, and consistently undermined her autonomy. Whenever she expressed her sorrow or tried to talk about their lost daughter, he would cut her off.

One evening, Kay tried to talk to Richard about her feelings. "Richard, I can't stop thinking about her. About our baby girl. We never got to—"

Richard interrupted her, his tone harsh. "We can't dwell on the past, Kay. It's out of our hands. We have enough problems as it is."

Kay felt a surge of frustration. "But she was our daughter, Richard. We lost her. Doesn't that mean anything to you?"

"Of course, it does, but what do you want me to do about it? Cry every night? We need to focus on Lucas and getting our life together. Another baby right now would have been a disaster." He sighed, looking at her with a mixture of annoyance and disdain.

"But she wasn't just another baby," Kay whispered, her voice breaking. "She was my sweet baby girl.

"Well, I need you to be strong. We can't afford to fall apart. Look, you need to stop being so emotional about this. We need to focus on moving forward."

Kay, trying to salvage their marriage and improve their lives, became more determined to find a way out of their dire situation. She believed that if they worked hard and got their own place, things might get better. Her mom's house, though a refuge, felt suffocating with Richard's increasing control and her mounting grief. She hoped that a change in their environment might spark a change in Richard.

Richard's behavior, far from improving after the loss, only sank into a deeper, more hostile regression. Though he finally secured sporadic part-time work, he showed a crushing lack of ambition, exhibiting little to no interest in finding a stable, full-time job. Instead, he became profoundly more controlling, channeling his failure into actively blocking every one of Kay's efforts to improve their situation. Whenever Kay broached the subject of finding a better job for herself or finally moving the family out of her mother's house, Richard would respond with immediate, savage hostility. This anger became their destructive pattern: his verbal defiance rapidly escalated, and their fights became not only more frequent but also brutally physical and volatile. Kay was living under an oppressive ceiling of violence, her hope for a fresh start now completely suffocated.

Weeks after the crushing loss of the baby, Kay's sole focus had been clawing her way out of the financial hole. She poured her grief into job searching, targeting roles with higher pay to ease the constant, crushing burden. The moment her doctor cleared her for normal activities, she'd secured a critical interview.

Kay stood at the kitchen counter, dressed in her best interview suit, a potential step toward a lifeline of financial independence.

Her mother eyed her, then the clock. "It's 101 degrees outside, Kay. The forecast says the heat index is higher. Take my car." She pressed a set of keys into Kay's palm, her gaze warm with concern. "You need to arrive looking composed, not like you swam there. Mine has AC."

From the doorway, Richard's voice cracked like a whip. "You are NOT taking her car!"

Kay spun around, the keys suddenly heavy in her hand. "Richard, please. Our car is a sauna. I need to make a good impression. Just this once."

He stalked across the room, his face a mask of escalating fury. "I said NO! Stop acting like a spoiled child. Our car is fine. Just deal with it. It's not like you're going to get the job anyway." The last phrase was a calculated strike, designed to wound.

"Why do you have to make everything so difficult?" Kay shot back, a surge of defiance momentarily overpowering her fear. "It's a simple request. I just want to arrive looking presentable."

Richard's face twisted, his jaw clenching. He leaned in, his voice a dangerous hiss. "You are not taking her car, Kay. End of discussion."

The argument shattered the tense quiet. Kay, propelled by desperation for the job and sheer frustration, ignored him. She gripped her mother's keys and bolted for the front door, her heels clicking rapidly across the hardwood floor.

She reached the driveway and slid behind the wheel of her mother's convertible, fumbling the key into the ignition. Before the engine could turn over, her door was ripped open.

A powerful hand clamped around her face, the fingertips digging into her skin, and Richard dragged her, thrashing, out of the car. Her feet tangled, and he slammed her to the ground. The jarring impact of the concrete driveway knocked the air from her lungs.

A searing, blinding pain exploded across her cheekbone as her face smacked the hard surface.

Kay's mom and boyfriend, witnessing the physical violence for the first time, erupted from the house. Her mother's scream was a raw, primal sound that sliced through the heat. Her boyfriend launched himself forward, punching Richard hard to break his grip on Kay.

Released, Richard stumbled back, then scrambled into their car. He threw the vehicle into reverse, screeching the tires as he shouted, "I'm getting Lucas! You won't beat me there!"

Kay pushed herself up, her hand pressing against the warm, rough concrete. Blood smeared her fingers. Bruised and shaking, she watched her son's father disappear down the street. A terrifying certainty washed over her: he was going to take their son. She collapsed, screaming, a sound ripped from the deepest terror in her soul.

Despite the searing pain in her face and the shock pulsing through her body, a single, primal instinct drove Kay: Lucas. Her legs, shaky and bruised, didn't fail her. She managed to get into her mother's car, the seat now a frantic, bloody blur, and sped toward the daycare center. She got there first.

She snatched Lucas, clutching him to her chest so tightly he squeaked, and raced back to her mother's house just as Richard's car was pulling onto the main road, the two vehicles passing without acknowledgment.

She spent the endless, silent night huddled on the living room sofa, her mom and boyfriend a constant, protective presence nearby. Richard never returned.

12

The Silver Shackle

The silence in the house was a suffocating pressure, heavier than the oppressive summer heat. Her cheekbone throbbed beneath a growing patch of swollen, dark purple, and the gritty feel of dirt and dried blood on her neck was a constant reminder of the asphalt.

The physical pain was nothing compared to the clarity that finally cut through the fear and shock. Looking at her sleeping son, the final, fragile walls of illusion she had desperately maintained around her marriage crumbled into dust. The man she had married was gone; only a dangerous, unpredictable stranger remained.

This was not a mistake. This was not a fight. This was the moment the danger became real, tangible, and lethal. She knew, with chilling certainty, that the escalating pattern of control and anger had finally broken into a full-blown assault.

The job interview, the financial struggles, the grief—all faded beneath the terrifying realization: she had to escape. Her priority had shifted from fixing the marriage to saving her son and herself.

The terror of the previous night had solidified into an overwhelming sense of urgency. Kay didn't need time to think; the decision was made the moment her face hit the pavement. She and Lucas were not merely unhappy—they were in immediate, physical danger. Richard had to leave.

Her solution was stark: she wanted him gone, banished to the only place that felt far enough away—back to Alabama. Distance felt like the only guarantee of safety, a physical shield against his volatile rage.

She sat with her mother that morning, the plan simple: when he called, she would tell him the marriage was over and he needed to go. She would hold her ground.

But Richard was always steps ahead, a master of emotional camouflage.

He didn't call. He simply returned the next afternoon, walking through the front door of her mother's house as if nothing had happened, except that his eyes were wide and red-rimmed. The monster of the driveway was gone, replaced by the broken, remorseful husband.

He approached Kay, but her mother stepped physically between them. Richard didn't argue. He stood a distance away, his voice thick with what sounded like genuine agony.

"Kay, I am so sorry. So unbelievably sorry," he pleaded, his head bowed. He didn't deny what he'd done; he used the act of violence as a backdrop for his performance. "I lost control. It was the stress, the heat, the job interview... I panicked. I will never, ever put a hand on you again. I swear it. Give me one more chance. Just let me come home."

His words were a calculated flood of apologies and false promises, manipulative bait designed to hook the woman who desperately wanted to believe in the good man she thought she had married. But Kay, seeing the purple swelling in her own reflection, recognized the game. The remorse was a trap.

She looked at him—at the man capable of dragging her across the concrete—and, for the first time, felt nothing but a cold, hard resolve.

"Kay, I'm sorry," Richard said, his eyes brimming with tears that Kay had come to recognize as insincere. "I've been under so much stress since we lost the baby. I know I've been terrible, but losing her affected me more than I realized. Please, just give me one more chance."

Kay, still bruised and emotionally shattered, found it difficult to believe him. But the manipulation was powerful. Richard played on her vulnerabilities, the grief of losing their daughter, and the hope that he could change. "I need you, Kay. We need to be a family for Lucas."

Richard's performance of remorse was a sickening charade, and Kay saw every thread of the lie. But knowing it was false didn't give her the strength to reject him. The barriers to leaving weren't just the man in front of her; they were immense, invisible walls built from her own pain and self-judgment.

The scene in the driveway—the shouting, the blood, the raw physical brutality—had been played out in front of the people she most respected. The shame was a scalding wash that made her cheeks burn hotter than the injury on her face. She felt like a public spectacle, a disastrous failure who had dragged her family into her chaos.

She used to be the bright promise, the young woman with so much potential. Now, every mirror of self-reflection showed her a mess: a bruised, dependent adult, forced back into her childhood home. She was trapped—not just by Richard's manipulative apologies, but by her own crushing reality:

No financial independence.

No college degree to open the doors she needed.

A mother living under her mother's roof.

She felt utterly diminished, her self-worth reduced to the terrifying math of her financial instability and her complete dependence on the very people she was meant to be comforting. Richard hadn't just punched her face; he had exploited the deep, raw wound of her perceived failure, leaving her paralyzed by the fear that she truly couldn't survive without him.

The air in her childhood home was thick not just with heat, but with unspoken expectations. Kay felt the weight of societal and familial pressure pressing down on her bruised shoulders. Her mother was a lifeline, yes, but her support came tangled with the values of their generation.

She was devastated by the sight of their injured daughter, yet the deep-rooted belief in the sanctity of marriage still held sway. They couldn't help but hope. They exchanged looks—a silent plea that perhaps, perhaps the incident was an aberration. She desperately wanted Kay to be safe and happy, but she also needed to believe that Richard, the man they'd welcomed into their family, was capable of redemption. This hope, while well-intentioned, became another heavy chain binding Kay to her misery.

Kay's internal landscape was a relentless battleground. One voice screamed, "Run! Leave him for Lucas and yourself!"—a primal, survival instinct. The other voice whispered the cold, hard truths of her reality: dependence, poverty, and failure.

Every single step toward independence felt like climbing a sheer cliff face. Where would she go? How would she afford rent, childcare, and food? She had zero financial stability and no job secured that could support a single mother. Richard's control wasn't just the memory of his hand on her face; it was an emotional and psychological vice.

His empty promises of change—I'll go to therapy. I'll get help. I'll be better.—were cruel, polished lies. Yet, they were the only things offered, and they preyed mercilessly on her desperate need for things to be simple again. She was an anchor dropped in quicksand, tethered to a man who was actively, slowly, and methodically destroying her life, paralyzed by the fear that leaving would destroy it faster.

As days turned into weeks, Kay's resolve wavered. The shame of her situation, the fear of judgment, and the lack of resources made her feel stuck. She knew she needed to leave, but the path to freedom seemed insurmountable. Each attempt to break free was met with Richard's manipulative return and the crushing weight of her own doubts and insecurities. The internal and external barriers to leaving were formidable, and Kay's journey to reclaim her life was far from over.

Kay's mind was a relentless echo chamber of pain. The questions spun endlessly, tearing at her core: Why didn't he love her? What was she doing wrong? How could she heal this marriage? She carried the burden of fixing a cruelty that wasn't hers to own.

But the most paralyzing fear was the specter of the future: raising Lucas alone. The thought was a stone in her stomach. She didn't trust her own capacity—to be the sole financial provider, the only emotional support, the flawless mother, all at once. The monumental task of independence felt impossible.

Then, a lifeline arrived. When her grandmother passed away, the small inheritance was a sudden, miraculous windfall. It allowed them to purchase a small house—a tangible beacon of hope. This wasn't just a change of address; it was supposed to be a fresh start, a clean slate away from the shame of her mothers' driveway.

But the walls of their new home offered no protection. In fact, they became a prison.

With no witnesses, Richard's behavior metastasized. Her mother was no longer there to hear the rising volume, to interrupt the verbal abuse, or to judge his increasing dependence on alcohol. He could now yell and berate her with impunity, his voice echoing through the empty rooms, turning the new house into an instant, private battleground.

He drank without restraint, his mood swinging wildly from cruel belligerence to sullen silence. The isolation amplified his control and made Kay realize the horrible truth: they had purchased not a sanctuary, but a cage, and the lock had just clicked shut.

Even within the constant, smothering atmosphere of the new house, a small, fierce spark refused to be extinguished. Despite the exhaustion, despite the shame, Kay found moments of profound, ice-cold resolve.

She would stand in the center of a room Richard had just stormed out of, the silence deafening, and whisper the absolute truth to herself:

she had to change the course of her life. This wasn't a wish; it was a mandate.

But the fear was a physical chokehold. The uncertainty loomed large and shapeless, a fog bank swallowing her future. Every empty promise Richard hurled at her was a psychological shackle, designed to keep her dependent. Her financial worries were a crushing, daily calculation: How much food money is left? Could she afford a single month's house payment? The calculations always ended in helplessness.

She didn't just want a better job or stability; she ached for it. She longed for anything—a tiny crack in the prison wall—that would allow her to break free from the suffocating, cyclical abuse.

The house, once a vision of hope, was now a stark, four-walled reminder of her entrapment. Every floorboard, every closed door, felt like a silent witness to her humiliation.

Kay's internal turmoil was a deep, churning ache, yet something else began to harden alongside it: her determination. It wasn't loud or dramatic; it was the quiet, terrifying resolution of a person pushed past their limit.

She would look at Lucas, sleeping peacefully, his small chest rising and falling, and she would make a vow. Pressing her lips together until they were white, Kay would whisper the final, defiant truth into the tainted air of her bedroom. It was a promise of war, not surrender.

"This isn't over."

13

The Unbreakable Cycle

Kay's quiet resolve was tested hourly. Her inner determination was a small, flickering light struggling against a daily torrent. Each day brought a new storm, and Richard's anger was no longer contained by mere words; it was a force seeking destruction.

One evening, after the long, soul-crushing hours of her first job, Kay pulled into the driveway, the car packed with groceries and a sleepy Lucas in the back. She desperately needed a brief, ten-minute respite before heading out for her second job. She barely managed to set the paper sacks on the counter when Richard's voice—raw, loud, and immediate—sliced through the air.

"Where the hell have you been?" he bellowed from the living room, his eyes wild and his body coiled with instant tension.

Kay took a slow, deliberate breath, trying to anchor herself. "I was at the store, Richard," she answered calmly, her hands still steadying the groceries. "I bought everything we needed."

His face contorted into a mask of pure, unwarranted rage. "You were gone too long! Who were you with?" Without waiting for a response, he grabbed a heavy ceramic lamp from the end table and hurled it across the room. The sickening CRASH of the lamp shattering against the wall made Lucas gasp and instantly start to cry in the next room.

Kay forced herself to hold his gaze. "I was at the store, Richard," she repeated, her voice now tight with barely controlled fear. "Someone has to purchase the food to feed us."

He advanced on her, his face inches from hers, his breath hot and reeking of stale alcohol. "You're lying!" he hissed. He shot out a hand and grabbed her arm, his fingers sinking into her flesh like claws. "You're always lying."

Kay flinched, but she stood fast. She knew the deadly equation: resistance fueled the fire. She had learned to become a silent wall, absorbing his fury to protect the only person she could. "Please, Richard," she murmured softly, her eyes pleading for a sanity he no longer possessed. "I am telling you the truth."

His grip tightened, cutting off the circulation. For a terrifying second, she felt the sickening inevitability of a slap, a punch. Then, he violently shoved her away, sending her stumbling back against the counter. "Get out of my sight," he snarled, his voice guttural. "Before I do something we'll both regret."

Kay stumbled to the kitchen, the adrenaline pulsing like poison. She knew his threats were not idle. The memory of the gun was a raw, fresh wound.

It had happened only a week ago, a confrontation ignited simply because she'd returned home empty-handed—the debit card had been declined.

"You think you can cheat on me?" he had screamed, the metal of the gun's barrel pressed ice-cold against her temple. "You think I'm stupid?"

Kay had felt the life drain out of her, reduced to a desperate, trembling animal. "Richard, please, the card didn't work. There are no funds in the bank—I called and verified there is no money left!"

His response was a brutal SLAP that sent her reeling to the floor, her ears ringing. He stood over her, the gun still in hand. "Liar!" he shouted. "You're all the same. Deceitful. Worthless."

Now, as she frantically put away the groceries, pushing the memory down, the lingering fear was a constant, icy companion.

Richard's abuse wasn't just physical; his psychological torment was the slow suffocation of her freedom. He began to steal her keys, turning their new house into an elegant cage. Each time she tried to leave, she felt trapped, her movements dictated by his petty, tyrannical whims.

One morning, dressed for work, she searched for the car keys. Panic tightened her chest as she tore through drawers. Richard was watching from the doorway, a sickeningly smug smile playing on his lips.

"Looking for something?" he asked, casually dangling her keys from his finger.

"Richard, please, I need to go to work," Kay pleaded, fighting to keep her voice steady.

With a mocking laugh, he tossed the keys across the room, watching her scramble on her hands and knees to retrieve them.

Every moment away from home became a source of crippling anxiety. She dreaded the wrath awaiting her return, knowing a simple errand was an invitation for a violent outburst. Each day was a brutal test of endurance, a frantic battle to maintain the last tattered remnants of her sanity.

Richard's manipulation extended far beyond the confines of their home. He meticulously crafted a public persona that painted him as the aggrieved party, a tactic that served to deepen Kay's isolation. To outsiders, Richard appeared as a misunderstood man, doing his best in an unwelcoming environment.

Richard perfected his final, manipulative plea, twisting his own toxic behavior into a shared persecution. He would slump in a chair, his face a mask of wounded martyrdom, his voice heavy with feigned sorrow—a performance Kay was now forced to witness daily.

"Everyone here hates me, Kay," he would lament, his eyes fixing on hers, forcing her to bear the weight of his perceived misery. "They just don't understand us."

The use of "us" was a chilling tactic—a verbal chain linking her to his persecution, implying that the outside world rejected them as a unit, isolating her further. He planted the seed of retreat, the idea that their only safety lay in an environment he controlled:

"We need to go back to Alabama, where I belong. That's where we can finally be happy."

It was the ultimate psychological trap: convince her that the abuse was the world's fault, not his, and that the only escape from the cycle was to move back to the place where she had no family, no support network, and no chance of rescue. He wasn't suggesting a move; he was proposing total captivity.

Kay watched him weave this narrative with a mixture of disbelief and despair. It was another layer of control, another way to make her feel responsible for his well-being. His constant refrain about moving back to Alabama became a drumbeat in their daily lives, a ceaseless reminder of how he manipulated perceptions to his advantage.

In public, Richard was the picture of charm and affability. He greeted neighbors with a friendly wave, engaged in small talk, and even volunteered to help with local fire department events.

Kay stood by, forced to smile and nod, her stomach churning. The man they saw was a facade, a carefully constructed illusion that bore no resemblance to the tyrant she faced at home. Richard's ability to switch between these personas was seamless, leaving Kay feeling trapped in a twisted game where no one could see the truth.

At home, Richard's isolation tactics grew more insidious. He constantly reminded Kay of how much he sacrificed for her and how he felt persecuted in Florida. "You know they talk behind our backs, right?" he said one evening, his tone conspiratorial. They think I'm the problem. They don't see what you're like when no one's watching."

Kay's heart sank as the isolation took its toll. She began to doubt herself, plagued by the gnawing fear that she might be the source of her own misery. The emotional burden was crushing, eroding her already fragile self-esteem with each passing day.

One afternoon, as Kay and Richard were sitting on the front porch, Kristy, Kay's neighbor, approached them. She had become a close confidante, someone Kay could trust amid the chaos.

"Kay, I was hoping we could catch up later," Kristy said, glancing warily at Richard.

Before Kay could respond, Richard interjected, his voice dripping with false cheer. "Oh, Kay's quite busy these days, Kristy. Maybe some other time."

Kay felt a pang of frustration. "Actually, Richard, I'd love to catch up with Kristy. It's been a while."

Richard's smile tightened, his eyes warning her not to push further.

Kristy noticed the tension and quickly said, "Maybe another time, then. Take care, Kay."

As they walked away, Richard tightened his grip on her arm. "You're always trying to make me look bad, aren't you?" he hissed.

"I just wanted to see a friend," Kay replied, her voice barely above a whisper. "Is that too much to ask?"

"It is when your friends are part of the problem," Richard snapped. "They're turning you against me."

The public facade Richard maintained made it even harder for Kay to reach out for help. He portrayed her as the irrational one, the one who couldn't be trusted. When she confided in Kristy about her struggles, Richard's manipulative tactics became even clearer.

"Kay, you know you can always talk to me," Kristy had said one evening over coffee. "I see how he treats you. It's not right."

Kay had felt a glimmer of hope, but it was quickly extinguished by Richard's constant surveillance. He made her feel like she was constantly being watched. The fear of his reprisals kept her from seeking the help she so desperately needed.

Richard's manipulation wasn't just about controlling Kay; it was about isolating her from any potential support system. By making her feel like an outsider, he deepened her dependence on him. Every kind word from a neighbor, every friendly gesture from Kristy, was turned into a weapon against her, reinforcing the narrative that she was the problem and he was the victim.

One morning, the atmosphere in the house shifted with a jarring, disorienting speed. Richard's demeanor changed abruptly, snapping from venomous cruelty to cloying sweetness without warning, catching Kay completely off guard. The storm didn't just pass; it was replaced by an artificial, suffocating calm.

Suddenly, he was kind and attentive, indulging her in ways she hadn't experienced in years—a terrifying reminder of the man he pretended to be during their courtship. He would prepare her favorite meals, the scent of comfort food feeling unnatural and suspicious in their battleground of a kitchen. He showered her with conversation and empty compliments.

"You deserve the best, Kay," he would say, his tone dripping with manipulative sincerity.

This sudden kindness was a poison. It didn't bring Kay comfort; it triggered profound suspicion. She watched him, constantly waiting for the mask to slip, her anxiety spiking higher than it ever did during his rage. The sweetness was not love; it was a psychological trap, designed to confuse her, erode her resolve, and make her doubt the clear danger she had just faced. She knew the cycle, and this deceptive peace was only the silent, chilling preamble to the next inevitable, brutal storm.

The stark contrast between his usual abusive behavior and this newfound kindness left Kay confused and wary, yet she couldn't help but feel a glimmer of hope.

Even at night, when they were intimate, Richard had become unexpectedly gentle. The harshness she had grown accustomed to was replaced with tender gestures that felt foreign, as if she were with a different person. It stirred something in her—a mix of longing for this to be real and fear that it was only temporary.

The brief, unsettling calm of Richard's "honeymoon phase" was violently shattered by a single, terrifying truth: Kay was pregnant again.

The realization hit her like a cold, crushing wave, instantly replacing the faint, artificial hope with pure dread. The memory of Richard's words from before—that they barely had the income to support themselves—flared vividly in her mind, turning her stomach to ice. A new life was not a miracle; it was an anchor that would drag her deeper into financial desperation and emotional captivity.

She watched him across the room, her hands trembling uncontrollably as she clutched the positive test result. She knew his volatility, knew that this news could ignite a fury far worse than any she had yet survived.

With a dry throat and a voice barely above a whisper, she forced the words out, confessing the life-altering truth as if it were a terrible crime.

"Richard, I'm pregnant," she finally managed, bracing herself for the inevitable explosion—the shouting, the accusations of financial ruin, the cold fury. Instead, the expression on Richard's face shifted instantaneously, lighting up in a way she hadn't seen in years.

"That's great news, Kay!" he exclaimed, his voice booming with forced, unearned joy. He even took a step toward her, his eyes shining with a strange, possessive excitement.

The reaction hit her with the force of a blow, perhaps more disorienting than the rage she'd expected. She could only stare at him, completely caught off guard, her body still coiled and waiting for the harsh, anticipated words. His happiness felt alien, a horrifying theatrical performance that made the pit of her stomach clench.

She knew the truth: this was not genuine excitement for their future. This was a man finding a new, stronger tether—another innocent life that would make it virtually impossible for her to leave. His sudden joy was just another layer of the trap.

Richard didn't wait for Kay to process the shock. The pregnancy was merely a trigger for his next calculated move. His voice was suddenly energized, bubbling with a false, relentless enthusiasm that made her skin crawl.

"I've been talking to my sister," he announced, the words tumbling out as if this were a shared, exciting plan, not a unilateral decision. "She says there's a great job opportunity in Georgia. It's the break we've been waiting for, Kay! The money is good—it'll finally give us the stability we need for the baby."

He paced the floor, completely ignoring her silence. "Here's what we'll do: I'll go ahead and secure everything—the job, the house, the whole setup. And then you, Lucas, and our new baby can join me."

14

The Final Surrender

The plan was delivered with the smooth finality of a predator closing a cage door. He offered hope and stability—the exact things she desperately longed for—but tied them to a new place where she would have zero support, zero resources, and be completely reliant on him. The move to Georgia wasn't about a better life; it was about achieving total isolation and control.

Richard's words—Georgia, new job, stability—were the precise, shimmering illusions Kay desperately needed to grasp. Despite the icy knot of dread in her stomach, a small, treacherous part of her heart couldn't help but flutter with cautious, agonizing optimism. The idea of a fresh start, a way out of the current toxic isolation, was a powerful temptation, a mirage of safety she could almost touch.

She looked at him, searching for honesty in his eyes, knowing she was inviting disaster by asking. The words, thin and laced with a terrifying vulnerability, betrayed her deepest longing.

"Do you really think it will work out this time?" she asked, her voice barely a breath, raw with desperate hope.

Richard seized the opening instantly. He approached her, his smile practiced and convincing, and took her hands in his—the same hands that had recently bruised her arm.

"It has to work out, Kay," he insisted, his voice low and intimate. "We have a new baby coming. This is our second chance. I promise you, everything will be different in Georgia. We will finally be a real family."

The promise was pure manipulation, but in the crushing chaos of her life, it sounded like salvation. He had successfully reframed the move from an act of control to an act of saving their family, and Kay, terrified of the alternative, felt her resolve begin to crumble.

Kay clung to a fragile hope that maybe leaving Florida might breathe new life into their struggling marriage. She imagined that a fresh start with a new child inside her could somehow turn the tide and transform the disappointment of the past few years into something better, something that might salvage their marriage and give them a renewed sense of possibility.

Despite the knot of internal doubt that tightened with every heartbeat, Kay agreed. Richard's charm offensive—that terrifying blend of false vulnerability and concrete promises—had landed its final blow. She wanted to believe in the possibility of a better future, needed to believe it for the sake of the life growing inside her.

Richard departed for Georgia, leaving behind a silence that was immediately and profoundly felt. He promised to send money and updates, words Kay filed away as fragile collateral.

In his absence, the house was transformed. The air, usually thick with tension and the expectation of rage, was suddenly quieter and less volatile. The simple act of moving around her own kitchen no longer felt like navigating a minefield. For the first time in months, Kay could take a breath that didn't feel supervised.

In that brief, borrowed respite, Kay allowed herself a dangerous indulgence: hope. It was a tiny, tentative thing, but it whispered that maybe, just maybe, things would finally change for the better. The fear was still a constant background hum, but for now, the overwhelming pressure was gone, replaced by the terrifying uncertainty of waiting.

Richard's promises, once sounding like salvation, quickly unraveled, revealing the cold, cynical manipulation behind his sudden kindness and his Georgia plan. The silence in the house, initially a relief, soon turned into a vacuum of worry.

Weeks bled into one another. There was no money, absolutely none, and only sporadic, cryptic phone calls from Richard. He offered vague updates and excuses—the job is delayed, the bank is slow, the wire transfer failed—each one a brittle lie designed to keep Kay passively waiting.

Richard's sporadic, empty calls and the silence where money should have been eventually strangled Kay's fragile hope, deepening into a suffocating despair. The sole, crushing burden of their financial survival rested entirely on her. She worked her exhausting jobs, the physical strain made worse by the life she carried, and still, she was sinking, the debt mounting like an avalanche. The temporary emotional relief of Richard's absence was cruelly offset by the crippling economic vice he maintained from hundreds of miles away.

But amidst the desperation, Kay remained fighting. She attended that critical job interview, the one she fought to make it to months ago, fueled by the terrifying need to survive.

Then, a sudden, blinding breakthrough: She landed the job at a wireless provider.

The offer was more than just a job; it was a lifeline. She was going to be making the most money she had ever earned—a salary that, for the first time, looked like it could actually cover her expenses and provide for them. A wave of transformative confidence washed over the crushing anxiety.

She could do this.

Standing alone in her quiet kitchen, the despair finally lifting, Kay felt a potent surge of power. She realized she could manage this life—the job, the pregnancy, Lucas—without Richard. The money was tangible proof that the walls of his financial prison were starting to crack. The fight was still ahead, but now, Kay had the tools to win.

Richard hadn't truly left; he had simply traded physical abuse for financial and psychological torment, tightening the leash until Kay was completely isolated and dependent. The new house was not a sanctuary; it was a waiting room for her total entrapment.

The new job was a lifeline, but it demanded everything she had. Kay was now driving 60+ miles one way to work, a grueling, time-consuming commute that ate up hours of her life. Yet, the steady pay made all the difference, creating a stable foundation she'd never had.

With an affordable sitter secured for Lucas, Kay settled into a punishing, necessary routine. She was managing it all: the long hours, the pregnancy, the housework, the sole responsibility for her son. She stayed diligent, fighting the exhaustion, forcing herself to keep a positive attitude—a desperate soldier fighting to keep their life afloat.

Surrender was a word erased from Kay's vocabulary. Giving up was not an option. Every bruise, every insult, every moment of paralyzing fear was now fuel for an unyielding, crystalline determination. She had seen the alternative—the dead-end of staying—and she chose the terrifying path of self-rescue.

Her success would not be measured in simple financial stability, but in total liberation. It was a path she was now prepared to carve out alone, powered by the love for her children and the cold, hard proof that she was capable.

She was done fighting Richard's battles; she was now fighting for her life. She would find the way, not just to survive, but to build a future defined by her own strength, securing a permanent, untouchable sanctuary for Lucas and the baby growing inside her. The grind would continue, but the goal was no longer keeping things afloat—it was reaching the distant shore of absolute freedom.

The bitter irony of her situation was a constant undercurrent: the stress was immense, but she was succeeding. The crucial realization crystallized with undeniable clarity: when Richard was home, he hadn't helped anyway. He had only created chaos, debt, and danger.

She was essentially doing the exact same difficult work now, but without his drama in the mix. The relentless grind of her independent life was a thousand times lighter than the paralyzing fear of his presence. Richard's absence was not a burden; it was a gift. She was finally, truly, in control of her own ship.

One evening, Kay found herself out of gas, stranded at a gas station with no money. The shared debit card was empty, and she had no way of getting home. Humiliation washed over her as she approached strangers, begging for enough money to fill her tank. "Please, just a few dollars," she pleaded, her voice trembling with desperation. Finally, a kind-hearted woman took pity on her and handed her a few bills. "Thank you," Kay whispered, tears of gratitude and shame mingling on her cheeks.

Richard's control didn't lessen with distance; it simply changed form, becoming an act of calculated, financial violence. He he had emptied their bank account, deliberately leaving Kay with a zero balance and no resources. This was not neglect; it was a cold, calculated move to guarantee her utter dependency.

Inside her mind, Kay was trapped in a crushing cycle of self-recrimination and desperate hope. She knew, logically, that depositing her new salary into the joint account—the same account Richard had repeatedly misused—was reckless. The outside voice in her head screamed, "How could you be so stupid?" Yet, the abusive dynamic forced her hand. She was desperately trying to buy peace; by demonstrating a willingness to commit to the "family plan" for Georgia, she hoped to delay his next inevitable explosion and secure a window of calm. She couldn't afford the immediate, certain violence that would erupt if she were caught opening a secret account. She was betting that the temporary stability of the new income, combined with the false promise of a better future, would keep Richard docile long enough for her to gather the resources and courage to finally escape his terrifying control. It was less an act of stupidity and more a terrible, calculated risk taken by a person in profound survival mode.

Even from hundreds of miles away, Richard continued his maneuvers. His sister's connections in Georgia weren't just a job lead; they were the most viable escape route to a place where he could re-establish total authority.

He was determined to exploit that connection, not for their "fresh start," but to rebuild his financial and emotional prison walls around Kay. She was working herself to exhaustion, fighting to fill a hole Richard had intentionally dug.

Despite his promises, Richard was living with his sister and job hunting, leaving Kay to fend for herself and Lucas. "I've got the job," he would say. "It's the most money I've ever made. We'll be able to live comfortably, and you can finally be a stay-at-home mom."

Kay wanted to believe him, but the reality of her situation kept intruding. She was falling behind on bills, struggling to provide for Lucas, and feeling the crushing weight of isolation. The temporary respite from Richard's physical presence did little to alleviate the mental and emotional strain. Each day was a battle to survive, her hope dimming with each unfulfilled promise.

In Richard's absence, Kay found solace in her friendships. They spent evenings playing cards, watching movies, and sharing meals. For a few hours, Kay could escape the relentless pressure and enjoy the simple pleasures of companionship. But even this brief respite was tinged with fear, as Richard's manipulative reach extended far beyond his physical presence.

Weeks turned into months, and finally, Richard called with the news.

"I got us a beautiful house here in Georgia," he said, his voice brimming with excitement. The promises of financial stability and a new beginning swayed Kay's heart.

The hardest reality of the Georgia move was the sacrifice demanded of her burgeoning self. Kay had to quit the amazing job she loved. She had been making the most money of her life, and while the high childcare costs consumed a chunk of it, the financial gain was secondary to the person the job allowed her to be. For the first time in years, she felt like a woman—not just a beleaguered wife and mother, but an individual with skills, competence, and a career. The office was a sanctuary where she could grow her skills and simply be herself, free from Richard's tyrannical gaze. Quitting was a profound loss of identity, a necessary surrender to staying with Richard. As she packed, she wasn't just losing income; she was burying the confident, capable woman she had just managed to resurrect.

"Please, Kay. Don't go," her friend Katie begged, clinging to her arm. "You have a job here. We can help you. We can make a separate account for you. Why are you choosing to walk back into this?"

Kay's eyes were wet, but her voice was steeped in a raw mix of shame and resignation. She felt the weight of the coming baby, the crushing financial need, and the insidious belief that she was the one who had to "fix" their family.

"I know, I know," Kay whispered, her throat tight. "But the money's gone now. I have to go. He promised stability for the boys. If I don't go, he'll just come back here, and then what? It's better if he's away, setting up the new life. I have to give him this chance."

Katie looked defeated. "A chance to do what, Kay? To finish what he started?"

But Kay was already retreating into the illusion. She squeezed Katie's hand one last time, turned to the boxes, and sealed the fate she believed was unavoidable.

As Richard arrived with a borrowed truck and horse trailer to move their things, Kay took one last look at the house that had once symbolized hope. She clutched Lucas close, whispering a silent promise to protect him no matter what lay ahead.

With her other hand resting on her swollen belly, she gently soothed the baby within, feeling the rhythmic movements that reminded her of the life she was carrying. The road to Georgia was paved with uncertainty, but in Kay's heart, a flicker of hope remained. She couldn't shake the feeling that this move was their last chance at finding the peace and stability she so desperately craved.

As they drove away, the future loomed large, filled with both promise and the shadows of past mistakes, leaving Kay to wonder if this new chapter would bring salvation or further heartbreak.

15

The Gated Canyon

In the dim light of early morning, Kay stirred awake, her body heavy with fatigue. The remnants of a restless night clung to her, an echo of the dreams that had turned into nightmares. She blinked slowly, her eyes adjusting to the half-light filtering through the curtains, but her senses were instantly alerted to the familiar presence beside her. Richard lay next to her, his arm draped over her as if claiming ownership.

The tension in the room was palpable, a suffocating weight that had become all too common since their arrival in Georgia. Moving here hadn't been the new beginning Richard had promised. Instead, the isolation and control that had once crept into their lives now dominated them entirely. He had grown more possessive and manipulative, as if the distance from friends and family had emboldened him. Georgia, meant to be a fresh start, had only deepened the cracks in Kay's life, leaving her more trapped than ever.

Richard stirred beside her, his presence invasive and oppressive. His hands moved over her skin with a sense of entitlement, a routine she had come to dread. He acted as though his touch was an act of affection, but it felt like anything but. This was not love, nor was it kindness. It was control, plain and simple. His feigned tenderness masked an ulterior motive, one that left Kay feeling hollow inside.

The act was mechanical now—his hands on her, his murmured reassurances, his breath hot against her neck—all of it scripted, all of it suffocating.

As he pressed closer, the warmth of his breath sent a chill through her body, a twisted contrast to the heaviness she felt in her chest. She lay still, her muscles tense, her mind racing through the familiar motions of fear and resignation. Richard's control over her had reached a suffocating crescendo. Every forced encounter left her feeling less like a person and more like an object, a vessel for his desires.

The walls of the bedroom, once a place of rest, had become a prison. She could feel herself shrinking, pulling inward, her spirit withdrawing to a place where he couldn't reach her. Her body was present, but her mind was far away, drifting to places where she could still feel something beyond fear and submission. Each time his hands moved across her, she felt a piece of herself slip further away, until all that was left was a shell, empty and cold.

Kay wanted to resist, to push him away, to say no. But the spark of defiance she once carried had long since dimmed, snuffed out by years of manipulation and fear. Confrontation had become a risk she wasn't willing to take, the consequences were just too heavy to bear. The last time she had tried to stand up to him, his anger had erupted like a storm, leaving her more isolated and frightened than ever before. His punishments weren't always physical, but they were always there, lurking beneath the surface, ready to strike at the slightest provocation.

She lay still as Richard continued his routine, his words dripping with the same sickly sweetness that masked his true nature.

The first morning in their supposed "fresh start" was a gut punch of brutal reality. Richard hadn't secured a comfortable house; he had secured a single-wide trailer nestled down a steep road in what looked like a literal canyon. It was basic, at best, and far from the "amazing, wonderful" life he'd promised. The crushing truth descended upon Kay: she had pulled Lucas and their unborn baby from a stable home near her supportive family and sacrificed her career, only to land in a rural trailer in the middle of nowhere.

She walked through the cramped rooms, the air thick with the smell of old dust and regret. Richard's sister was genuinely great, offering a brief, warm welcome, but Kay already felt the tearing ache of loneliness. She was already missing her family and friends, and a cold, sinking certainty settled over her: she had made a horrible, catastrophic mistake.

Just as Kay tried to steady her breathing, a sharp knock at the door shattered the fragile silence. Richard stepped outside, his posture immediately defensive, exchanging curt words with a man Kay didn't know. He returned seconds later, his face tight with familiar, venomous anger, but this time, it was directed at the world and at her.

"We have to move out," he spat, throwing his hands up.

Kay stared, utterly bewildered. "Move out? Why? We just got here! What's going on?"

Richard relayed the hurried, flimsy lie: the man who rented the place was divorcing and needed the trailer for himself. "He needs this place for himself, Kay. I can't argue with the guy!"

"Richard, we just moved all this stuff in! Boxes are everywhere! Where are we gonna go? Lucas is going to be so confused!" Kay cried, her voice rising in panic.

He cut her off instantly, unwilling to absorb the consequences of his chaos. "I'm going to my sister's. I'll figure out what to do next. Don't be so dramatic!"

Richard stormed out, leaving Kay stranded amid the disaster. She sank onto the floor, pulling Lucas tight against her chest, and the tears finally came—hot, wrenching sobs. This can't be happening. She couldn't believe she had fallen for his pathetic lies, sacrificing her job, her home, and her safety for this immediate, devastating failure.

Every time she thought she was doing the right thing, trying to build a future, her life completely spiraled. They were surrounded by towers of half-unpacked boxes, a mountain of mess, and now they had to leave and go where?

The reality of their isolation was immediate: Richard's sister and her husband were living with extended family; there was absolutely no room for Kay, Lucas, and the new baby. Kay was utterly alone, broke, and stranded in a desolate canyon, watching the last threads of her security burn to ash.

Richard finally returned an hour later, but not with a solution—he came with a sentence. His face was a mask of false resignation.

"There are no other places to rent. Nowhere to go," he announced, the words ringing with finality. "We have to go to Alabama, to my mother's."

The name Alabama was the sound of a prison lock clicking shut. Kay stood motionless, the terrifying certainty blooming in her chest: This was his plan all along. The job in Georgia, the trailer rental, the eviction—all a grotesque, elaborate piece of theater to maneuver her into the one place where she would be completely and utterly alone. The immediate collapse of their "new start" wasn't a failure; it was a devastating success for his control. This must be some sick nightmare, she thought, dizzy with disbelief. How in the world did I let myself get here?

Richard, abandoning his "so-called" amazing job without a second thought, immediately secured his brother's help. Within hours, Richard's brother arrived with the same borrowed truck and trailer. In a desperate, humiliating blur, they emptied the messy, canyon trailer, repacking the same boxes and pulling out the same day. Kay watched the dismal scenery recede, her heart heavy with the devastation of being led directly to the very place she had prayed never to return.

After the grueling, four-hour drive that felt like a journey to the end of the line, they finally arrived at Richard's mother's small trailer. Richard's mother was genuinely happy to see them, offering a brief, immediate respite from homelessness. The home was small, but it was salvation from the street, and Kay mechanically expressed her gratitude for the hospitality.

However, the relief was immediately overshadowed by the brutal logistics. Because Richard's mother had no space, they had to shove their entire life into a storage unit in the nearest town—a final, painful act that rendered Kay completely possession-less and further destabilized her.

Richard immediately launched into his next empty plan, announcing his intention to "find leads" on places to rent. Kay gave him the benefit of the doubt, but only because the exhaustion and the terrifying lack of options had left her with no other choice but to pretend. She was now entirely dependent on the man who had stolen her money and driven her to this place of absolute isolation.

Richard's mother was loving toward Lucas, but Kay was paralyzed by mounting anxiety. The small trailer was quaint, but claustrophobic. The real terror was the woman who ran it: Richard's mother was short-tempered and demanded that things be kept a certain way. Richard, as the baby of her children, could do no wrong in her eyes, a fact that insulated him completely from consequences.

Kay vividly remembered the conversation from earlier in their marriage—a memory that now slammed into her with sickening force. She had once confided in his mother, tentatively sharing the terrifying secret that Richard had hit her.

His mother's response, delivered without hesitation, was the crushing proof of her isolation: "What did you do to deserve it?"

In that moment, standing in the cramped trailer, Kay knew with chilling clarity that she was in a truly bad spot. She was trapped with her abuser and the one person on earth who would justify his violence.

The stay with Richard's mother was tragically short-lived. One evening, a fiery argument erupted over something utterly insignificant—a misplaced chore, a comment about the bills—but the underlying rage of their situation turned the small trailer into a powder keg. Richard and his mother were shouting, the noise ricocheting off the thin walls, and Kay found herself desperately trying to mediate the chaos.

In the heat of the moment, as Kay desperately pleaded for calm, Richard's mother turned her blinding rage away from the men and focused it entirely on Kay. The attack was sudden and shocking: she snapped out and clamped her hand around Kay's arm, her fingers digging in with surprising strength. Kay cried out in pain, the act fueled by a vicious, protective rage for her son. She wouldn't let go, forcing Kay to endure the prolonged agony, a clear message that in this house, Richard was sacrosanct and Kay was the enemy.

Kay recoiled, the shame and the terror instantly crystallizing into absolute clarity. This is it. She looked at the woman who had asked, "What did you do to deserve it?" and knew she was at the end of the line.

"I'm done," Kay whispered, the simple words carrying the weight of years of torment.

16

The Scrambled Road

Kay stumbled outside with the cordless phone, tears streaming, and dialed the number of Marcy, an old friend and former coworker from the insurance company, who lived in Alabama.

"Marcy, please," Kay sobbed into the phone, her voice raw. "I know this is a huge imposition, but is there any way you could lend us a room for a week or so, until we can find a place to rent?"

Marcy, a true Southern Christian woman, was the answer to a desperate prayer. Her husband, a builder, had constructed them a beautiful, sprawling home on twenty acres. Marcy already juggled six children, and the house was chaotic, but she welcomed Kay, Richard, and Lucas with open arms.

"Stay as long as you need, honey," Marcy insisted.

Kay apologized a million times for imposing, vowing to help with anything. Marcy gave them two rooms on the first floor to create some sense of normalcy. Kay retrieved the basics from the storage unit, enough to set up their temporary rooms. Richard quickly fell back into routine, spending his days at the firehall, leaving Kay and Marcy hours to catch up. Marcy was genuinely shocked to hear the full drama that led them there, offering a supportive, non-judgmental ear as Kay recounted the stories.

The peace lasted less than a few weeks. One afternoon, all hell broke loose at Marcy's house. Richard returned home from the fire station and announced, with casual certainty, that they were doing a controlled burn training exercise.

"I'm taking Lucas with me," he stated, grabbing the boy's hand.

Kay's internal panic exploded. "No! Absolutely not!" she snapped, stepping in front of her son. "That is no place for a two-year-old kid! Fires are dangerous, and he is not going!"

Marcy wisely stayed out of the escalating fury. The argument spilled into the driveway as Richard's brother, Ben, pulled up in the truck to pick them up. Richard was insistent, blinded by the need to exert his control and show off Lucas to his buddies. Kay begged and reasoned, but he wouldn't listen.

The confrontation turned physical when Richard tried to forcefully snatch Lucas from Kay's arms. It became a terrifying tug-of-war with Lucas's body caught between them. They struggled violently, and before Kay knew it, she was on the ground with Lucas still clutched fiercely against her.

The feeling of the hard gravel hitting her body, all over, a little boy who was crying in terror, finally shattered every remaining thread of compliance. Kay had had enough.

The minute Richard drove away, Kay ran inside, breathless. She quickly apologized to a stunned Marcy. "I can't do this anymore. I'm done. I'm going back home."

17

The Fragile Redemption

She called her mother, her voice thin with desperation. Her mother, hearing the raw fear in Kay's tone, instantly offered to Western Union her cash to drive home.

Kay and Lucas quickly gathered the few necessities they could carry. She loaded their small truck with what fit, leaving everything else—all their stored belongings, all the physical evidence of her marriage—behind.

Kay was terrified. She could not drive fast enough. How long until Richard returned home to find her gone? Though she knew the way home to Florida like the back of her hand, fear clouded her judgment. She bought a map and took different, winding roads, constantly checking her rearview mirror, convinced Richard was not far behind.

She did not feel safe, did not truly breathe, until she was finally sitting on the sofa in her mother's home. Once again, she was home—a failure, a mess, drama. The shame was crippling. What must my family think of me? she agonized. This girl can't get her life together with a kid and one on the way—how can this be happening?

The next morning, Kay woke up in her bed to a profound, blessed silence. Richard was gone. He hadn't called, he hadn't shown up—he must have been utterly furious that she had left him with no warning, no transportation, and no control. That anger, however, was now hundreds of miles away, and it no longer had the power to paralyze her heart.

Reaching out to Marcy for an update, Kay learned Richard had immediately moved back to his mother's trailer that night, leaving most of the couple's remaining belongings at Marcy's house.

Kay didn't feel a pang of loss; she felt a vast, cold indifference. She didn't care about anything she left behind. The storage unit filled with their possessions, the clothes, the furniture—it was all worthless junk compared to the lives she had saved. Her focus had narrowed to a fierce, protective point: Lucas and the baby growing inside her were all that mattered. Nothing else was even remotely comparable, not a job, not her possessions, and most certainly not the broken, terrified woman she had been.

The shame of returning home as a perceived failure was utterly dwarfed by the burning, quiet conviction that she was done. Done with his abuse. Done with his control. She would start over from scratch, and if that meant living with her mother again, dealing with the judgment of her family and the anxiety, then she would do it with fierce gratitude. This time, she wasn't running to a lie; she was running for their lives, armed with an absolute, unshakeable determination to build a sanctuary for her children.

Safely back in Florida, Kay wasted no time. She enrolled Lucas into a pre-school program and immediately plunged into the job hunt. Despite being heavily pregnant, her urgency was primal: she needed money fast, as her mother couldn't afford to support them all indefinitely.

Richard's calls began immediately, persistently, and suffocating. He switched tactics from rage to desperation, pleading with her to come "home."

"Kay, please. You have to come back," he begged. "I'll get things together. I want us to be a family. I was just stressed out, worried about money, no place to live..."

Kay stood firm, her voice steady and edged with cold clarity. "I am not going back to Alabama, Richard. And I'm not coming back to live with other people. I am done."

Richard, a master of flattery and false sincerity, poured on the empty promises. "You are the center of my world, Kay. I only want to make you proud. When I feel like I'm not doing that, I lash out. I swear, I didn't mean to hurt you. It was the last thing I wanted!"

Kay's frustration finally broke through the polite wall she had built. "Stress? You get stressed, and I get beat! You apologize, and then it happens again!" she shot back, her voice tight with fury and sorrow. "We had a place to live right here in Florida, Richard! My inheritance paid the down payment for that home, and you made us walk away from it! You promise a million things and never deliver. How much more do you think I can take? How much more trauma can we inflict on our children? The baby is about to be born! I can't raise children in this environment, not for myself, but I owe them better. Not this shit."

Richard immediately scrambled, promising marriage counseling. "I swear, we'll go this time! We'll fix it!"

"You said that last time!" Kay snapped, throwing his words back at him. "We did go, and what did you tell me? You told me to get out of the car! You said I was the problem, not you! Remember that?"

He offered a rushed, hollow apology, blaming the meltdown on the loss of the baby and the stress. Kay simply stated, "I am not leaving my mother's." Richard, defeated but not giving up, desperately assured her he would find a way to "show her" that his promises were real and that she could believe him this time.

Kay listened, took it with a grain of salt, and hung up the phone. She was no longer waiting for his change; she was building her own escape route.

She took a job at a local Penske dealer. It wasn't the career she loved, but it was a paycheck, a necessity.

The second crucial step was fortifying her defenses. She enrolled into college online, turning the small, borrowed hours of the evening into an investment in her liberation. Studying every night after Lucas went to bed, working days while he was in pre-school, Kay was starting to see the first fruits of her labor pay off. It wasn't easy, and living back at home felt like a setback, but it was a thousand times better than living in hell with him.

Richard's calls began weekly, a steady drip designed to erode Kay's resolve. He didn't demand or scream; he was soft, checking on her, Lucas, and the baby. Though he still hadn't found work, he insisted on being present.

"I want to be there when the baby is born, Kay," he pleaded. "You owe me that much."

Kay, exhausted by the constant fighting and clinging to the hope that distance was truly healing them, agreed. The calls felt different; perhaps the separation was helping them both. Within days, Richard was back at her mother's home.

Kay established firm ground rules: "You can stay, but you sleep on the couch, and there will be no arguing or yelling. I'm not going back to Alabama, and I'm not going back to that life.

Simultaneously, Kay's sister offered to rent her house down the street to Kay. Grateful, Kay accepted, and they moved in, creating a private space. Richard played the perfect partner, helping with the move and showering Kay with praise. "I'm so proud of you, Kay," he'd say. "Getting Lucas into pre-school, starting college, working full-time... you're amazing." He recognized the immense strength she had mustered up to fight for a better life, and his flattery was an attempt to co-opt her victory.

Richard kept his distance, sleeping on the couch and spending his days job hunting. He soon took a job on the maintenance team at a local golf course. With both of them working, money was coming in, and bills were getting paid. Kay thought, We're doing it. This time is different.

But the fragile peace was shattered when Kay went into premature labor. The doctor gave her a shot of tocolytic to stop the contractions, his tone grave. "You need to go on bed rest," he advised. "That job is too physical. You need a few more weeks before you can deliver safely."

Fear—cold, stark, and absolute—gripped Kay. The memory of her sweet baby girl, whom she had lost, was a terrifying weight. She couldn't bear to be the cause of losing this baby, too.

Richard, sensing the moment of vulnerability, seized the opportunity. He was loving and supportive. "Don't worry, Kay," he insisted, holding her hand. "We will be fine with my income. You stay home, rest, take care of yourself and Lucas. That's the priority now."

Relieved but terrified, Kay resigned from her job, sacrificing her independence for the baby's safety. She stayed home, tending to the house, cooking, cleaning, and going to school, trapped once again in the role of dependent spouse. Richard had successfully removed her income and placed her back under his financial control—all under the guise of love and necessity.

It didn't seem like any time had passed at all since she went on bed rest. One moment, Kay was engaged in the simple, mundane task of moving the kitchen table to sweep and mop underneath it; the next, she felt a sudden, unmistakable gush. Her water broke. She was home alone, terrified, with Lucas safely at preschool and Richard at work. She needed to get to the hospital, and she needed to move fast.

The panic was immediate and absolute. She managed a frantic call to her mother, who lived thankfully close. Her mother rushed her to the hospital, but couldn't stay—she had to attend to staff and patients waiting, leaving Kay alone just as she was being admitted. Richard was still at work, unreachable, and someone needed to get word to him.

Kay was scared and profoundly alone. Every white wall, every antiseptic smell of the delivery ward, triggered a wave of paralyzing memory: the last time she was in this hospital, things had not gone as planned. The quiet dread of loss settled over her, chilling her despite the urgency of the moment. She was quickly admitted and found she was already dilated—it wouldn't be long. Her primary worry now was a desperate, anxious plea: Where was Richard? Did he know? Was he on his way?

Within an hour, just as the delivery team was preparing, the door swung open, and Richard arrived. He had made it, showing up just in time for her to give birth. It all happened with blinding speed.

A brief, overwhelming rush of pain, and then a profound, disbelieving silence. Kay was handed her new baby boy, Aiden.

Later, Kay's friend arrived, having picked Lucas up from preschool, and brought him into the room to meet his new brother. Lucas, wide-eyed and quiet, looked at the tiny, peaceful infant. Aiden was small, quiet, and perfect—a new life that felt like a miraculous, fragile redemption after the trauma of the past year. Kay held her new son, relief flooding her system, thankful for this tiny, quiet being who represented a new, hopeful future she was determined to protect.

18

The Vegetative Verdict

Kay stirred awake slowly, her body heavy and sluggish from the drugs and exhaustion. The sterile scent of the hospital room mingled with the distant hum of machines, slowly drawing her foggy mind back to the present. Her eyes scanned the room, landing first on the bulky, worn armchair in the corner where Richard was slumped over, fast asleep.

Then, her gaze shifted to the small bassinet beside her. A tidal wave of feeling—relief, exhaustion, and a fierce, primal love—washed over her. There, swathed in white blankets, was a tiny, perfect bundle. Aiden. Her baby boy. His quiet presence was a miracle, a precious, fragile new beginning salvaged from the brink. Despite everything, she had held on, and he was here.

As Kay slowly sat up, every movement felt disconnected, as though she was moving underwater. A soft rustling came from the bassinet, pulling her attention. Aiden was awake, making soft little noises that reminded her of a kitten. Her heart swelled at the sight of him—perfectly formed, with delicate features, tiny hands curled into fists.

Standing up, her legs shaking from exhaustion and the emotional weight of it all, she approached him. Bending down, she took in his little face, calm and still, eyes fluttering beneath closed lids. But as she watched him breathe, an unsettling thought gnawed at the back of her mind. He was so quiet—almost too quiet.

Her firstborn, Lucas, had filled the room with his cries from the moment he was born. Aiden, however, seemed different—almost unnaturally still. His skin, though soft, carried a yellowish tint that unsettled her. The nurses had mentioned the jaundice, a simple clinical word that belied the heavy weight it carried in the small, sterile room. As Kay gently reached down to stroke Aiden's cheek, the yellowish strangeness of his skin weighed heavily on her. The nurses had assured her it was common, but the image of her healthy baby looking subtly ill was deeply unsettling. They offered a simple piece of advice before she could even ask: "At home, just make sure you set him in the sunlight. He'll get better." It was a small instruction meant to ease her mind, but it added yet another concern to the long list Kay carried—a reminder that even now, she was solely responsible for her baby's fragile health. His tiny body moved so little. Deep inside, she sensed something amiss—something only a mother could know.

Just as she reached out to brush her fingers gently over Aiden's cheek, the door creaked open. She looked up to see the nurse walk in, followed closely by her mother.

Her mother leaned down over the bassinet, her expression transforming into one of pure, unadulterated happiness. Richard, however, seemed distant. Seeing them both now felt surreal, as if they didn't fully belong to this quiet moment between her and Aiden.

The nurse smiled briefly as she checked Kay's vitals and glanced at the baby. "He's doing well," she said. "Just a touch of jaundice, but we'll keep an eye on it. Nothing to worry about."

Kay nodded, but her thoughts were elsewhere. As the nurse continued her routine, she glanced at her mother, then Richard, searching for the words to express the gnawing worry in her gut.

"I... I think something's wrong," Kay finally managed to say, her voice shaky. "Aiden's so quiet... and he's not like Lucas. I just feel like something's off."

Her mother sighed at the familiar sound that came when she thought Kay was overreacting. "Honey, every baby is different. Lucas was loud from the start, but that doesn't mean anything's wrong with Aiden."

Richard, standing by the door, glanced at his phone and shrugged dismissively. "Yeah, he's fine. Don't stress so much."

Kay's heart sank. She looked at the nurse for validation, but the nurse simply smiled and said, "It's common for mothers to feel anxious after birth. You're still recovering. Try to rest."

Silenced by their dismissals, Kay swallowed her unease. Maybe they were right. Perhaps she was just being paranoid, feeling overly protective and anxious in her post-birth haze. She nodded along, but the hollow pit in her stomach remained.

Back to their home in Florida, Kay and Aiden were welcomed warmly by friends whose love provided some comfort. The last few months had been tough, but their excitement at meeting Aiden lightened Kay's heavy mood. Lucas had stepped into his role as big brother with maturity, proudly helping and showing love to Aiden. Kay felt proud watching him grow into such a caring and thoughtful boy. Yet, despite the picture-perfect family they presented to others, Richard was retreating to his old behavior. In public, he was the doting father, but in private, his abusive, controlling behavior resurfaced, deepening Kay's isolation. Still, for her children, she pressed on.

Kay, though, couldn't shake the growing pit of worry gnawing at her. Aiden was different. He was quieter, more reserved than Lucas had been as a baby. He didn't cry much and barely made a sound unless he was hungry. Something about his stillness, the way he gazed off without truly focusing, left her feeling unsettled.

She tried to talk to her friends. Over coffee and casual chats, she would carefully bring it up.

"Aiden doesn't cry or move much," she mentioned one afternoon, stirring her coffee absentmindedly. "He's so different from Lucas at this age."

"Oh, don't worry about that!" Lisa, her friendly neighbor, replied. "Each child is different. Lucas might have been a handful, but Aiden's just laid-back. Enjoy it while it lasts!"

"Exactly," chimed in another friend, Jenna, leaning forward with a smile. "Some babies are just quieter. You can't expect them to act the same."

Kay nodded along, forcing a smile. "Yeah, I guess you're right."

But deep inside, she felt something was wrong. She couldn't explain it, couldn't pinpoint exactly what it was, but it gnawed at her, a persistent whisper in the back of her mind. Even her mother, during their phone calls, insisted Kay was just overthinking things in her postpartum haze.

"Kay, honey, you're just tired. Newborns all have their quirks. Just give it time. You'll see—he'll start making more noise as he grows."

"I hope so," Kay would say, feeling the weight of her mother's words but still haunted by her concerns.

The more they brushed off her worries, the more Kay withdrew into herself. She stopped bringing it up, swallowing her fears and doubts every time Aiden would stare blankly at the ceiling or lie still in his crib for hours. One afternoon, while rocking Aiden in in the nursery, she whispered to him, "I just want to know you're okay, baby. You can tell me if something's wrong." His wide eyes gazed past her, and the pit in her stomach tightened.

Later, while folding laundry, Kay found herself lost in thought. Lucas burst into the room, his energy filling the space. "Mom! Can we play outside?"

"Of course, sweetie. Just let me finish up here," she said, forcing a smile. When Richard walked in, she tried to shake off her worries. "Lucas wants to play outside. I think I'll join him in a minute," she said, trying to sound casual.

"Can you look after Aiden while I take Lucas outside?" she asked, her voice tight with suppressed anxiety.

Richard didn't even look up from his chair. "Sure. He's just sleeping, right?" he replied, dismissing her concern with a careless wave of his hand.

Kay hesitated, the crucial instruction—don't let him lie flat because of the jaundice, keep an eye on his breathing—catching in her throat. "Yes, he is. But I—"

"Just let the baby be, Kay. You worry too much," he interrupted sharply, his tone hardening into the familiar, dismissive command. The sudden sharpness in his voice made her instantly shrink back, the unspoken maternal warning immediately swallowed by the old, instinctive fear of crossing him.

As he left the room, Kay stood frozen, clutching a small onesie in her hands. She told herself maybe they were right. Maybe she was being paranoid. Maybe all babies were just... different. But the hollow pit in her stomach never went away.

Kay returned to work almost immediately. With two boys to care for and a life to rebuild, there was no time to rest. Fortunately, she secured a job at another phone company, a stable position with decent pay and benefits. It was a small victory—something solid amidst the shifting uncertainty that had followed her since Aiden's birth.

The daycare near their new place was affordable, and Aiden was enrolled. Each morning, as Kay dropped him off, she felt a pang of guilt at seeing Aiden's tiny face so quiet and still. "Why aren't you a little more like your brother?" she would whisper, brushing a gentle hand across his cheek. But she reminded herself it was necessary. This job was their chance at a better life, a way to keep moving forward after the chaos of being evicted and the whirlwind of starting over.

Her new car—a used but reliable sedan—had become Kay's lifeline. Although old, with worn seats and a touch of rust around the edges, it was her trusted companion on the long commute from home to work in Tampa, an hour each way. Each morning, she would pack up the boys, drop them off, and brace herself for the day ahead.

As the weeks passed, Kay found herself juggling work, both boys, and managing the house. The demands of her new life left little room for conflict, and she tried to sidestep Richard's simmering frustrations. One evening, while she was unloading groceries, Richard slammed the door behind him.

"I can't keep doing this, Kay!" He shouted, his voice echoing in the small kitchen. "You're always too busy with your job and the kids. What about me?"

Kay was busy in the kitchen, carefully measuring out ingredients, her mind on stretching their meager budget. She took a deep breath, setting a can of beans down on the counter—a gesture of pure, domestic labor and financial worry.

"I'm doing this for all of us, Richard. We need this money," she said, the words a weary justification for the hard choice she'd made to leave the baby so soon and take the job.

Richard scoffed loudly and shoved his chair back from the table. "This place feels like a prison.

"A prison?" Kay countered, turning to face him. "We have a roof over our heads and healthy kids. What's wrong now?"

His face twisted with self-pity. "I was looking online. The golf course is seriously underpaying me here, Kay. I found courses that pay double for the same job! I feel totally taken advantage of "The hours I'm working aren't enough. I'm going to look for courses that pay what I'm worth."

The declaration wasn't a promise of proactive change; it was a preemptive strike. Kay knew the cycle: Richard would quit the one stable job they had, plunging them back into financial uncertainty and giving him a justification for his impending rage.

Richard's announcement was simply the prelude to the inevitable storm. He was the perpetual victim of the "greener grass" syndrome: nothing was ever good enough, and the stability they had was immediately dismissed as a personal insult.

His expectations were wildly unrealistic, fueling a cycle that drove Kay to the brink of madness. It wasn't just about money; it was about instant success without effort. He wanted the high-dollar job and the prestige, but he adamantly refused to work his way up from the bottom. The money wasn't coming in fast enough, the job wasn't prestigious enough, and the fault, by extension, was always laid at Kay's feet for somehow forcing him into this miserable situation. This constant, toxic loop of dissatisfaction and blame was a dizzying prison, and Kay knew exactly where the next escape attempt would land them: in total chaos.

Kay placed her hands flat on the counter, leaning into the exhaustion of their shared burden. "Richard, we can't just run away again! We finally have a roof over our heads and food on the table. You're talking about quitting a job when our bills are just starting to get paid."

Her voice rose, edged with desperation. "I'm doing everything I can to heal our finances—you have to hold up your end! If we chase another fantasy, we'll be homeless again, and I won't do that to our kids. I'm trying to give us stability, and we both need to fight for it."

His face twisted with anger, and in a sudden, terrifying burst of rage, he didn't strike her—he lunged toward the table. He snatched the heavy tape measure sitting there and hurled it across the room. It smashed into the wall just inches from Kay's face, the plastic casing exploding on impact with a sharp, violent crack.

He stood breathing heavily, his chest heaving as he pointed at Lucas. "The boys live a life far better than I ever had!" he snarled, using the danger he'd just created to justify his self-pity.

Kay staggered back from the near miss, the sound of the shattering tape measure echoing in the sudden, ringing silence. Her shock quickly gave way to a searing anger born of exhaustion and disappointment.

"Yeah, that's how to handle this!" she shot back, her voice shaking but suddenly loud. "Tear up our house! That's really being a man, Richard!"

Her voice cracked as the question that haunted their life finally spilled out, raw with despair. "Why can't we ever just have a discussion? A simple conversation? Everything with you is always a conflict! It's always yelling, breaking things, hitting me, or running away! I'm tired of living like this. I'm tired of walking on eggshells waiting for you to explode."

He stormed out of the kitchen, slamming the front door behind him. The pressure of their life together crashed down on her, and she couldn't hold back the tears any longer.

Slumping against the counter, Kay broke down, her sobs echoing through the empty house. She felt the weight of the world pressing down on her, the fear of their unstable lives, the worry for Aiden and Lucas, and the suffocating isolation of her situation. But after a while, she took a shaky breath, wiped her tears, and forced herself back into her daily routine. She had to be strong for the boys, even if it felt impossible.

The next morning, as Kay worked diligently at her job, putting in extra hours to pay off past due bills and prove her worth for a promotion, the phone rang, pulling her attention away from the computer screen. She answered it, and the voice on the other end sent her heart racing.

"Hello? Is this Aiden's mother?" The voice on the other end, belonging to the pre-school worker, was tight, thin, and laced with a terrifying degree of concern.

Kay's stomach immediately dropped, sinking like a stone. "What's wrong? Is he okay?"

There was a gut-wrenching pause that felt like an eternity. Kay could feel her worst fears creeping in, a cold, tightening vice around her chest, stealing her breath.

Then came the clinical horror: "We're calling to let you that an ambulance is on its way for your son," the woman stated, her voice striving for calm but failing. "Aiden is turning blue, which raises serious concerns about his oxygen levels. If you can, please meet us at the hospital as soon as possible."

Kay didn't hang up the phone; she dropped it—the plastic clattering uselessly on the desk. Her heart immediately began pounding in her chest like a violent drumbeat of dread. She managed a choked, breathless explanation to her boss about the emergency before bolting out of the office, the urgency overriding all composure.

When Kay's desperate call reached Richard at the golf course, his initial reaction was a chaotic mix of disbelief and self-preservation. But the terror in Kay's voice—" He's turning blue!"—cut through his usual self-absorption.

He didn't hesitate. For once, the gravity of the situation was too great for scheming. He immediately marched into his boss's office, delivered a terse, frantic explanation, and left.

As she slammed herself into her car, every second felt like a cruel eternity. The drive to the hospital blurred into a frantic, high-speed rush of terror. She shot onto I-75, the speedometer needle climbing past 90 miles per hour. Her knuckles were white as she gripped the steering wheel, pushing the small car to its limit. The world outside became a hazy, desperate streak of colors—trees and buildings whipping by in a dizzying blur. Her mind spiraled through the worst-case scenarios, each one a sharp, icy terror: Was he breathing?

Despite the hour-long journey under normal circumstances, she barely registered the distance as she navigated through traffic like a storm. The sirens of her anxiety drowned out everything else. Finally, she screeched into the ER parking lot, where a chaotic scene greeted her like a nightmare come to life. Without wasting another moment, she darted down the corridor, the fluorescent lights above flickering ominously. The sound of her footsteps echoed off the sterile walls, each step amplifying the dread coiling in her stomach.

She rushed toward one of the staff members, her voice trembling with urgency. "Excuse me, do you know if a baby named Aiden was brought by ambulance from the daycare?"

"I'm his mother," she added, her eyes frantically scanning the area for any sign of her son. "Can you tell me what's happening?"

"I'm sorry, we don't know much yet," the desk clerk replied, trying to maintain a calm demeanor. The doctors are still assessing the situation. If you go down this hallway, you'll reach the room where your baby is being treated."

Clinging to the hope that someone would soon explain what was happening with Aiden, she hurried toward the indicated room. Her heart raced with each step, and when she arrived, she found him with Richard happy, though discolored, with no signs of struggling to breathe. But as she waited for news, the first round of tests revealed nothing. They checked his heart, examined his stomach, and ran scan after scan—but everything came back normal. Each dead end deepened her frustration and fear. Why couldn't anyone tell her what was wrong with her son?

Kay's hope began to slip away, not with a sudden crash, but with the slow, agonizing erosion of weeks blurring into a desperate maze of appointments and tests. The medical community treated Aiden's blue spells like a puzzle no one could solve, passing Kay and her fragile baby from one specialist to the next across different cities. Each new doctor offered little comfort, leaving Kay to manage the terrifying logistics of shuttling a sick newborn while fighting the suffocating dread of the unknown.

The exhaustion was compounded by the constant, crushing cycle of hope and failure. They first saw a Pediatrician and a Pulmonologist and a Pediatric Cardiologist in Tampa to investigate After every invasive test, the result was the same: No issues found.

After exhaustive, high-tech tests, the doctor delivered the final, devastating news: Aiden's heart was structurally perfect, and there were no issues found. Kay left the hospital with her hope shattered, her checkbook empty, and the terror of the undiagnosed ailment only intensified. The vast network of specialists had only confirmed one terrifying truth: Aiden was still turning blue, and no one knew why.

Next, a lung specialist conducted an array of tests, but again, they came up empty-handed. With each passing day, Kay's anxiety deepened, and her frustration mounted as they continued to search for answers that never seemed to come. Eventually, they admitted Aiden to the Children's Hospital for further evaluation, including consultations with gastroenterology and neurology.

It was during that stay, after a seemingly endless series of tests, that they finally found his first diagnosis. The relief mixed with dread as she grappled with the implications, desperate for clarity in the storm of uncertainty.

Finally, after what felt like hours of waiting, the doctor returned with the news and a tennis racket and bag in hand.

The doctor didn't look up from the chart revealing the MRI results; the grave medical news was delivered with the casual air of announcing a weather report. Kay felt her world tilt sideways when she heard the first words.

"It's a rare condition," he said, glancing dismissively at his watch as if calculating how much time he had left before a scheduled golf game. "Partial Agenesis of the Corpus Callosum."

He offered the explanation mechanically, not meeting her eye. "It's a neurological condition where there is an incomplete formation of the corpus callosum—the main structure connecting the two hemispheres of the brain. Communication between the halves is affected, which can lead to a range of developmental and cognitive challenges. Symptoms can vary widely, but expect developmental delays, learning disabilities, or difficulties with motor skills. Some individuals have milder symptoms, others are asymptomatic."

The words—incomplete formation, developmental challenges, rare condition—struck Kay like a series of physical blows. The doctor spoke of brain hemispheres and medical terms, but all Kay heard was the shattered promise of her son's future, delivered by a man who couldn't wait to leave the room.

Kay blinked, her vision momentarily blurring as she struggled desperately to absorb the torrent of cold, complicated medical terms. She pushed herself upright in the chair, her voice thin with disbelief and raw terror.

"What does that mean?" she finally managed to ask, pleading for a translation that might offer a single shred of hope.

The doctor, already halfway to the door, didn't bother to soften the blow. His expression remained utterly dismissive, and his final words were a casual, brutal execution of her hope.

"Basically, a vegetative condition," he said.

The words didn't just land; they struck her like a heavy, crushing stone dropped directly onto her chest, stealing her breath and shattering the last vestiges of her composure. He offered absolutely no elaboration, no clarification, no path forward—just that cruel, final verdict that left her breathless and reeling. Without another word, without a look of empathy or care, he turned his back on her and her precious, sick son, and left the room. Kay was left in the sterile silence, clutching her tiny baby, the devastating sentence echoing endlessly in the small, empty space.

Richard was pacing the small hospital room, ignoring the fact that his son had just been diagnosed with a rare, complex neurological condition. He wasn't focused on Aiden's future or Kay's terror; he was focused entirely on the doctor who had delivered the news.

"What an asshole," Richard sneered, his voice tight with disdain. He gestured toward the door the doctor had just exited. "He's useless. All those specialists he just drop a bomb like that and walk out."

Kay looked up from her baby, exhaustion blurring her vision, struggling to process his words. "Richard, he just told us Aiden has something seriously wrong with his brain..."Kay was left grappling with the harsh implications of his statement. What would this mean for Aiden? Would he be confined to a life devoid of connection and growth? The fear that her son might never know the joys of life beyond mere existence threatened to engulf her, and at that moment, the weight of uncertainty felt almost unbearable.

She glanced over at Aiden, his tiny body resting peacefully in his crib. He was always so quiet, so content. Was this the future that awaited him?

As the searing shock of the P-ACC diagnosis morphed into a gnawing, steely resolve, Kay felt something harden inside her. She refused to accept the cruel fate the last doctor had so callously dictated. Aiden was more than a neurological challenge; he was more than a doctor's cold, dismissive words.

During that same traumatic hospital stay, while specialists shuffled in and out, the Gastroenterologist finally delivered a second, critical diagnosis that explained the terrifying blue spells: "Silent Aspiration." This explained why Aiden was continually turning blue and struggling with his oxygen levels—he was inhaling tiny amounts of food or liquid into his lungs without coughing or showing obvious distress.

The news was a double-edged sword: another severe diagnosis, but one that offered a clear, immediate solution. This was the reason a feeding tube had been placed—not just to address inadequate weight gain, but to keep the very thing that sustained him from becoming lethal. Kay now had two enemies to fight: the long-term struggle of the P-ACC and the immediate, deadly threat of aspiration. She left the hospital with a heart heavy with grief and fear, but utterly determined to fight for every breath and every milestone her son deserved.

The realization of Aiden's medical needs immediately slammed the door on her fragile plan for stability. The panic was raw and immediate: how would Aiden go to daycare? The terrifying truth hit her—daycares won't care for a child with a feeding tube. They weren't equipped, they weren't staffed, and they certainly wouldn't take the liability of a baby who could aspirate silently or turn blue at any moment.

This single, crushing logistical hurdle threw Kay's entire life into jeopardy. With no one else to provide the intensive medical care Aiden needed, the knot in her stomach tightened into a vise: She was going to lose her job. The income, the college classes, the fragile sense of independence she had fought so hard to build—all of it was about to evaporate. She was facing total financial collapse, forced back into complete dependency just when she had achieved a glimpse of freedom. The medical diagnosis wasn't just a threat to Aiden's health; it was an execution order for Kay's future.

After the surgery, she sought out Richard, hoping for some comfort or support. "Can we talk for a minute?" she asked. She needed reassurance that they were in this together and that he cared for Aiden as she did.

"What's on your mind?"

Her heart sank at his dismissive tone. "I just thought... maybe we could figure things out together with Lucas and Aiden now," she ventured, searching his face for a glimmer of understanding.

"How will I continue to work and take care of Aiden with these tubes and medical needs?" Lucas is fine in pre-school, but Aiden won't be allowed to go back with all these medical issues. He is going to need skilled care, constant monitoring against aspiration, and a liability no standard childcare facility would accept.

The hospital was offering a lifeline: "They're going to get us a social worker to help me figure this out," she told Richard, but that help was abstract and distant. "It's gonna take time, and I've already taken off way too much time from work. I'm going to lose my job." The financial and logistical cliff she faced was absolute.

It was in this moment of pure desperation that Richard offered his terrifying solution: "I'll stay home with Aiden until we can figure out some sort of skilled care for him."

The offer should have been a relief, but it scared Kay rigid. Richard was not a great caretaker; he was neglectful, moody, and volatile. He spent most of his free time glued to the internet, claiming he was doing "research," but the fleeting images of naked girls on his screen told another story of his focus and his commitment. Leaving her fragile, medically complex son in the hands of the very man she had fled—the one who needed constant supervision himself—felt like trading one medical crisis for a disaster of psychological and physical neglect. She was trapped: lose her job and financial footing, or leave Aiden alone with Richard.

19

The Cedar Sanctuary

In the weeks that followed, Richard's commitment to staying home with his sick son was half-hearted at best—a facade quickly crumbling under the weight of real responsibility. He viewed the arrangement not as a necessity, but as an annoying obligation that interfered with his internet browsing and self-pity.

Every morning, before leaving for her ten-hour shift at the Penske dealer, Kay meticulously performed the duties Richard ignored. She moved with frantic, silent urgency, setting up a life support system for Aiden: she prepared the specialized medical supplies, carefully filling the precise feeding bags and running the formula through the tube, ensuring the pump was charged and ready. She laid out clothes, organized a towering stack of diapers, and wrote exhaustive, detailed notes on feeding schedules, medication times, and warning signs for the Silent Aspiration. This frantic, preemptive effort to create some semblance of order and safety was Kay's insurance policy, her desperate attempt to mitigate the neglect she knew was inevitable when she was gone. She was essentially pre-caring for Aiden, hoping her meticulous routine could compensate for Richard's utter lack of focus or commitment.

With no choice but to leave her baby with Richard, she felt a gnawing anxiety each time she walked out the door. The uncertainty of Richard's care loomed over her, and the weight of responsibility pressed heavily on her shoulders as she hoped for the best.

Yet each evening, Kay returned home from her ten-hour shift not to rest, but to a crushing wave of domestic and medical chaos. The house was not merely untidy; it was in a state of deliberate disorder. The kitchen was a total disaster, with dishes piled high in the sink, dried formula smeared across the counters, and Lucas's toys strewn across the floor, ignored.

Worse than the mess was the fear for Aiden. She would rush to the baby, checking the feeding pump and the medical supplies she had so meticulously organized. The sight of the disarray—a bottle left uncapped, a supply bag discarded haphazardly—sent a spike of cold panic through her chest.

"Did you give him a bath?" she would ask Richard, her voice a low, strangled mix of utter exhaustion, disbelief, and fear for her son's health. The question wasn't about the housework; it was about the survival of her medically fragile child.

"He's not dirty!" Richard snapped, his focus was clearly elsewhere. When Kay pointed out Aiden's needs, he shrugged it off. Richard spent most of his time on the internet, ignoring everything and everyone around him. The computer was set up in the baby's room, so he was physically present, but he might as well have been a world away, lost in his distractions. Meanwhile, Aiden lay in his bed, alone and vulnerable, needing the attention, care, and love that Richard seemed unwilling to provide. He craved interaction and comfort, yet he was left in his crib all day, deprived of the nurturing touch and connection every child deserves.

"Why can't you help more around here?" She implored one evening, her voice weary. "I'm doing everything alone!"

Richard rolled his eyes, his frustration palpable. "I'm doing the best I can." With that, he retreated to the couch, turning on the TV to binge-watch his shows, as if escaping into another world would somehow absolve him of his responsibilities.

The more complicated Aiden's care became, the more involved Kay had to be. Trusting Richard to care for him was no longer an option. Aiden now required regular visits with seven different specialists, as well as intensive therapies for speech, occupational skills, and physical development to address his developmental disabilities. Kay was overwhelmed by the demands on her time and energy, taking care of their oldest son and making sure he was loved and cared for on top of everything else. Each appointment and therapy session filled her days and left her exhausted.

As they finally got high-speed internet, it was as if the floodgates had opened for Richard—he dove headfirst into a new obsession: porn, chat rooms, and women.

The deeper he sank into this online world, the more distant he became. It was like a double-edged sword: while Richard occupied himself with virtual distractions, he neglected his responsibilities at home. Kay found herself navigating the chaos alone, juggling the kids, work, bills, and home upkeep with no one to lean on.

With Aiden's increasing reliance on machines to monitor his health, Kay knew securing nursing services was essential. The feeding pump, pulse oximeter, and heart monitor were vital for Aiden's well-being; however, the logistics felt overwhelming. How could she manage two kids while working full-time an hour away?

Kay, feeling trapped with a medically fragile newborn and facing total financial collapse, launched a desperate, frantic campaign for survival. She devoured the internet, spending every precious minute at night while the boys slept, researching resources, options, and programs that could help her care for him and keep her family afloat. She wasn't searching for miracles; she was searching for a financial lifeline—any support that could help get Aiden proper care and get Richard back to full-time work.

Kay knew she had no choice but to get help. She plunged into the daunting process of applying for Supplemental Security Income (SSI) for Aiden immediately following his diagnosis. This was not a simple form; it was a mountain of confusing, complex paperwork designed to be overwhelming. Unable to afford the necessary guidance of an attorney, she was forced to navigate the labyrinthine requirements entirely by herself, fighting for her son's right to support. From meticulously gathering every single medical record from the blur of specialists across multiple cities, to attending intimidating Social Security appointments alone, Kay took on the relentless bureaucracy. Her fierce determination to fight the system matched her resolve to fight for Aiden's health.

Kay found her most immediate and vital weapon: organization. She immediately started creating dedicated binders for each doctor and specialist. These weren't just random folders; they were meticulous, color-coded records where she logged every single medical appointment, every change in medication, every proposed treatment, and every cryptic note from the specialists. There was simply too much to juggle, too much at stake, and organization became her frantic necessity.

She needed to keep it straight; this intense level of detail was the only way she could manage the chaos of Aiden's care while dealing with the chaos of raising two kids, her job, and everything else on her plate.

Richard, predictably, viewed this diligence through his lens of contempt. Watching her laboriously compile charts and schedules, he scoffed and dismissed her effort. "You're going completely over the top, Kay," he'd sneer, dismissing her life-saving vigilance as neurotic excess, simply because it was effort he refused to expend on himself. Her organization was a direct challenge to his disorder, and he hated it.

Kay's life became a brutal, relentless calculation of minutes and miles. Overwhelmed but unyielding, she managed to organize morning medical appointments and therapy sessions around her work schedule, allowing her just enough time to clock in by 3 p.m. for her second shift at the phone company. She would work until 11 p.m., return home, and begin the next shift: cleaning the house, meticulously doing laundry, and preparing all the specialized meals and medical setups for the next day. This domestic labor often kept her awake until 2 or 3 a.m. By 7 a.m., she was awake again, already getting Lucas ready for pre-school and checking on Aiden, the physical exhaustion a constant, dull ache.

Eventually, Kay's relentless persistence and bureaucratic fight paid off. The notice arrived: Aiden's Supplemental Security Income (SSI) application was approved. This success was immediate, profound, and life-changing. With the SSI approval, Aiden immediately qualified for state medical coverage that included essential LPN nursing services. This provided six hours of skilled care each day right in their home. This wasn't just help; it was a lifeline. It was the crucial gap filled, the margin of safety secured, and the only thing that allowed Kay to maintain her job, her sanity, and the delicate balance of their survival.

The daily reality of Aiden's care was a constant, terrifying symphony of technology. With the feeding tube, the beeping pulse oximeter, and the heart monitors all attached, Aiden required relentless, moment-to-moment attention. Kay was intensely grateful for the LPN nurses, viewing them as absolute saviors. They managed the complex medical equipment with ease, offered Kay critical instruction, and—most importantly—gave her a brief, profound reprieve from the suffocating weight of her responsibilities.

The six hours of skilled nursing care were Kay's ultimate salvation, creating an unexpected pocket of peace that allowed her to truly focus at work. With a medically trained professional managing Aiden's vital signs and the terrifying risk of aspiration, the knot of crippling anxiety that followed her everywhere finally loosened. Knowing that Richard was effectively displaced from his role as primary caregiver during those crucial hours gave her the ability to breathe freely for the first time since Aiden's diagnosis. It was the absence of Richard's neglect that was the true gift.

The nursing services provided a temporary, vital escape in another crucial way: when the nurses were present, Richard immediately transformed into the "perfect" father. He would suddenly be attentive, speaking gently to Aiden and Lucas, asking appropriate questions, and even tidying the house. It was a calculated, transparent performance designed to maintain the facade of a loving, functional family for the medical professionals. Kay knew it was a lie, but she was grateful for the hours of peace, safety, and real care it afforded her son. She could pour her full, desperate energy into her job, without the constant, draining fear of a medical emergency caused by his indifference.

"Hey, Lucas! Want to help me with this?" He'd say, his tone light and jovial as he engaged with their older son.

"Sure, Dad!" Lucas beamed, eager for his attention, if only for a brief moment amidst the weight of reality.

Kay watched, a knot twisting in her stomach as Richard reveled in the attention of the nurses, using them as his audience. He leaned into the drama of their marriage, spinning tales of her long hours and absence, painting himself as the martyr while she struggled to hold everything together behind the scenes.

"Honestly, I don't know how she manages it all," he said, a smirk playing on his lips. "It's tough being the one left at home while she's off working all the time."

Kay felt the sting of his words. In Richard's narrative, she was always the villain, the bad guy who prioritized work over family. What he conveniently omitted was the truth: she had no choice but to work tirelessly to feed them, to keep the lights on, and to pay the bills. His part-time job wouldn't even cover the car payment, yet he painted a picture of a mother who was neglectful, which left her feeling like the worst kind of monster.

As the nurses would nod sympathetically, Kay's heart would break. She wanted to scream that she was doing this for them, that every late night and early morning was a sacrifice for their future. But all she could do was smile tightly, knowing Richard's version of their story would linger long after they left.

As December rolled in, the air grew colder, and with it came the familiar warmth of the holiday spirit, a stark contrast to Kay's current reality. Christmas was approaching, and she had secretly put everything on layaway, carefully setting aside small amounts from every paycheck to ensure her boys wouldn't go without.

The quiet effort Kay poured into her secret layaway plan was a direct battle against the shadow of the first Christmas she spent with Lucas—a memory that still held the chill of pure, unadulterated violence. The incident had occurred in Alabama.

That year, the dream of a joyful family holiday had been completely shattered. Gifts provided from a local church charity sat innocently under the tree, but there was nothing from her or Richard for their baby, the stark visual proof of their chaos. The night ended not in cheer, but in a brutal fistfight. Kay's broken nose served as the immediate, painful reminder of that night's end, forcing the cancellation of the planned Christmas dinner. Richard, obsessed with maintaining his facade, had refused to allow anyone to see his handiwork, insisting they tell family that Kay and the baby were too sick to host. Every flash of tinsel and every holiday carol now felt tainted by the memory of that Alabama trauma, fueling Kay's desperate need to provide a safer, happier celebration this time.

As December dragged on, the mounting external cheer became a relentless torture. The festive lights outside glimmered mockingly at her through the window, a stark contrast to the emotional bleakness that enveloped their home. The laughter of children playing outside pierced her heart, reminding her of the simple joy that felt impossibly far away.

Christmas also dragged forth the raw, unhealed wound of her past. December was the anniversary of losing her beloved brother, Brandon. The combined weight of the family trauma from Richard's abuse and the silent grief for Brandon was suffocating. She was fighting so hard for the living, yet she was constantly pulled back by the memory of the dead.

The tinsel glittered, but all Kay saw was the shadow of two devastating Christmases: the one broken by Richard's violence, and the one marked forever by the absence of her brother.

The night Kay managed to sneak the final items home from layaway, Richard was utterly shocked. The sheer volume of gifts triggered his immediate, possessive anger.

"Where did all this come from?" he demanded, his voice low and accusatory, his focus already shifting from the festive scene to the money he felt was stolen from him. "The money, Kay. Where did you get the money for all this?"

Kay felt the familiar dread, knowing he saw her effort not as love, but as financial insubordination. He paced the room, gesturing dismissively at the carefully chosen presents. "They don't need all this stuff! They're small kids. This is too much, Kay! We could have paid the bills with this! You have no idea how much stress this puts on me!"

His judgment was swift and brutal, dismissing her months of sacrifice and secretive planning. He couldn't recognize her fight for normalcy; he only saw her independence and the money she had hidden from his control.

Kay faced Richard's accusatory glare, her carefully constructed holiday joy rapidly turning to ash. She stood her ground, her voice strained but firm, determined to defend her small act of defiance.

"I took a little bit out of each paycheck to make payments," she explained, emphasizing the sacrifice and planning involved. "I wanted the kids to have a great Christmas, Richard. Life has been so hard. This year has been nothing but hospital visits, moving, and fear. They deserve some joy."

Her voice cracked with the painful truth. "It's not their fault we financially struggle! We could have gone through another year with nothing under the tree, or we could make them happy, because it's Christmas." She was arguing not for the gifts, but for the principle:

the children deserved normalcy, and she was the only one fighting to provide it.

With the crushing weight of grief and hardship surrounding her, Kay fought back with sheer will. She was fiercely determined to carve out a pocket of unadulterated joy for her sons. She cranked the Christmas music loud, forcing a bright, happy face onto her exhaustion. The kitchen filled with the nostalgic scent of baked cookies, and she worked tirelessly to make Christmas morning special—an act of defiant love against the bleakness of their reality.

The chaos of the past months was temporarily suspended by the magic of the holiday, and for a few precious hours, Lucas and tiny Aiden were simply boys enjoying the wonder of gifts and a mother's devotion.

The precarious balance of Kay's life finally broke: she had missed too much work. Between Aiden's nonstop medical appointments and the nurses frequently calling in sick, the absences piled up. One afternoon, she was quietly released from her job. She was now home full-time, and they were desperately struggling on Richard's golf course maintenance income alone.

Richard, sensing his advantage, immediately found his angle out. After months of "research," he announced, "I've landed an interview in Atlanta, Georgia, at a high-end golf course. I'm leaving tomorrow."

Kay was shocked, but utterly defeated. She knew the truth: "I can't argue, Richard. We do need more money, and you're not getting a better job here."

He drove to Atlanta for the interview, then drove straight to his mother's in Alabama, avoiding returning to Kay. He called, promising he would send money, which, of course, he did not.

Finally, he called with the triumphant news: "I got the job! I'll send money soon, and we'll get you moved to Georgia." Even though she dreaded the isolation, the truth was undeniable: two kids, no job, nothing. She was powerless. She needed Richard, and he knew it.

With grim determination, Kay began researching schools for Lucas (who was starting kindergarten) and doctors and therapists for Aiden in the Atlanta area.

Less than two months later, Richard's promise of a new life—something much better than a trailer or a rental home—came true with shocking grandeur. He sent Kay a exterior picture for a home that made her jaw drop.

"Look at this, Kay!" he boasted over the phone, his voice happy, upbeat, and full of intoxicating hope. "It's a full cedar home, huge, with high ceilings! It looks like a mansion!" He rattled off the details: "Beautiful wood floors, a fenced backyard for Lucas, tons of room, a double-oven kitchen!"

"I'm making a ton of money, Kay!" he exclaimed. "You won't have to work. You can just care for Aiden and go to school. This is it! This is the beginning of everything!"

Kay was shocked, amazed, and profoundly impressed. Was this the turning point? Was this finally real? His entire demeanor had changed; he seemed genuinely loving and hopeful, promising a new life and an improved marriage.

Kay, once again, packed their belongings, rented a U-Haul, and drove both boys alone to Atlanta. When they arrived, it was even better than he had described. It was early fall, and the tall trees lining the long, winding driveway were turning beautiful shades of gold and crimson, leading up to the most stunning home she had ever seen.

She stepped inside and gasped. It was breathtaking, like something ripped from a magazine.

"Richard, how can we possibly afford this?" she whispered, overwhelmed.

He embraced her, his confidence absolute. "It's all taken care of, Kay. I have it under control. The home is close to the golf course where I'm working, so I can even come home for lunch."

The house was a physical embodiment of success, a stunning, palpable reality that Kay was finally allowed to inhabit. The space itself was luxurious and affirming: each boy had his own bright, dedicated room, ending years of cramped, chaotic sleeping arrangements. The house centered around a large, standing stone fireplace. The kitchen was massive, boasting double ovens—a far cry from the tiny spaces where Kay had fought to prepare meals. There was a separate, elegant dining room, and perhaps most importantly to Kay, a massive office/playroom. This room was a dual sanctuary, perfect for her to resume her college studies and big enough to create a safe, huge play area for the boys.

Kay was ecstatic; it felt like a true new start. Lucas was instantly happy, running through the house in his socks, skating across the hardwood floors, laughing and giggling.

Life settled into a rhythm of stability she'd never known. Lucas started kindergarten, Kay happily resumed college, and without the grueling job, she had more precious time to spend with Aiden, time she loved and treasured. They were, impossibly, happy.

20

The Unyielding Resolve

Every day, Kay poured her heart into Aiden's care, refusing to let any diagnosis define him. The doctors had spoken of limits and boundaries, outlining a future where Aiden would never crawl, never walk, never speak, and might never even eat on his own. But Kay saw something else. She saw strength, a spark in his eyes that defied every expectation placed on him, and with unshakable faith, she began her mission to help him reach beyond what anyone thought possible.

She found herself slipping into the rhythm of appointments. Every week she reached out to new programs, consulted with doctors, and connected with social organizations. She learned the language of his needs, listening not to words but to the quiet communication in his hum, in the small, bright expressions on his face. Aiden's world unfolded slowly, each milestone feeling like a victory carved out of persistence and prayer.

And then, one day, Aiden did the impossible. Determined as ever, he wriggled forward on his belly, his little body working out a way to move. One arm lay to the side, while the other arched, using his elbow to pull himself forward, inching toward a toy on the floor. At times, he would lie on his back, using his legs to push himself backward or roll over to reach something he wanted.

Each movement wasn't without frustration—he would cry out when he couldn't quite reach, but his determination was unwavering, shining through the tears. And then, with a triumphant giggle, he tried to chase after Lucas by using his one-armed crawl, giggling as he went, his laughter filling the house like sunlight breaking through clouds. It was unsteady, imperfect, but it was his, and in that moment, Kay felt her heart lift with pride. She knew this was only the beginning.

Aiden found ways to make himself known even without words. He learned a few basic signs, pressing his hands together to signal "more," laughing when he got his way. And while he didn't speak, the sounds he made had their own language, which Kay grew to understand instinctively. The way he'd hum when he was content or his high-pitched squeal when he was excited became as familiar as any word. His eyes sparkled with a mischief that words couldn't contain, his expressions brimming with the joy of small discoveries.

Some days were hard, weighed down by frustration and exhaustion. But those days were overshadowed by the sheer beauty of seeing him overcome each hurdle. She prayed over him every night, whispering words of love and strength as he drifted off to sleep in her arms. The promise in his eyes, the triumph in every small achievement—each one was a testament to his spirit and her unwavering faith.

Kay immersed herself completely in the world of Aiden's special needs, transforming from an overwhelmed mother into a relentless, self-taught expert. Every minute she wasn't studying for college or tending to her family, she spent on the computer, her desperation fueling her diligence. She pored over site after site, consuming detailed medical articles and complex neurological journals. Her focus wasn't just on the cold medical facts of Partial Agenesis of the Corpus Callosum (P-ACC) and Silent Aspiration; she was hunting for practical solutions, for hope. She reached out to different organizations for support, connecting with foundations and parent groups dedicated to

P-ACC, finally finding voices who understood the isolation and the daunting road ahead. For Kay, this research was her shield and her sword—the only way to truly fight the cruel, silent verdict the doctor had delivered.

Kay had once been told to prepare for all the things Aiden would never do, but she had found a way to celebrate all the things he was doing every single day.

For as young as she was when she became a mother at twenty-one, Kay lived a life of devotion that profoundly transcended her years. She never indulged in the typical, carefree outings of youth—there were no nights out, no late dinners, or no careless drinks with friends. That world simply evaporated the moment her first son was born.

Instead, her children were the undisputed center of her world. Their needs, their activities, and their well-being always came first, a fierce, protective commitment that left no room for selfishness. She didn't mourn the loss of her youth; she traded it for an intense, rewarding purpose. Every moment spent together was infused with value: school events and kindergarten drop-offs for Lucas, endless therapy sessions and critical doctor appointments for Aiden. Whether they were spending time at the park or simply huddled together at home, those moments were Kay's reality, her sanctuary, and her greatest source of unwavering strength.

There was a simple yet profound comfort in knowing her love for her children was unconditional and absolutely steadfast—the single, truest, and strongest connection she had ever known. This deep, bedrock certainty filled the massive emptiness left by the constant chaos and betrayal of her marriage.

She didn't just love them; she immersed herself in nurturing the best relationships she possibly could. Every hug, every bedtime story read to Lucas, every tiny developmental victory celebrated with Aiden, was an active decision to repair the damage and build a future rooted in safety and affection. Their innocent, unwavering devotion was the only thing that had never faltered, and in return, Kay poured all her fierce, determined energy into them, allowing their pure love to be the anchor that held her steady amidst the swirling uncertainty.

Joyful moments weren't grand, orchestrated events; they were found in the smallest, most fiercely protected things. They were found playing ball in the fenced yard, the sheer physicality releasing tension; in blasting music while cooking and cleaning, the volume a defiant counterpoint to past silence; and in dancing wildly around the living room, the hardwood floors Lucas loved turning into a private stage.

Lucas, with his big, magnetic personality, was always at the center of this warmth, eager to be a super helper around the house and always looking to make her laugh with silly jokes and cute antics. His innocent, unwavering affection was Kay's constant lifeline. These moments—this shared, raucous laughter over funny shows or silly games—transformed ordinary, exhausting days into cherished memories, filling Kay's heart with a profound, stabilizing warmth.

Kay and Lucas were far more than mother and son; they were an unspoken alliance, forged in the crucible of chaos. With the number of times she and Richard had separated, and the vast stretches of time Richard spent absent from the house, it had become Kay and Lucas against the world, with tiny Aiden in tow. This history had created a bond so profound it transcended normal family ties.

At just five years old, Lucas was wise beyond his years—a miniature sentinel of emotional support. He was loving, caring, and funny, instinctively eager to fill the vast emotional space Richard left empty. Lucas was special in his own way, operating with an almost adult awareness, as if he knew exactly how much his mother needed him to hold the center steady. His affection wasn't a childish need; it was a steadfast source of strength that helped Kay keep fighting for their small, fiercely protected world.

Watching movies together, surrounded by the love and laughter of her boys, made even the toughest days a little brighter. In those precious instances, her heart was full, and everything felt perfect. Both boys had a love in their hearts that was so evident and vast, wrapping their little family in a sense of belonging and joy.

Her days ran with relentless precision, a series of endless tasks Kay tackled like a machine—well-oiled and utterly efficient. She'd rise before dawn, preparing breakfast, meticulously checking Aiden's medical supplies, and organizing her entire day down to the minute. But this was not mere maintenance; it was a fierce, daily mission. Her work was to care for her family, dedicating every ounce of her strength to ensure her boys would grow stronger and wiser. It was a silent, unbreakable vow: she would shield them from the chaos and hardships she had known, channeling her trauma into a determined, unshakable future for her sons.

As the days blurred into weeks, as usual, Richard's insatiable hunger for quick, dishonest money had taken over. He began using the high-end golf course shop for his side hustles, taking advantage of the company's expensive tools and supplies without permission. It was a fatal, arrogant gamble, and it wasn't long before management caught him and fired him on the spot.

She was sitting at the kitchen table, meticulously trying to stretch their meager grocery money, when he stormed through the front door, rage simmering just beneath the surface.

"They fired me!" Richard growled, slamming his fist on the table. "Those assholes—out to get me from day one. I knew they were looking for a reason to screw me over."

Kay whispered, her heart dropping like a stone. "Fired? What happened?"

"They said I was using the shop for personal stuff," he spat. "Didn't even give me a chance to explain. Just kicked me out, no warning, no nothing."

Kay stood up slowly, her mind spinning with terrifying clarity. "But... Richard, you were using the shop for your side hustles. We talked about this. You knew it was risky."

He stopped pacing and turned on her, eyes blazing with pure, redirected fury. "Are you taking their side now? Is that it? You think this is my fault?"

The truth felt like a physical object stuck in her throat. "I'm not saying it's your fault," she said softly, clutching the counter edge. "I just—"

"Just what?" he snapped, looming over her. "You think I'm the bad guy? You think I wanted this? They were out to get me, Kay, and you know it! I did everything right!"

Kay recoiled, fear mixing with stark desperation. "Richard, we're going to lose the house. We have hardly any money. What are we supposed to do?"

He let out a bitter, self-pitying laugh, venom filling the air. "You think I don't know that? I'm doing the best I can!"

"We can't keep doing this!" Kay finally cried, her voice cracking as frustration and fear bubbled over, no longer contained. "We're always on the edge of disaster, always broke, always struggling, constantly moving! Where are we going to go this time, Richard?" Her plea was laced with the terrifying reality of their situation: "Lucas just started kindergarten, I finally got Aiden set up with a new set of doctors—and Thanksgiving is in two days!" The imminent holiday, meant for family and stability, served only to underscore the depth of their latest, most devastating collapse.

Richard stared at her, his face a mask of cold dismissal. Then, without warning, he grabbed his keys. "I'm going out," he muttered. "I can't deal with this right now."

Kay watched him storm out, leaving her trembling in the kitchen, the weight of everything crashing down. They were days away from being kicked out of the cedar mansion—a fantasy turned nightmare.

Once again, the only constant in her collapsing life came through: her mother. When Kay called, her voice shaking with shame and desperation, her mom had wasted no time. She found them a new place to rent in Florida and covered the deposit and the first three months' rent—yet again saving them from drowning.

Kay felt the guilt tighten in her chest, a physical vice. She had promised herself she would never ask for help again. But here they were, about to move back to Florida with nothing to show for Georgia but more debt.

21

The Reckoning Drive

Richard, of course, was furious, and his anger intensified when the conversation shifted to their escape. "I can't believe you called your mother!" he snapped, his voice tight with humiliation that someone else had stepped in to fix his disaster. "I don't want to go to Florida again, Kay!"

Kay met his blazing eyes with a terrifying weariness, no longer bothering to argue the fault. Her voice was flat, carrying the full weight of their impossible situation. "What else can we do, Richard? Be homeless?" She gestured around the house, the walls of the beautiful mansion mocking their situation. "We are out of options because of what happened here. This is the only way we survive."

Kay watched him with a numbness that was becoming all too familiar. She was exhausted physically and mentally from the endless stress. Richard filled every corner of their life with his selfishness, and she was suffocating.

Late that night, as they packed the last of their belongings, the exhaustion bled into a quiet, cold resolve. "We can't keep doing this, Richard," she said, her back to him. "Something has to change. We can't keep moving, can't keep living like this."

He scoffed. "What are you even talking about?"

Kay turned, "I'm talking about the fact that we have nothing. No money, no home of our own, no stability. And it's not just bad luck, Richard. This keeps happening because of our choices."

His face darkened instantly. "You really want to do this right now? You want to start blaming me?"

"I'm not blaming you," Kay whispered, blinking back tears. "But I'm scared. I'm scared for us, for our kids. I'm scared that we're never going to get out of this cycle."

Richard sneered, shaking his head. "You think it's that easy, huh? You think I don't want things to be different? You think I'm not trying?"

Kay felt the final thread of hope snap. "I don't know what to think anymore, Richard. All I know is that we can't keep doing this."

He stared at her, his jaw clenched, the silence heavy and malicious. Then, without a word, he turned, and his heavy footsteps echoed down the hall, each one pulling him further away from her and from their collapsing family. Kay remained motionless, trembling, the weight of the coming move and the absolute failure of their marriage crashing down around her.

The stunning Atlanta fantasy dissolved into the humiliating reality of yet another emergency move. Once again, they loaded their life into a rented U-Haul, driven by failure and despair, returning directly to Florida. Kay felt the shame of her situation like a physical sickness; she was embarrassed and profoundly guilt-ridden that her mother had, yet again, been forced to bail them out of a disaster entirely of Richard's making.

The rental home her mother secured was a double-wide trailer—a vast step down from the cedar mansion, but perfectly situated right on the river. Despite the chaotic move, the location was a small, immediate blessing. Lucas was ecstatic when he saw the water, and the sight of the covered back porch with its swing offered Kay a flicker of peace. The trailer itself was clean and respectable: three bedrooms, two bathrooms, a decent kitchen and dining room—a safe, small refuge.

Kay immediately plunged into unpacking, fighting exhaustion to complete the boys' rooms first, desperate to restore some sense of normalcy. Thanksgiving had come and gone without celebration, a casualty of the Georgia collapse.

She was self-motivated, resilient, and unyielding in her resolve to make sure Richard's bitterness didn't ruin the kids' joy or their childhood. Even though Richard barely made time for them, she wanted her sons to feel like he was there.

The gravity of their situation was crushing: neither Kay nor Richard had a job, and they were operating on a terrifying two-month grace period before the first rent payment was due. Richard began a sporadic job hunt, while Kay remained at home—a necessary captive, as they did not have the nursing care yet secured for Aiden in this new location. Adding to the upheaval, poor Lucas was immediately enrolled in a new kindergarten, forced to shift schools again just weeks after starting. Kay pushed forward, organizing the chaos, praying that this location—this modest haven by the water—would finally be the place where she could build a wall strong enough to keep the disaster out.

The quiet refuge by the river quickly curdled into a new kind of tension. Richard seemed far more focused on finding a job elsewhere—a better, higher-paying, more prestigious escape route—than securing immediate work in the local area. He spent hours behind the computer, claiming he was diligently applying, but Kay knew better. The reality was that he had certainly not found a job, and the hours were often wasted on pursuits she dared not question, adding another layer of anxious secrecy to their strained life.

The pressure of unemployment and financial insecurity inevitably led back to the familiar, terrifying cycle. The arguments returned, sharp and sudden, escalating until they broke the physical boundary Kay could no longer tolerate. Arguments, fights, and his hitting her continued, the violence a grotesque punctuation mark on their daily despair.

Then, one night, after a particular violent outburst, the emotional dam inside Kay finally shattered. Kay sat alone in her bedroom, bruised and bleeding, with the boys tucked away in their room. She thought they hadn't seen, hadn't heard. But in the quiet, Lucas tiptoed in, his little face a mask of concern. "Don't worry, Mommy," he whispered, crawling into bed beside her. "It's okay, I love you. I'm here." His small arms wrapped around her as if he could somehow shield her from the storm outside.

That night, as she lay in the dark with Lucas still beside her, Kay knew something had to change. The life she'd built for her children couldn't continue this way. For her boys, for herself, she would have to find a way out of the chaos.

It was moments like these that made her see the damage all too clearly. She couldn't ignore it any longer. She couldn't go on pretending that her love alone would be enough to protect them from the ugliness creeping into their lives. The man she had once thought she'd share a life with was no longer just hurting her; he was hurting them all. The sacrifices she'd made, the joy she'd fought so hard to preserve for the kids—they deserved better. She was left with a cold, absolute clarity. She had finally had enough.

She faced Richard, her voice quiet but carrying the final, undeniable weight of her resolve.

"I want out, Richard," she said, the words falling into the silence like lead. "I want a divorce."

Richard's reaction was immediate and theatrical. He was shocked, his eyes welling up as he launched into a desperate, manipulative performance. He was crying, begging her not to destroy the family.

"No, Kay! Please, don't do this!" he sobbed. "We can figure it out. We just got here! Don't throw everything away!"

Kay refused to break. The memory of the black eyes and the stolen money gave her strength. "I'm done, Richard. It's over. We need to figure out how to separate."

His sadness instantly warped into familiar rage and self-pity. "Separate? You can't do this to me!" he yelled, his hands flying up in frustration. "I have no job! No place to go! You brought me back here with nothing! This is your fault, Kay! You ruined me!"

Kay stood motionless, meeting his desperate gaze with an unshakeable resolve. She was no longer afraid of his anger; she was only afraid of letting him stay.

Richard's shock and rage over the divorce demand were immediate and explosive. He screamed, grabbed his keys, and immediately left the house in a rage, tearing out of the driveway toward the river. Kay stood trembling, knowing that in his current state, his destination could be anywhere, and the outcome could be anything.

It was only a short while later that the phone rang, the caller ID showing her mother's boyfriend, Mike. His voice was grave and urgent.

"Kay, listen to me. Richard is down by the river. I need you to stay inside and lock the doors. He has a gun, and he's threatening to kill himself."

Kay felt the blood drain from her face. She sank against the wall, the breath leaving her lungs.

(Voice shaking with cold disbelief) "What? A gun? Are you serious, Mike? Is he okay?"

"I'm coming over now. I'll handle it. Just stay inside."

Mike arrived and spent a terrifying period talking down Richard. Richard confessed his desperation to Mike: he would "rather die than be without her and the boys." Mike, acting decisively, managed to talk him down and secure the weapon.

Richard eventually returned to the house, broken, but safe. He fell to his knees in front of Kay, sobbing uncontrollably, begging for grace and another chance to save their marriage.

Kay looked at him, utterly exhausted, enumerating the long, devastating litany of betrayal: "I can't do this anymore, Richard. I can't. The empty promises, the lies, the deceit, the porn, the cheating with women online—it's destroying me. It's affecting my mental, emotional, and physical health."

Her voice hardened with finality. "I am tired of this rollercoaster life. There is no way for these two precious boys to live. They deserve a safe, healthy home, not this train wreck. Stability is important to raise healthy children, and all these years have been one storm or tragedy after another."

Richard promised to show her, not give her lip service. He swore he would be the husband and father they all needed. Under immense, agonizing duress, Kay told him yes, she would give him another chance, but only because she was terrified. She knew in her heart she wanted the divorce, but she could not live with the guilt of pushing him into killing himself.

Unsurprisingly, Richard's desperate job searches turned up nothing. The grace period for their new trailer quickly vanished; the rent was past due yet again, and they were facing eviction.

But Richard, ever the opportunist, had been communicating on golf maintenance forums and announced a new, dazzling prospect: "I got an interview in Nashville, Tennessee, at one of the largest courses in the state. Kay, this is it. This is the gig that will change everything." The cycle, fueled by chaos and financial despair, was back on, forcing Kay into yet another terrifying move driven by a phantom hope.

Richard was on to his next "get rich quick" idea. He had joined several online groups claiming to know the secret path to success, each one dangling the promise of wealth and freedom just within his reach. It was like an addiction for him—this constant search for the "big break" that would lift them from struggle to prosperity.

"Once I get this job in Nashville, everything will change. Money will solve every problem we have."

His eyes glinted with a feverish obsession; nothing else mattered but getting there, as if Nashville held the key to a life, he had convinced himself was waiting.

With his sights set, Richard threw himself into the pursuit, brushing aside any concerns or objections as if they were merely details to be ignored. His determination was as fierce as it was familiar; Kay had seen that single-minded focus before, and it always meant change was on the horizon, whether they were ready for it or not. Even a major hurricane, threatening to upend the area with relentless rain and howling winds, couldn't sway him from his path.

As the storm warnings grew louder, most people were hunkering down, gathering supplies, and preparing to wait out the weather. But Richard made light of it, laughing off the idea of staying put. He dismissed the threat with a wave of his hand, claiming it was "just a bunch of overblown forecasts." His mind was already in Nashville, imagining the opportunity, the fresh start. Nothing could keep him from leaving to secure that job, the first step in what he was sure would be a life-changing move.

Watching him pack, Kay felt the familiar ache of apprehension settle over her. She held Aiden close, his small form warm against her chest, as if somehow his presence could steady her in the face of yet another upheaval. She looked over at Lucas, his brow furrowed in worry, and felt a surge of protectiveness.

"Richard, are you sure it's a good idea to leave before the hurricane? What will me and the boys do?" Kay asked, her voice trembling slightly with concern.

"Come on, Kay! It's just a bit of rain and wind," he replied, rolling his eyes as he stuffed clothes into a suitcase. "You will be fine at your mothers." His casual dismissal stung, a cruel reminder of how little he seemed to care about their situation or the safety of his family.

Kay felt a mix of relief and despair wash over her as she turned back to her children. She began preparing the resources they would need to ride out the storm, all the while bracing herself against the emotional tempest that was Richard's departure. He was supposed to go up, interview for the job, and send for her and the kids once everything was settled.

The final desperation of their situation was palpable. Because they were facing imminent eviction, the plan was stark and humiliating: Kay and the boys had to move into her mother's home while Richard went ahead to Nashville to "lay the groundwork." He promised he would quickly find a place and then move them all there for a true, fresh start.

Just as Kay was trying to organize this chaotic, temporary retreat—and starting to feel the smallest sense of control over the logistics—another devastating bombshell dropped. The owner arrived unannounced, his face set with cold determination, demanding they vacate the premises immediately. There was no grace period, no last chance.

The evacuation was swift, brutal, and humiliating. Kay and Richard packed everything they owned—furniture, clothing, the remains of their previous lives—and once again, shoved it all into a rented storage unit in town. They left behind only the bare essentials needed for Kay and the boys to survive in a single, cramped bedroom at her mother's: a few changes of clothes, medicine, and the medical equipment for Aiden. This final contraction of their world meant Kay, Lucas, and Aiden were forced to move into a single bedroom in her mother's home. Stripped of their possessions and their privacy, the room became their entire universe, a final, painful testament to the complete, catastrophic failure.

Before he left, Richard played the concerned husband for the final time. He made sure Kay and the boys were "settled" in the single, cramped bedroom at her mother's house. It was a cursory show of attention, designed to leave Kay feeling obligated rather than secure. Then, without fanfare, he took their only car—the sole means Kay had of achieving any independence—and left for Nashville. His departure was marked by the familiar, empty promise: he would call, he would get the job, and he would send for them soon to start their elusive new life. Kay was left completely reliant on his word, stranded once again, and her entire future was dependent on a man who had never kept a single one of his promises.

As he pulled out of her mother's driveway, taking their only means of transportation, Richard offered one last, thin assurance, tossing it over his shoulder like a handful of cheap confetti. "It's just for a short time, Kay. Don't worry." He delivered the command to stop worrying, yet left her staring at the gaping, immediate reality of her life: two children, no car, no job, and all their possessions locked in a storage unit—all dependent on his next move. That simple sentence, intended to soothe, only amplified the terrifying precariousness of her existence.

"Thank you, Mom. I know this isn't easy, and I just—thank you. I don't know what I would do without you."

Her mother gave a small nod as she reached out, placing a reassuring hand on Kay's shoulder. "We'll get through this, Kay. Just focus on the kids and getting some rest."

With Richard gone and their world temporarily contracted to a single room, Kay desperately tried to settle into a new rhythm. The next two days were a haze of anxious stillness as she focused solely on making her children feel safe in this temporary haven. She kept Lucas close, answering his endless questions about the move and his father's absence with as much patience as she could muster.

Kay's mother did her best to make them comfortable, but the storm clouds looming outside only added to the tension inside. Then, as predicted, the hurricane hit—its winds howling and rain pouring down like a wrathful tide. They huddled together as the power went out, plunging them into darkness.

The meager sense of stability was brutally short-lived. Two massive hurricanes followed in quick succession, a devastating one-two punch that shattered the quiet refuge. The roar of the wind was deafening, uprooting trees, tearing at rooftops, and turning the streets into deep, brown rivers. Then came the silence of the aftermath: they were left without power for eleven endless days.

This was a crisis, made slightly less lethal only by her mother's foresight. Kay's mother had a generator that provided just enough electricity for life's necessities. This allowed Kay to keep the refrigerator running and, crucially, to charge the batteries for Aiden's feeding pump in short, desperate bursts. The power was limited, but the generator was the only reason Aiden's lifeline remained operational.

The terrifying reality was Richard's complete silence. He hadn't called once—not to check if they were safe, not to see if they needed help. Eleven days passed with no word.

By the fifth day without power, Kay's nerves were utterly frayed. The darkness amplified her fear for Aiden; despite the generator, she was still forced to manually watch every single breath and color shift, battling exhaustion and the constant, crushing dread of a silent event. Richard's utter, selfish neglect was the final cruelty in the midst of a natural disaster.

Kay raced to the phone when it finally rang—a sound that sliced through the anxious quiet. Her heart leapt with a painful mix of hope and terror.

"Richard!" she answered instantly, the name tasting like a desperate prayer. She tried, unsuccessfully, to mask the raw exhaustion and pleading desperation in her voice.

"Listen, Kay," he said, his tone shockingly cold and distant, utterly devoid of any concern for the hurricanes or their safety. His voice sounded miles away, clinically detached from their reality. "I just called to let you know I'm not coming back."

The words hit her with the sickening force of a physical blow, a direct strike to the center of her chest. Her world fractured. "What?" she whispered, barely able to form the sound. "What do you mean you're not coming back?"

"I mean, I'm moving on, Kay. This isn't working for me, alright?" he said flatly, the explanation as shallow as a puddle. The true horror wasn't his absence; it was the total lack of feeling in his voice, proving her entire fight—the job loss, the moves—had been for a ghost.

"Not working for you?" Kay repeated, her voice rising to a raw, disbelieving cry. The sheer audacity of his selfishness was staggering. "Richard, I'm here in the middle of a hurricane with two young kids, no power, and no way out! You deliberately left us with nothing. You didn't even call to check on us for eleven days!"

Kay's initial shock quickly turned to a cold, burning fury when the immediate, brutal question of survival surfaced. She remembered the urgency that had driven her to the ATM.

"Also, where is the money? I went to the ATM to get some cash for gas, and it says zero balance! What did you do?"

Richard's voice, already distant, became defensive and dismissive. "Oh, that. I needed it for my hotel and gas money to get around Nashville. I've got a lot of ground to cover."

Kay felt the air leave her lungs, the realization of the deliberate cruelty hitting her like a fresh wave. "You left us with no money! Nothing! You cleaned out the entire account! How could you do that, Richard? How could you take our last dollar?"

Richard trying to shift the blame, "Look, Kay, it's not a big deal. You'll be fine with your mom. She's got money, right? You guys don't need it right now."

Kay, shaking with rage and despair, "Need it? We need it to survive! Aiden's Social Security payment was in there! You stole money meant for a special needs child!"

Richard, hardening his tone, completely indifferent, "I don't know what to tell you, Kay. You'll be fine with your mom. I have to take care of myself out here. Don't worry about it."

His response was delivered with chilling, flat finality, a testament to his utter lack of empathy. "Look, I don't see the point in dragging this out. I've got my own plans now, and they don't include running back to pick up the pieces every time something goes wrong for you."

The implied blame—that her crisis was an imposition on his new freedom—sent a bolt of white-hot fury through her. Her hand gripped the phone so tightly her knuckles turned white, the plastic digging into her palm. "After everything I've done to make things work—the moves, the jobs, the doctors—you're just gonna... leave?"

"I'm done, Kay," he said, unmoved, his voice already moving on to his better, unencumbered future. "I have my own life to live."

Kay lowered the phone, her hand trembling uncontrollably, fighting back the urge to scream a primal, wounded sound. Tears streamed down her face, mixing the bitter sting of anger with the profound ache of heartbreak.

"How could you leave me after everything I had done?" The internal question was a crushing weight. She thought of the countless hours spent caring for Aiden's medical needs, managing the household, and working to provide for their family—all while he remained oblivious to her sacrifices. She had stayed by his side through the darkest moments, enduring his abuse, neglect, and indifference, only to find herself abandoned in the wake of a literal disaster when she needed him most. The betrayal felt like a knife twisting deep in her heart, deepening the wound of his departure into an absolute, final devastation.

By the time the power returned and the roads cleared, Kay's fury had only grown.

That evening, Kay sat with her mother, her face hardened with determination. "I'm going to Nashville," she said simply.

Her mother's eyes widened. "Are you out of your mind, Kay? What about the kids?"

"Will you keep them for me?" Kay replied, her voice steadier than she felt. "Just for a few days. I need to confront him, Mom. I can't let him have the last word after everything he's done to us."

Kay's mother stood watching, her arms folded tightly across her chest as deep frustration and disbelief washed over her face. Her voice, though strained, was firm with desperate conviction.

"Kay, you all have been through enough!" she insisted, shaking her head. "Don't give him any more power by chasing after him. Just let him go! This is the moment you stop the madness." Her eyes searched Kay's face, pleading for understanding. "Why would you even want to go after him? This is your chance to be free! You have Aiden's SSI, and you have the boys safe. You are so much better off without him!" The words were a direct challenge to the manipulative fear that still bound Kay, urging her daughter to finally choose survival over a toxic promise.

But Kay shook her head, the exhaustion and betrayal finally hardening into pure, unyielding resolve. Her voice was quiet, but it carried the weight of a definitive decision.

"No, Mom. He doesn't get to walk off and leave us with nothing and just vanish," Kay insisted, her face set. "He left us stranded in the middle of a literal disaster. He owes me better than this, and he is going to face me. I'm done being the victim." Her eyes met her mother's, pleading not for intervention, but for validation. "I'm going, and I am begging for your support. I can't do this without knowing you're backing me up."

Her mother definitely thought she was insane, but after a long silence, she relented, however hesitantly: "Fine. I will keep the boys with me."

Kay nodded slowly, her resolve hardening into an unyielding wall of steel. She pulled Lucas into a fierce hug, kissing the top of his head and whispering promises of immediate safety. Then she shifted her focus to Aiden, holding him close to her chest. The small, fragile body of her baby, still fretful and needing constant attention, was the weight that gave her the final push.

"Mommy's going to make this right, sweetie," she murmured into his soft hair, her voice thick with emotion but absolute certainty. I'm going to end this chaos, and I will make sure of it." The promise was a silent oath to herself: she would retrieve what Richard had stolen, and then she would ensure their future was one defined by her strength, not his neglect.

The next morning, Kay did not wake up with grief; she woke up with a cold, driving fury. She set out toward Nashville alone, her mind a dangerous storm of rage, fear, and unyielding determination. This journey was no longer about clinging to a dead marriage for the children's sake or hoping for some fleeting miracle of change. This was a reckoning.

Richard had made the profound error of not just abandoning her, but of stealing her last hope—and dismissing her as weak, dependent baggage. Kay was going to drive hundreds of miles to make sure that Richard knew the true, terrifying strength of the woman he had so callously cast aside. She wasn't just coming for the money; she was coming for justice, prepared to look the man who broke her in the eye and prove that she would be the architect of his consequences.

22

The Six-Month Lie

Kay's fingers gripped the steering wheel tightly, her knuckles white as the road blurred beneath her. The miles between Florida and Nashville stretched out like the years she'd spent in this marriage—endless, suffocating, and full of moments she couldn't take back. She hadn't stopped once during the drive, her mind spinning, calculating, mapping out a plan that would change everything.

The tires hummed against the asphalt, carrying Kay toward the inevitable. She knew, with bone-deep certainty, that this was it. This was the final, non-negotiable chapter in the story she'd been forced to live—the one she'd kept pretending had some possibility of a happy ending. That fantasy was dead.

She had spent too many years swallowing the pain, playing the role of the dutiful, naive wife while Richard got to live his life without any real consequences for his destruction. But now, the exhaustion and the betrayal had distilled into a cold, unbreakable resolve. She was ready. She wasn't going to keep walking through this storm blindly; she was driving into the chaos with a plan of her own—a plan rooted in justice and a fiercely protected future for her sons. The time for pretense was over.

She had contemplated this moment for days, running the confrontation over and over in her mind. But now that she was finally driving toward Nashville, the initial surge of excitement was over-shadowed by a cold, steely determination. There was no room left for doubt, only a grim focus on the mission. She was no longer running from disaster; she was moving toward her future, ready to execute her meticulous strategy. She was going to get everything she needed: the last remnants of their financial stability, legal clarity over the chil-dren, and the first clean steps toward the future she would build alone. She had planned it all down to the smallest detail, and Richard was about to face the consequences of dismissing a woman with nothing left to lose.

The plan that hardened in Kay's mind during the long drive to Nashville was brutal in its simplicity and chilling in its resolve. It was a six-month strategy for total liberation.

This journey was not about confrontation; it was about perfor-mance. Kay would get Richard back in line, making him genuinely be-lieve she was still willing to fight for their family, for their life. She would move the boys up to Nashville, settle them in, and play the role of the perfect, compliant wife once again. She would act as if every-thing was normal, as if she were still that woman he could easily ma-nipulate, control, and push around. She would give him the illusion of the "real family" he constantly craved and the stability he immediately sabotaged.

But all along, Kay would be setting the stage for the real ending. Six months. That was all it would take to establish residency, secure legal footing, and ensure Aiden's medical transfers were complete. In six months, she would file for divorce, walking away with everything she could legally take, ensuring their future was finally secured on a foundation built by her, and her alone. This time, there would be no going back.

Finally reaching the cheap motel Richard was staying at, Kay sat in the parking lot, trying to calm her emotions from running wild. She was sure she'd catch him inside with someone—a woman from one of his chatrooms, maybe someone local he'd charmed into letting him crash at her place. But no.

When she knocked on his door, it was just him, disheveled and tired. No other woman in sight. The surprise was brief, and then the anger simmered just under the surface. He had left her and the kids with nothing, cleaned out her bank account, and now he was here, looking like he didn't have a care in the world. But she swallowed it down. Not now, not yet. This wasn't about settling scores today.

"Kay," he said cautiously. His expression flickered between irritation and wariness. "What are you doing here?"

She stepped forward, her voice soft, pleading. "Richard, can we just talk. Please."

His eyes narrowed slightly. "We already talked, Kay. It's over."

She forced a small, broken smile and ignored the pang in her chest. "We did. But I've had time to think, and I just... I know we can fix this. For us. For the kids. I'm willing to try—if you are."

He hesitated, glancing back into the small, dimly lit room behind him. Finally, he stepped aside. "Come in."

The room smelled of stale smoke and cheap beer. A duffel bag sat in the corner, half-unzipped with clothes spilling out. Kay perched on the edge of the bed, her hands clasped tightly in her lap. Richard leaned against the dresser, arms crossed, waiting for her to speak.

"I know things haven't been good for a long time, Richard," Kay began, her voice carefully measured and laced with a deceptive sincerity. She had to sell the lie. "But I truly believe we can get back to where we were. We've been through too much to just throw it all away. Think of all we've overcome—the moves, the children, the diagnosis. We can fight for this marriage. Let's make it work, for the boys."

Richard scoffed, shaking his head with a show of weary exasperation. "Kay, it's not that simple," he insisted, his tone hardening with false resistance. "Things are different now. I've got a really good job here, starting tomorrow. I'm finally trying to start over, and I can't just throw that away to run back to Florida. You need to understand I have commitments now."

Kay quickly leaned forward, her voice dropping to a persuasive, sincere tone, fully committed to her performance. "And I'm proud of you for that, Richard. I truly am—landing a job like this is exactly what you needed." She paused, ensuring he felt her validation. "But starting over doesn't have to mean leaving your family behind."

She widened her gaze around the area, selling the illusion. "This city... I agree it's a fresh start, a real opportunity. Think about the boys: the schools are better here; the medical care is phenomenal. Aiden could finally get the comprehensive treatment he needs without us worrying sick about how to afford it. There are more opportunities here, Richard, for all of us. This is the chance to build that real life you always wanted."

Her voice softened, but there was urgency beneath it. "I can move the kids up here. I'll find a job, whatever it takes to make this work. We don't have to keep struggling like we did before. We have a chance to build something better."

His eyes narrowed. "Why go so far?"

Her breath hitched, but she steadied herself. "Because I realized what I stand to lose. I can't let that happen—not to Lucas, not to Aiden. They need their father, Richard. And I... I need you." The words tasted bitter, but she said them anyway.

"It's not as easy as you say," he sighed, rubbing the back of his neck.

"Then let's make it easier," she pleaded. "We can do this together. I'll do better. I'll be a better wife, a better partner. I'll support you in everything. Just... give us another chance. Please."

He studied her for a long moment, his expression unreadable, as Kay held her breath.

Richard slowly dipped his head, the gesture looking less like acceptance and more like reluctant surrender. The fight drained out of him, replaced by the selfish lure of stability and the convenience of having Kay manage his life.

"Alright," he finally conceded, the word tight and grudging. "We can try one more time, I guess. But you make sure this works, Kay. You handle the moving." He wasn't agreeing to a partnership; he was delegating a chore, fully stepping into the trap Kay had just meticulously set.

"Thank you, Richard. You won't regret this. I promise," Kay whispered, her voice laced with the sweetest relief, her face a carefully constructed picture of happiness and surrender. The performance was flawless. She had secured his agreement.

But beneath the surface of that gratitude lay an undertone of cold, unwavering determination—a silent vow of betrayal Richard would never see coming. She knew this was the final act of her captivity, and the moment he agreed to her move, he signed the warrant for his own ruin. Kay smiled, a predatory, chilling certainty in her eyes: He won't forget me. I'll make sure of it. This was not a chance to fix their marriage; it was the start of the six-month clock toward her absolute freedom.

Kay looked at Richard, feeling a chilling sense of strategic satisfaction. For now, she had him exactly where she needed him. But she knew better than to trust this fragile truce.

The hotel room in Nashville had been sterile and empty—no visible trace of another woman, no misplaced perfume, no forgotten receipt. Yet, Kay didn't believe for a second that he had been faithful. Richard was a man who thrived on having options, and she knew in her bones that there was someone else—a clean slate he was already contaminating. He probably planned to have his cake and eat it, too: the security of a wife and family, subsidized by her effort, and the freedom of an affair, subsidized by his lies.

But Kay looked at the man who had stolen everything from her, the man she was now pretending to love, and a cold certainty settled over her. She wouldn't let that happen. She was the architect of this deception, and she was the only one who would write the final, devastating ending.

Together, they began scouring listings for a rental home that would suit their family. Richard seemed halfhearted about the process, often brushing off her suggestions, but she pressed on, taking the lead in their search with a quiet determination that masked her inner resolve.

The children stayed with her mother during the interim, giving Kay the space to solidify her next steps. Twenty-two days later, they secured a modest house in a quiet Nashville neighborhood. It wasn't much, but it was enough—a stepping stone toward the life she was carefully crafting, one move at a time.

With the new rental house secured, Kay made the long, exhausted drive back to Florida to retrieve Lucas and Aiden. The moment she walked through the door and saw her sons, the crushing weight of the past weeks—the lies, the manipulation, the terrifying solo drive, the constant fear—seemed to lift, if only for a breathless, suspended moment.

She dropped to her knees, immediately wrapping her arms tightly around Lucas, who hugged her back with a fierce, childlike devotion. She held Aiden close, inhaling their familiar, comforting scent. In their embrace, Kay felt her purpose renewed; this reunion was the fuel she needed for the difficult performance that lay ahead.

"I missed you so much, Mommy!" Lucas exclaimed, his small hands gripping her shoulders tightly.

"I missed you too, baby. So, so much," Kay whispered, her voice cracking as she kissed his cheek. Aiden, perched on her hip, babbled something unintelligible but heartfelt, his little hand patting her face.

"Are we going to live with Daddy now?" Lucas asked, his wide eyes searching hers for answers.

"Yes, sweetie," Kay said, forcing a smile. "We're going to start fresh, all of us together. It's going to be good, I promise."

The journey back to Nashville was a mix of chatter and occasional laughter. Lucas chattered about his toys at Grandma's house and the things he would like to share with his Dad.

"Do you think Daddy will like the drawing I made?" Lucas held up a crumpled piece of paper he'd carefully kept.

Kay glanced at Lucas in the rearview mirror. Richard hardly paid any attention to Lucas anymore. She knew better than to lie, but she also couldn't bear to break her son's heart, "You worked hard on it, didn't you?"

Lucas nodded solemnly. "Uh-huh. It's a picture of all of us, happy."

Kay swallowed hard, gripping the steering wheel. "That's a wonderful picture, Lucas. It's perfect."

Aiden, still in his car seat, made happy hums, kicking his feet. Kay reached back during a stoplight to squeeze his tiny hand, her heart clenching at the sight of his toothy grin. For a few hours, the car was filled with the kind of hope and joy Kay hadn't felt in a long time. It was enough to bolster her determination to see this through—for them, if not for herself.

But the journey wasn't easy—every once in a while, she had to pull over to tube-feed Aiden, carefully administering his nourishment the way she'd learned after his surgery. It was second nature by now, but each feeding was a reminder of how much he had already endured.

Once back, she threw herself into establishing stability for her children. Lucas was enrolled in a nearby school, and Kay navigated the web of phone calls and paperwork to set up nursing care, doctors, and therapy for Aiden. It was a grueling process, but each step completed felt like another small victory. The sight of her boys settling into their new routines gave her a sense of purpose, even as she continued her delicate balancing act with Richard.

Her own life was falling into place, too. Within weeks, she landed a job at another major telephone company in Nashville. The pay was significantly better than what she'd earned in Florida, a financial buffer that gave her the independence she desperately craved. For the first time in years, Kay felt a glimmer of control—over her career, her children's futures, and her own destiny.

23

The Breaking Point

Yet, the marriage remained a battle she fought behind closed doors. Richard was more distant than ever, throwing himself into work with an intensity Kay hadn't seen before. He spent long hours at work, sometimes not coming home until late at night, and when he did, his presence was anything but comforting. This, she thought grimly, was the one silver lining: the less he was home, the less she had to see him.

But when he was home, it was like navigating a minefield. He was irritable, quick to lash out, and visibly exhausted. His words were sharp and cutting, filled with a bitterness that Kay had stopped taking personally.

One evening, as she placed a plate of food in front of him, he barely looked up from his phone.

"You're late again," she said, her tone carefully neutral.

"Work," he muttered, stabbing at his food without enthusiasm.

"You 're working lots of very late nights and not seeing the boys hardly at all."

Richard glanced up, his expression hard. "You think I'm out there for fun? I'm doing what I have to do. Someone has to."

Kay bit the inside of her cheek, keeping her voice steady. "I know. I just worry about how tired you seem. That's all."

He scoffed, shoving his plate away. "Don't start, Kay. I don't need this tonight."

Without another word, he stood, grabbed his keys, and headed for the door.

"Where are you going?" she asked, masking the frustration bubbling beneath her calm facade.

"Work," he snapped, slamming the door behind him.

The lie was obvious, but Kay didn't press. It wasn't worth the fight, and truthfully, she didn't care where he went. His absences gave her more freedom to focus on the boys.

Still, the volatility of his time at home kept her on edge. When he wasn't ignoring her, he was pushing her buttons, making passive-aggressive remarks about her spending, or criticizing the kids' behavior.

Kay adopted an unshakable focus, determined to appear completely unbothered by Richard's presence and behavior. She carefully kept her voice neutral and her demeanor perfectly accommodating, playing the part of the devoted, easily manipulated wife to keep his suspicions at bay. She endured his dismissive comments, his growing emotional detachment, and the internal storm of fury and fear that swirled inside her.

Every conciliatory word she spoke, every meal she cooked, every moment of shared silence was not an act of surrender, but another brick in the foundation of her exit strategy. She was quietly building her case, setting her timeline, and waiting. This forced intimacy was her final, agonizing performance before she delivered the ultimate consequence he deserved.

It wasn't easy, but Kay had become an expert at wearing a mask. She smiled when she wanted to scream, laughed when she wanted to cry, and played the role of a wife desperate to mend her marriage. All while knowing her days in this life were numbered.

One night, as they sat at the dining table, Richard offhandedly mentioned that his new position was more demanding than he'd anticipated. "I didn't think they'd have me running all over the place like this," he muttered, spearing a piece of overcooked chicken.

"Maybe that's a good thing," Kay replied. "It shows they trust you. It's a chance to prove yourself."

He gave her a sidelong glance, his expression unreadable. "I guess."

"I'm proud of you, Richard," she added, forcing a smile that didn't reach her eyes. The compliment was a calculated lie, delivered with clinical precision. It was not genuine admiration for his job; it was necessary fuel for his inflated ego, a transaction designed to keep his guard down.

She seized every opportunity like this, feeding his ego just enough to keep him invested. The sacrifices were small compared to what she stood to gain. Each word she spoke, every gesture of submission, was a calculated move, a means to an end.

In the quiet hours of the night, when the house was still and the kids were asleep, working in her dedicated office, Kay's pursuit of financial independence became an open, relentless hustle. She researched side work, actively marketing her skills to small businesses online during the day, using the time Richard spent at the golf course.

Kay sat at her desk, openly pitching virtual marketing services, web design, graphic work, and administrative help. She even leveraged her voice and musical skills for her most unusual gig: DJing music for an online radio station and recording voice-over commercials at night. Richard was fully aware of the stream of work coming in, though he dismissed it as harmless "hobby money." Kay, however, took on every shift she could manage, turning her skill into currency. She was not just earning money; she was diligently creating a solid professional following and networking with other professionals, openly building a robust personal brand that was completely separate from his control. This visible, focused effort was Kay's insurance policy, her undeniable act of building a future defined by her own success.

The money from Kay's side hustles, though small, was her proof of concept: it trickled in at first, just enough to confirm that she was capable of standing on her own two feet. Her first decisive move was securing a financial sanctuary: she opened a secret bank account, using a separate institution and taking meticulous care to ensure Richard wouldn't suspect a thing.

To handle the cash from her DJ and voiceover gigs, she developed a clandestine system. The hidden checkbook was tucked away inside old photo albums stored in the back of a closet, blending seamlessly with forgotten memories. Any cash she earned was hidden in plain sight—rolled and stuffed into dishes and bowls inside the china cabinet. She would only deposit and spend small increments, saying she had made "twenty dollars here or there," keeping the amounts small enough that his neglectful eye wouldn't notice, and his raging greed wouldn't be triggered. Every dollar saved was a defiant act of self-rescue.

Richard claimed to be working two demanding jobs—golf course maintenance during the day and security detail for the same course at night. His schedule was punishing: most nights, he did not return home until after 2 a.m. He insisted he was pouring every ounce of energy into providing for the family, but the math simply didn't add up. The hours he claimed were impossible, the exhaustion seemed performative, and the money that should have been flowing into their account never materialized. Kay watched him, the suspicion cold and hard: he insisted he was working, but none of his story held together. The long nights were just another opaque layer of control and deception.

She had to get creative because Richard's spending habits were spiraling out of control. It was as if the more money he made, the more he found ways to squander it. He'd come home with expensive tools, new clothes, or receipts for lavish lunches or dinners he never mentioned.

The financial pressure was unrelenting, made worse by the crucial decision Kay had been forced to make: her entire paycheck went directly into their joint account. This wasn't a choice she made out of trust, but out of necessity and fear of Richard's wrath. This vulnerability was now being exploited: Richard's failure to pay bills meant every dollar Kay had earned was now at risk. She was fighting to keep the collector calls at bay and the eviction notices off the door, all while knowing their shared account was bleeding dry due to his neglect.

The house was shrinking, its walls closing in under the crushing weight of overdue bills. When the doorbell rang, Kay would often pretend not to be home, her heart hammering against her ribs as she heard the muffled voices of bill collectors outside. She couldn't afford a confrontation—she had enough on her plate trying to manage Lucas and Aiden's care.

Money grew impossibly tighter, and the arguments with Richard became frequent, sharp eruptions fueled by his reckless financial disregard. The final breaking point often came over a crumpled scrap of paper.

One evening, Kay spotted a familiar receipt Richard had carelessly dropped on the kitchen counter. Her composure snapped.

"What is this, Richard?" Kay demanded, her voice shaking with suppressed fury as she held up the slip. "A three-hundred-dollar charge from Snap-on Tools? What exactly did you buy that was more important than the power bill?"

"Oh, that? It was a couple of tools I needed for work. I have to be able to do my job, Kay."

"Your job? Your spending is gonna make us homeless!" Kay's voice broke, the disbelief curdling into bitter, desperate anger. "Richard, that money was for bills! We are getting disconnection notices, and you're buying three hundred dollars' worth of tools?"

Yelling, his voice rising in manufactured anger, Richard advanced on her. "Stop acting like I'm the only one spending money! You're always so goddamn negative! Why do you always have to bitch about the bills the minute I walk through that door? Is that your purpose, Kay? I told you, I will take care of it! Now drop it!"

But Kay knew the truth: Richard's commitment was useless. Their life was not defined by his promises; it was defined by the bills he refused to pay.

Kay devoted every spare minute to becoming an unshakeable expert in her son's care. She spent hours researching different support groups, special needs programs, and therapeutic interventions. The phone became her primary weapon; she would spend hours on calls, and when one person couldn't help or didn't know the answer, she would immediately pivot, asking for referrals: "Who do you think can help or point me in the right direction?"

She never took no for an answer, driven by a fierce, maternal belief in Aiden's potential. She felt he was capable of so much more than just sitting in a chair all day, connected to a feeding pump. Kay was driven to find the precise resources Aiden needed to learn, improve, and be better. Her vision for her son transcended his diagnosis: she wanted to see him learn to walk, learn to eat, laugh, or sing—to experience all the simple joys that his complex condition threatened to steal.

The boys were slowly adjusting to their new reality in Nashville, though the transition had been difficult. For Kay, securing a new team was a massive task: Lucas had to transition to another new school, new LPN nurses had to be secured for Aiden, and a fresh set of specialists and doctors had to be established. Despite the upheaval, they were starting to find their routine. Lucas, though initially uncertain, was settling into his new environment, finding neighborhood friends and activities that gave him some sense of normalcy. Aiden, on the other hand, was still mostly withdrawn, his small world revolving almost entirely around Kay and his critical medical team of doctors and therapists.

Meanwhile, Richard continued his elaborate, chilling charade of being the perfect, engaged father, reserved exclusively for the benefit of the home health nurses. He was invisible during the real battles: he never attended Aiden's actual appointments, never sat through the grueling, long waits, and never listened to the specialists' complex concerns.

But the moment the nurses arrived at the house, he materialized. He would flash an exaggerated, plastic smile, nod precisely at the right moments, and ask just enough superficial questions to construct the illusion of an involved partner. He was performing for an audience of one—the LPN nurse—seeking external validation and ensuring no one documented his true, utter neglect of his son's life-threatening condition.

As soon as they left, the act dissolved, and the distance between him and Kay settled back in, thick with unspoken resentment. The financial strain only added to the tension, stretching their already fragile truce thinner with each passing day.

Despite the overwhelming emotional and financial strain, Kay kept fighting for Aiden. She transformed her pain into advocacy. Hoping to find connection and comfort, she designed a website to blog their journey through his complex diagnoses, meticulously documenting each step, struggle, and small victory. She became the resonant voice for Aiden's future, pushing for every opportunity, no matter how small, to make his life better.

It was during this period of relentless advocacy that the severity of Aiden's condition was compounded by further devastating news. The doctors confirmed he had additional disabilities, delivered with the same blunt, clinical finality. First, they diagnosed partial heterotopia—the presence of gray matter in areas of his brain where it shouldn't be, explaining his unpredictable neurological symptoms. Then came the diagnosis of cerebral palsy, a congenital disorder that severely affected his movement, muscle tone, and posture. His symptoms were varied and difficult to manage: exaggerated reflexes, rigid limbs, and involuntary motions.

The combination of these conditions was overwhelming, a mountain range of challenges piled atop the original diagnosis. Yet, Kay refused to back down. Her resolve only hardened; she was now driven by a singular, fierce vow: she would find the best care, the most effective therapies, and the greatest opportunities, no matter the cost or the obstacles Richard or life threw in her way.

Although Nashville offered better care and more resources than they had back in Florida, getting Aiden into school remained a challenge. The feeding tube, the constant wires, the appointments, the therapies—every day felt like a race against time. Aiden still had not spoken a word, just sounds and gestures, making it even more difficult to connect with the world around him.

Kay shouldered the colossal burden of her son's complex medical reality completely on her own. She became a solitary pillar of strength, making every appointment, sitting through every agonizing evaluation, and meeting with more than eleven physicians and therapists—all without a single ounce of support from Richard. The long, fluorescent-lit waiting rooms, the dense medical jargon that felt like a foreign language, the exhausting, infuriating back-and-forth with insurance companies and state aid—it all fell squarely on her. She managed the logistics, the emotional devastation, and the crippling fear, alone. Her resolve wasn't just determination; it was a desperate, fierce act of survival for her child, undertaken in complete isolation.

And yet, despite Kay's fierce, solitary resolve, the system itself seemed to be working against them at every turn. The mountain of paperwork, the baffling denials, the endless hoops she had to jump through just to secure Aiden's basic medical needs—it was relentless, designed to wear down the exhausted and the poor. The burden was heavy, suffocating at times, amplifying her terror that a single misplaced document could cost her son his care.

But she never stopped fighting. The chaos of the bureaucracy was just another form of abuse she had to endure. Aiden needed her, and Kay had long since accepted the role of warrior. She would move mountains for him, no matter the emotional or physical cost to herself.

But then, there were moments when the weight of it all pressed down so hard that Kay felt the fragile structure of her resolve cracking. One evening, the tension of her double life—the meticulous schedule, the relentless medical advocacy, the secret side hustle—hit its breaking point.

After work, Kay picked up Lucas from school, relieved the nurse watching Aiden, and headed straight to the grocery store. She pulled into Walmart, her mind running a frantic, continuous calculation. She had carefully calculated every item before leaving the house, double-checking prices and sales to ensure she had just enough to cover the essentials. She still remembered the searing shame of having to return everything during a previous shopping trip and vowed never to endure that humiliation again.

The cart filled up slowly, each item placed with desperate precision. No extras, no impulse buys. Just the necessities. When she finally reached the checkout, she knew the total before the cashier even read it back to her. Taking a steadying breath, she swiped her card.

DECLINED.

Her heart stopped. That wasn't right. She swiped again, more forcefully this time, her pulse hammering against her ribs. INSUFFICIENT FUNDS.

A cold, sickening wave of panic washed over her. That wasn't possible—she had done the math; she knew exactly how much was in the joint account. Or at least, she thought she did.

She turned to the cashier, her voice tight and desperate. "Can you please try it again? Just one more time?"

The cashier hesitated, her eyes dropping briefly to the long line forming behind Kay. "Sorry, ma'am, but it's definitely not going through."

Kay's blood boiled with humiliation and fury. Her grip tightened on the shopping cart until her knuckles were white. She could feel the hot, judging eyes of the other customers on her as she forced herself to nod, trying to hold her composure. She left the full cart right there, a monument to her failure, the humiliation sinking in with every step she took toward the exit. As she stumbled out the door and started the car, the weight of Richard's deception and her endless struggle crashed down. The silence in the car was broken by a single, shattering thought: She was done being the one to suffer in silence.

Kay stormed home, the engine roaring in the background of her thoughts, the humiliation of the grocery store fueling a cold, focused fury. She walked through the door to find Richard slumped on the couch, mindlessly flipping through TV channels, a picture of self-absorbed idleness. He barely spared her a glance.

"Richard," she snapped, her voice harder and sharper than she had intended. "Why is there no money in the account?"

He sighed, his expression already settling into the familiar, bored look of an uninterested victim. "What's the problem now, Kay?"

The words rushed out, hot and fast, frustration finally spilling over the edge. "My entire paycheck just deposited! I just got paid two days ago, and now—it's gone! Every single cent! Where did it go, Richard?" She pointed toward the counter. "It didn't go to the bills—they're all still past due. So, what was it? More tools? Eating out?"

Richard just stared at her, his expression momentarily unreadable, before he sighed dramatically and stood up. "I have to eat Kay!"

"Eat! You can take a lunch, I offered to make it for you," she shot back, her voice rising to a raw cry. "I'm working as much as I can. I'm trying to make sure the kids have what they need and that we have food on the table! But you're just... spending it faster than we can make it!"

Richard's eyes darkened, his thin patience dissolving into rage. "You're being ridiculous."

"Ridiculous?" she repeated, incredulous, taking a step toward him. "I'm trying to take care of us, Richard! You are the one who's checking out of this marriage, who's throwing everything away!"

The accusation was out, raw and unfiltered. For a moment, the air seemed to freeze, thick with tension. Richard stepped forward, his face reddening with violent anger, looming over her.

"You think I don't have enough on my plate without you nagging me all the time?" Kay?" he growled, his voice low and menacing.

Kay's heart pounded, but she wasn't backing down this time. The shame of the Walmart checkout was the armor she needed. "I'm not 'nagging,' Richard. I'm trying to get us out of a hole, and you are actively making it worse!"

The room seemed to close in around them, the tension suffocating. Richard's rage flared instantly, and before Kay could take another breath, his hand shot out and clamped down hard on her arm.

"You always think you know better, Kay," he growled, the pressure tightening. "You don't."

Kay yanked her arm back, fueled by a new, cold defiance. Her heart was racing, but the old, familiar fear, the doubt, the hesitation—it was all gone. She was done letting him control everything. But in that moment of final resistance, the dam broke.

Richard shoved her hard. She stumbled, hitting the ground directly on her arm with a sickening force. A sharp, sickening crack split the air, and pain—pure, blinding agony—exploded through her entire limb. Kay's scream tore from her throat, raw and involuntary, as her vision blurred with tears. The physical agony drowned out everything else.

Richard stepped back, his eyes wide, but there was no regret in his gaze—only simmering frustration. He didn't seem to process the severity of the damage he'd inflicted.

"You started this," he muttered, immediately shifting the blame. "You won't let it go. You're constantly bitching."

Kay barely heard him. She was on the floor, clutching her arm, the sharp, relentless pain radiating up her shoulder. But the real, crushing weight of it was the humiliation—the agonizing fact that she was here, in this moment, in this marriage, with a broken body and absolutely no one to turn to but herself.

The boys were in the other room, and Kay knew they had heard everything—the shouting, the crash, and her primal scream. But she couldn't worry about them right now; the blinding agony in her arm demanded all her focus. She had to get through this single, immediate crisis.

The next few hours were a terrifying blur. She found herself in the Emergency Room, the harsh fluorescent lights illuminating the brutal reality of her situation. Richard sat beside her, perfectly composed, the boys silent and wide-eyed in tow. When the doctor asked the inevitable question—What happened?—Richard delivered the lie with chilling composure: "She tripped over a tub of Legos."

Kay did not contradict him. There was no point. The narrative was already set; the truth would only invite chaos she couldn't afford. She allowed the nurses to place the heavy plaster cast on her arm, the weight of it feeling almost symbolic—like a chain wrapping around her own body, one more physical tie to the man who broke her, one more devastating lie she had to live with.

But as Kay sat there, her body broken and her life spiraling, she knew she was staring directly at her absolute breaking point. The six-month clock had run out of time. She prayed desperately that things would improve, but even as she made the wish, a cold, hard certainty gripped her: she was wrong. The next few months would only bring more turmoil, and she was no longer willing to wait for the final disaster.

The tension that had been building since the hospital climaxed brutally one morning. Kay woke up to find that all of her jewelry was gone. The shock was immediate, followed by a cold wave of realization: Richard had taken it all—the wedding ring she'd worn since their vows, the class ring her parents had gifted her, and the promise ring her father had given her at the age of thirteen. All gone.

The loss hit her like a punch to the gut. The rings meant more than just precious metal; they were potent symbols of love, of promises made, of a past she could now never reclaim. This was not just theft; it was the obliteration of her personal history.

Anger surged through her veins, a pure, white-hot blaze. She found Richard on the couch and confronted him, her voice trembling with disbelief and fury.

"Where's my jewelry, Richard?" she demanded.

"I pawned them to catch up on the bills," he stated flatly, as if discussing a minor chore. "The power company was gonna disconnect the power today."

Kay couldn't believe it. Even at this point, with her arm in a cast from his previous assault, he had found a way to turn the blame onto her. Her hands were shaking with rage at his calculated destruction of her most cherished memories.

"You don't get to blame me for your wasteful spending!" she shouted, her voice breaking. "You're the one who eats out every damn day, buying new tools we can't afford! You stole from me!"

His eyes instantly darkened, and the final barrier of control dissolved. Before she could react, he was on her, shoving her against the wall. He hit her once, twice, his hands like iron clamps around her neck. Kay fought back with every ounce of strength she had, her cast making her defense clumsy, her fists landing weakly against his chest. But every move she made seemed only to fuel his escalating rage, and the blows kept coming. This was the end.

In the midst of the chaos and the violent, terrifying assault, Richard's words became the final, coldest weapon. His voice was a venomous hiss, his breath hot and repulsive against her skin as he leaned in, his hands still clamped around her neck.

"You think anyone will care if you're gone?" he spat, the question a calculated strike at her identity. "You're nothing. You're not even worth it."

Then came the deathblow, the threat stripped bare of all pretense. Richard's eyes were cold and focused, and his voice dropped to a low, chilling certainty.

"We're not far from Alabama—I know just where to put you where no one would ever find you," he hissed, the threat laced with local knowledge that intensified the terror. "You think anyone will care? You're nothing." Kay stumbled back, clutching her side as she gasped for air, the vile threat striking her like a physical knife. He'd said horrible things like this before, threats veiled in drunken anger, but now, delivered with cold, surgical clarity, they felt terrifyingly real. The realization slammed into her: He was absolutely capable of it, and she was trapped. Her body might be broken, but her mind instantly shifted to one, primal mandate: survival.

24

Isolation and Betrayal

Richard was a hero.

At least, that's what everyone said.

Richard had been a volunteer firefighter since high school, throwing himself into the role with a restless, intense dedication that consistently earned him admiration. Wherever they moved, he immediately found a department to join, integrating himself into the community's structure. He wore the title like a badge of honor, like it was the most essential part of his identity—a role that, in his mind, excused everything else: the violence, the neglect, and the financial ruin he inflicted at home.

Initially, when they were dating, even Kay was impressed by it. She admired his community service and the way he rushed into danger for others. She had seen him in his uniform, standing tall with a quiet confidence, and believed she had found a man who was selfless, brave, and good. But over time, she realized it was just a show—a way for him to feel powerful, to be adored by everyone around him while keeping her trapped in the shadows.

People loved him. The guys at the station would pat him on the back, buy him drinks after long shifts, and call him one of the good ones. At community events, he was the first to step up, to man the grill, to shake hands. If someone's house caught fire, Richard was the one charging in, braving the smoke and heat, emerging with a soot-streaked face and a reassuring grin. Women in town whispered about what a good man Kay had married and how lucky she was to have a husband who put others before himself.

They didn't know the real Richard. They didn't see the man who came home from a shift reeking of beer and bad decisions, slamming doors and hurling insults like they were just part of the nightly routine. He was a terrifying specter of volatility, always focused on himself. The boys were an afterthought, never receiving affection, love, or even dedicated time. When he was home, he was often silent and sullen, never seeking out Lucas for simple conversation or a game.

This was the man who drained their bank account, called his wife "dramatic" when she questioned where the money had gone, and pawned her wedding ring and cherished mementos, watching her crumble without a flicker of remorse. He performed commitment for the public but reserved only neglect and chaos for the family he claimed to protect.

Every time Kay had dialed 911, it was an act of desperate, raw hope—foolish enough to believe it would finally change something. She had been gasping for breath, a fresh bruise blooming across her ribs where Richard had shoved her into the kitchen counter. She had dialed the numbers with shaking hands, pressing them as though salvation, in the form of impartial justice, waited on the other end.

Every time Kay had dialed 911, pressing the numbers with desperate, shaking hands, the subsequent arrival of aid became another layer of her humiliation. When the sirens finally cut through the night, it wasn't objective strangers who arrived, but Richard's buddies from the fire department and local law enforcement.

The men in uniform, who shared loyalty and shifts with Richard the volunteer firefighter, would take a quick look at the scene—the tear tracks on Kay's face, the frantic state of the house—and immediately confer with their friend. They'd end up hanging out in the front yard with Richard, casually talking and laughing, completely dismissing her desperate plea for safety.

To Kay, trapped inside, it was clear what they were discussing: her. She was the hysterical wife, the one always causing the drama. The lifeline she reached for was nothing but another tether back to the chaos he created, instantly undermining her credibility and reinforcing the horrifying truth that Richard's identity as a public servant excused his private abuse.

Anytime they fought, he would remind her, his voice low and full of certainty, "No one will believe your nonsense." And she knew he was right. He had already made sure of that.

It happened again. And again. Different states and cities, different departments, different men who wore the same badges but played the same roles. Every time she called, it was Richard's friends who showed up. Every time, they dismissed it.

Despite the humiliation and the certain knowledge that her calls were being dismissed by his friends, Kay never stopped dialing 911. It was not just a plea for immediate rescue; it was a desperate, calculated act to create a record. She endured the contempt and the front-yard conferences to ensure that official records and reports existed—physical evidence of the violence and Richard's volatility. This paper trail was her shield and her future witness, a silent, documented case against the man whose respectable public image masked a private terror.

But she knew one thing with absolute certainty—Richard had made sure she had nowhere to turn.

And now, she had to figure out how to survive on her own.

The collapse wasn't immediate. It happened in small, deliberate ways—so gradual that she didn't realize she was losing everyone until she was already alone.

At first, it was subtle. Richard would make offhanded comments about her work friends, planting seeds of doubt. "Did you notice how Jenna always changes the subject when you talk about your promotion? She's jealous, babe." Or, "I don't think Sarah really likes you. She only comes around when she needs something." It was so casual, so convincing, that Kay found herself second-guessing things she had never questioned before.

Then, he made it harder to see them at all. He'd sulk when she made plans, guilt-tripping her until she canceled. If she insisted on going, he'd call and text nonstop, manufacturing some crisis at home that required her immediate attention. But the worst part was the condition he attached to her leaving: she'd have to give him sex before she could go anywhere, before she could leave the house. It was a bribe, a trade-off—a twisted bargain she agreed to, hoping he'd be in a better mood afterward, hoping he'd treat the kids with some decency or give her a moment of peace.

When Kay would return, often apologetic for her mere absence, Richard would punish her with a cold, calculated precision. He didn't need to yell; he used silence as a weapon, making the house feel frozen and menacing. When he did speak, it was only in sharp-edged remarks designed to make Kay feel utterly incompetent and guilty. He'd deliver these judgments with a sneer: "Lucas doesn't listen when you're gone—you need to handle him better." Or, twisting the knife further, he'd complain, "Aiden cried too much; you need to figure out what's wrong with your own son." Every word was a deliberate attempt to undermine her maternal capability and ensure she felt that her simple act of leaving the room was a transgression deserving of punishment.

Richard's sabotage wasn't confined to the home. In public, he didn't bother with subtlety. When Kay introduced him to her colleagues, he immediately launched an aggressive, humiliating campaign. He flirted so crudely and made offensive jokes in front of them, laughing loudly when their discomfort was obvious. "Relax, I'm kidding," he'd sneer, but Kay saw the truth in her coworkers' strained smiles, the way their eyes subtly avoided contact. The result was inevitable: invitations stopped coming. No one wanted to be around him, and by extension, no one wanted to be around her.

His cruelty was most effective with Kay's female friends. He was relentlessly vulgar and disgusting, making suggestive comments that left them visibly squirming. Then, he'd quickly play it off, flashing that practiced, phony grin. "Come on, you know I'm messing with you," he'd insist, forcing them to accept his behavior. Kay watched, helpless, as their expressions shifted from discomfort to genuine fear, and their visits became less frequent until they stopped altogether. All Kay wanted was company, people to laugh with and lean on, but every single attempt at connection was sabotaged.

In the end, she was left profoundly alone, exactly how Richard wanted her: no friends, no one to call, no one who would believe her when he inevitably called her "dramatic." But in the complete, devastating emptiness of her isolation, a new, cold clarity emerged. She looked at her empty phone and her silent house, realizing the terrible truth: if there was absolutely nothing left to lose, then there was nothing holding her back. The ultimate isolation became her ultimate freedom.

The divorce had been Kay's final, desperate chance because leaving on her own had become logistically impossible. She had secretly tried to explore options for escape, but every door slammed shut because of Aiden's complex medical needs.

The domestic violence shelters, her intended safe haven, had turned her away, sympathy laced with absolute finality. "We're not set up for that," they had explained. With Aiden dependent on a feeding pump and tubes, his constant monitors, and the necessity of scheduled LPN nursing care, the shelters lacked the medical staffing and facilities to ensure his survival. Kay was forced to face the brutal truth: her son's needs, which she fought so hard to meet, had paradoxically locked her into the marriage. She was trapped, the system designed to help women escape, providing a clear, heartbreaking path back to her abuser.

So, she did the only thing she could—she began the search for an attorney. This was not a plea for help; it was a quiet, desperate act of war, executed entirely in secret. She met him downtown, slipping away from Richard like a fugitive, her heart pounding with the risk of discovery.

In the sterile, quiet office, she poured out the whole truth, a raw, chronological inventory of abuse and betrayal. And for the first time in years, someone listened—someone powerful, impartial, and capable of fighting back. The attorney agreed to take payments, small amounts each week, allowing her to chip away at the retainer using the secret money from her side hustles. She clung to those payments like a lifeline, counting down to the moment when the last dollar would be paid and the papers would be filed. Her freedom had a price, and she was determined to pay every cent.

When the time finally arrived, Kay didn't know it was coming. She hadn't been keeping a meticulous tally of the secret retainer payments, nor did she have a running chart marking the countdown. Instead, she had been making small, desperate deposits—a constant, anxious act of survival driven by hope, not mathematics. The moment the attorney called, the final payment complete, it arrived not as a scheduled triumph, but as a sudden, stunning pronouncement of imminent freedom. The long, silent period of waiting was abruptly over.

It was the day before Thanksgiving when she got the call.

The phone rang, slicing through the quiet hum of the office. Kay almost didn't answer. Her stomach twisted as she saw the unfamiliar number, her pulse hammering against her ribs.

"Hello?"

"Mrs. Thompson?"

The voice on the other end was detached. Professional.

"Yes," she said, gripping the armrest of her chair.

"This is Paralegal Daniel from the Myer's office. I'm just calling to give you a heads up—your husband is about to be served with divorce papers, along with a restraining order."

Kay gripped the phone, her breath catching in her throat. Her heart, which had been racing since the moment she answered, felt like it momentarily stopped.

"It should happen within the next couple of hours or so," Daniel finished, his voice calm and precise, completely unaware of the earthquake he had just triggered in Kay's world.

Kay's breath caught in her throat, his words landing like a sudden, unexpected punch to the gut. She hadn't prepared for this moment to arrive today—not now, not on the day before Thanksgiving. The world around her tilted, the hum of the office vanishing as a wave of paralyzing shock washed over her. All her careful planning had ended instantly, violently. For a terrifying, beautiful moment, she struggled to catch her breath, realizing the long, silent siege was finally, spectacularly, over. The risk was immediate, but the promise of freedom was absolute.

"They're... they're serving him already?" Kay's voice was shaky, a terrified whisper of disbelief. The immediate reality of the threat—Richard receiving the papers—was paralyzing.

"Yes, ma'am," the paralegal confirmed, his tone professional but grave. "We just wanted to let you know beforehand, in case you needed to take any precautions."

The subtle warning resonated with brutal clarity. Precautions meant escaping the immediate, violent rage that would follow the sight of the divorce papers. Kay knew she was standing at the edge of the final, most dangerous confrontation. Her meticulous plan required her to move now.

Kay could hear the cold, professional clarity in Daniel's tone, but it did nothing to anchor her. Instead, she felt herself spinning, drowning in a sudden flood of thoughts and emotions. The question was primal and immediate: *What should she do? What could she possibly do now?*

Her heart was hammering against her ribs, the adrenaline kicking in with the force of a panic attack. She had prepared for this moment for six agonizing months, rehearsing the escape again and again in the quiet hours of the night. But now that the lawyer had pulled the trigger, it felt as though the ground was being ripped out from under her. The plan was executed, but the reality was absolute terror. She had mere hours to evacuate her entire life before Richard's fury detonated.

She wasn't ready. The stunning news—you are about to be free—was too much, too fast. She hadn't even finished processing the fear of the last beating, the humiliation of the past six months, or the crushing reality of Aiden's complex needs. She had spent half a year meticulously plotting, telling herself she was a warrior, prepared for this moment, but now that the lawyer had pulled the trigger, she was terrified. The fear was cold, absolute, and immediate. The meticulous plan she had built in theory suddenly felt impossible in practice, leaving her questioning the very core of her resolve: *Was I really ready? I thought I was, but now it's here, and I'm just so scared.*

And then there was Richard. The thought of him finding out—of him receiving the papers that demanded his accountability—shot a fresh wave of paralyzing fear through her chest. He wasn't the kind of man to go quietly, not now, and certainly not when his carefully constructed life of comfort and control was being dismantled.

Kay knew the truth: Richard might not have wanted to raise their boys, not really, but that didn't mean he wouldn't fight. He would fight for control, for the financial power he believed she owed him, for the right to look like the victim, and for anything he could hold onto. His reaction wouldn't be sadness or acceptance; it would be a violent detonation of rage, and Kay had mere hours to evacuate before the shockwave hit.

The panic clawed at her. She needed to get to them—needed to get to her oldest son before he could do anything rash.

"Okay," she whispered, trying to steady her breathing. "Okay, thank you for calling to let me know."

But as she hung up, the sense of disbelief stayed. She wasn't ready. She didn't have time to brace herself for the reality of what was coming. Her mind flooded with images—of Richard's anger, of his threats.

Her hands shook violently as she gripped the steering wheel, barely able to focus as she drove to the school to pick up her son.

Kay's heart pounded as she drove home, the thoughts of the restraining order pressing on her chest. Richard was banned from coming near her or the kids. She didn't know where Richard would go but she knew that nothing would stop him from trying to regain control in whatever way he could. It wasn't about violence—never had been. It was all about manipulation, about keeping her off balance.

For the next thirty days, Kay lived in a state of paralyzing, hypervigilant fear. The anxiety was a physical force, eating away at her; every sudden noise, every unexpected knock at the door, sent her heart skyrocketing into a frantic panic. She didn't know what Richard would do, but she knew, with grim certainty, that it would come.

The hearing was only thirty days away, and each day felt like an eternity, her mind trapped in a crushing loop of dread. Even with the restraining order—a piece of paper meant to ensure her safety—she couldn't shake the terrifying feeling that the worst was yet to come, that he would find some new, twisted way to hurt her. It was all she had ever known, and that familiar expectation of violence was now her constant, suffocating reality.

On the day of the kids' visitation, Kay drove to the local Police Department—the designated, neutral location for the swap, a necessary precaution for her safety. She went there expecting the usual tension, maybe a veiled threat or an ugly outburst, but she certainly didn't expect this.

There stood Richard, laughing easily, his arm casually draped around the shoulders of a woman she'd never seen before. The sight hit Kay with cold, sickening finality. He didn't seem upset at all—didn't even seem phased by the divorce, the hearings, or the children. He had already found his new distraction, his new victim. The six months of agonizing pretense she had endured, the lies he had sworn to, the promises he had broken, all culminated in this single, brazen display. He had already moved on, just as Kay had suspected, proving that his life had always been a series of disposable women and discarded commitments.

Kay gripped the steering wheel, her knuckles turning white against the plastic. The sight of Richard with another woman knocked the breath from her lungs. She had braced herself for his violent rage, for bitter retaliation, for some grand, twisted reaction that showed he cared enough to fight. Instead, she was met with pure, stunning indifference.

Richard glanced up as she parked, his expression unreadable. For a split second, their eyes met across the cold, asphalt distance of the police parking lot. He didn't look guilty; he didn't even look angry about the divorce papers that had just shattered his life. If anything, he looked relieved—as if she had finally done the difficult, messy work of dissolving the marriage that he had long resented.

Her stomach twisted with a sickening realization.

Kay finally stepped out of the car, her legs unsteady beneath her from the shock and the trauma of the last thirty days.

Richard let out a short, dismissive laugh, shaking his head as if she were a pathetic joke. He turned to the woman beside him and smirked. The woman—brunette, entirely plain, the kind of forgettable beauty that didn't even warrant a second look—leaned into him, her unmanicured nails trailing down his arm. She shot Kay a fake, brittle smile, as if they were old friends enjoying a casual reunion.

Kay's pulse roared in her ears. Ignoring the woman, she focused on the only thing that mattered. "Where are you staying, Richard? Where are you taking the boys?" she asked, her voice cracking with maternal panic.

Richard shrugged, the casual arrogance slicing through her fear. "I am at a hotel. Don't worry about where it is. I don't have to tell you shit, Kay." His refusal was the final, stinging proof that he viewed the law, the court order, and her maternal rights with utter contempt.

Kay focused on the legal necessity, steeling herself against Richard's callous indifference and the presence of the other woman.

"Yes, you do have to tell me. The temporary custody papers state I need an address where the boys will be staying. I have a restraining order, Richard. You can't just vanish with the children."

"Stop acting like a crazy person, Kay. I told you, I'm at a hotel. Fine, I'll be at the Holiday Inn off the interstate. Happy? Now stop being a bitch." He dismissed her with a vague, likely false location, clearly infuriated that she had called him on the legal terms.

Richard's final move was to ignore her entirely, using the children as his immediate escape route. Kay knew this was the end of the conversation. She knelt down quickly, hugging Lucas fiercely.

Lucas, wide-eyed and silent, nodded, already sensing the deep, unspoken crisis unfolding around him. Kay placed Aiden, fragile and connected to his portable monitors, directly into Richard's arms.

She stared at him, waiting for something—regret, shame, even a flicker of acknowledgment—but there was nothing. He had already set up a new life, a new person. He had stripped her of everything and moved on as if she was nothing more than an inconvenience he had finally shaken off.

Richard quickly bundled the children into the car, the new woman sliding into the passenger seat without a glance back. Kay watched the car pull away, taking her sons and her financial stability with it. She stood alone in the sterile police parking lot, the cold indifference of Richard's betrayal having done more damage than any physical blow. Her mission for the day was complete, but the war for her children was just beginning.

Why cheat when he could have simply left? What was the sickening point of dragging out the devastation? The question was a raw wound in Kay's mind.

The answer felt crueler than any final blow: Richard hadn't stayed for the marriage; he stayed for the control. He prolonged the agony not because he needed her, but because he needed the structure she provided—the home, the childcare, the meals, the financial lifeline she created with her hustle—all while keeping her emotionally shackled. He destroyed her slowly, methodically, because destroying her was easier than being responsible for himself. He had been ready to go all along, but leaving meant forfeiting his power. By cheating and abandoning her, he got the final, ultimate reward: total freedom without ever having to admit failure or face a single consequence for the wreck he left behind.

The final, sickening questions hammered relentlessly in Kay's mind, each one a hammer blow to the foundation of her past: Were they behind on bills because he was courting this new woman?

The deepest horror was the realization of the timeline: Was he never really working those double shifts at night, but instead with her? Was his exhausting schedule, his impossible hours, his constant exhaustion—was it all a meticulous cover story?

Kay was left facing the terrifying, inescapable truth: Was everything—the Nashville job, the remorse, the promise of a future, one gigantic, calculated lie? The answer was yes. He had systematically destroyed their home, not because of bad luck, but to finance his own escape, proving that their entire life together had been a stage for his elaborate, selfish deception.

The last, fragile remnants of Kay's illusion didn't just crack—they shattered entirely. She had foolishly, desperately held onto the belief that at the end of it all, she would at least see Richard on his knees, begging for forgiveness, that her sacrifice would culminate in one moment of satisfying, undeniable victory.

But she didn't even get that. She was met instead by his cold indifference and the sickening sight of the new woman. Her meticulous plan to inflict consequences on him was completely nullified by his easy, immediate escape. His composure, his lack of shame, proved that he hadn't lost anything; he had simply discarded her. The final, crushing blow was the realization that her suffering had never even registered on his scorecard.

The ultimate, crushing realization was that Richard didn't fight. He didn't fight for her, he didn't fight for their boys, and he certainly didn't beg for the marriage. He didn't even bother to pretend to care enough to manufacture a final, dramatic scene. He had simply moved on before Kay even had the chance to officially leave, slipping into a new life—complete with a new woman—with the same chilling ease with which he had discarded an old appliance. His composure in the police parking lot wasn't courage; it was the total indifference of a man who had already mentally replaced his entire family.

The divorce papers were only the beginning—just the first step in what would become a five-year battle for freedom.

And suddenly, she was truly alone.

No support.

No safety net.

Just her, the kids, her job, and the nurses who came in shifts to care for her youngest, Aiden. And the fear—the constant, suffocating fear—of what Richard might do to her next.

She had no answers. Only exhaustion. Only dread.

She didn't have the luxury of breaking down. There were no soft landings, no one to lean on. So she did the only thing she could—she worked.

She threw herself into survival because there was no other choice.

She picked up a second job, juggling shifts that left her running on fumes. She put her oldest in after-school care, fought for extended nursing hours for the youngest, and scraped together what little she had to make ends meet. Every hour was accounted for. Every decision was made with one goal in mind—keeping them afloat.

The cold indifference Richard showed did not crush Kay; it stripped away the last, toxic layer of guilt, leaving behind a core of pure, unyielding resolve. Richard had taken everything she owned—her jewelry, her savings, her safety, and her peace—but she now focused on the final, absolute, undefended line: He would not take the boys.

She was the one raising them. She was the one showing up for every appointment, every therapy session, every flag football game and every midnight panic. She was the one fighting for their future, for Aidan's complex medical needs, and for their safety. Richard could claim them, but he could never replace her.

Kay pursued the divorce with a terrifying certainty, knowing her fight was just and her cause sacred. Yet, even as she prepared for the victory she had painstakingly purchased, a cold dread whispered a warning she couldn't ignore: the worst was yet to come. The battle was won, but the war was only just beginning.

25

Struggle For Safety and Autonomy

K ay sat in the quiet of their old home; the silence felt louder than anything Richard could have said. She thought she had prepared herself for the battle ahead.

What she hadn't anticipated was the life that came after. A phone call came from her office to deliver the news that shook her world to the core.

"Kay, I'm afraid we're going to have to let you go. It's a downsizing, you understand. You've been with us a while, but we just can't keep everyone."

Her mind didn't immediately register the words. For a moment, she thought she was still in some dream, stuck in the haze of a busy morning. But now, she was also losing her job?

"I'm so sorry," the voice on the other end continued.

Kay managed a weak smile that no one could see, though she suspected she heard her own heartbeat through the phone.

"I understand," she whispered before hanging up.

The emptiness that followed settled deep into her chest. There was no time to break down. She still needed to take care of Aiden and Lucas. And with no support system—no family close by, no real friends—Kay had to dig deep.

Her parents were in Florida, a world away, but she could call them. They tried their best to reassure her, but there wasn't much they could do from thousands of miles away. Kay had always been the strong one. Her mom would say, "You'll be fine, sweetie. You always have." But Kay wasn't so sure anymore.

Every day, she was juggling the endless unpaid bills, Aiden's appointments, Lucas's schoolwork, and somehow trying to keep the house in one piece. Sometimes, all of it crumbled together and crushed her, but what else was there to do? She couldn't afford the rent on her own, and she knew it was just a matter of time before she would need to move, probably to some cheap, rundown place that would barely fit the three of them, but it was all she could do.

The legal battle with Richard was its own distinct brand of misery—a deliberate extension of his control. Every time Kay thought she could finally take a breath, there he was, fighting her on every single technicality. It wasn't about the division of property, because there was nothing of value to divide—no house, no car, nothing except the towering pile of unpaid bills.

When she received a copy of his official reply to the motion for divorce, she was shocked by the sheer pettiness of his demands. He wasn't seeking assets; he was demanding revenge. He requested the court to award him the towels, the silverware, the plates, the rugs, and the lamps—items she of no value. These objects were not important to him; they were weapons. His only motive was to inflict pain, to prolong the agony, and to ensure Kay knew he would fight her to the absolute last, bitter end.

"Are you serious, Richard?" she had asked once when he sent back his list of demands, including towels, sheets, and even the silverware.

"I want what's mine," his response was terse, detached.

Her frustration boiled over. "What's yours? We don't have any-thing! All we have is debt. And you want to take the damn towels? The dishes the kids eat from? The forks they use for their cereal?"

He didn't respond. He didn't need to. This wasn't about kitchen-ware or linens—it was about power and control. About making sure she stayed small and scraping, right where he'd left her. He just wanted to win.

And in some twisted way, taking the towels and the silverware from his own children was part of that win.

Kay didn't know how she was still standing most days. The fear of the unknown clung to her like a second skin—this deep, gnawing doubt that maybe she wasn't cut out for life after divorce. Not like this. Not with no job, no partner, and two little boys who needed more than she could give.

Especially Aiden. Her youngest was a sweet soul, but his care was nonstop—a carousel of doctor's visits, therapies, and medications, al-ways reminding her of what was at stake. There was no such thing as rest. Her plate wasn't just full—it was spilling over, and there was no one else to help carry it.

And then there was Lucas. He was only seven, yet he had somehow become the little man of the house, a miniature sentinel of emotional labor. He never complained. Instead, he meticulously helped with Aiden. He would quietly bring Kay tissues when he found her weeping silently in the kitchen and would tenderly pat her back like he'd seen her do for his brother during a meltdown.

His words were always the most devastating: "It's okay, Mommy. We're okay," he would say, and every single time, his simple, profound reassurance broke something open inside her.

No little boy should have to carry that kind of immense, adult weight; no child should be so acutely aware of disaster. But Lucas did, because he saw her fighting to stay strong. He was scared too, and maybe, Kay realized, his fierce devotion was his way of holding their shattered world together—not just for himself, but for her. He was a silent participant in her war for stability.

And Kay... she was profoundly grateful. She was fiercely proud of the small, seven-year-old man who held her hand and helped secure their chaos. But beneath the gratitude, a terror pulsed. If she finally allowed herself to fall apart, if the exhaustion won, who would catch them?

The answer was a terrifying, absolute silence: No one.

So, she did the only thing she could in the face of that unbearable solitude: she locked the fear away. She stopped acknowledging the pain, refusing to allow any crack in her armor. She tried, with every ounce of physical and psychological strength she possessed, to hold herself rigidly together, knowing that her survival—and the survival of her two precious boys—depended entirely on her not breaking.

They couldn't afford cable anymore—just one of the many luxuries that had quietly slipped away in the aftermath. The house was quiet most nights, the occasional burst of laughter from one of the old VHS tapes the boys loved. But once the boys were tucked in, Kay would retreat to the couch with a blanket and a book.

During that period, her reading was relentless and utilitarian. She sought no escapism in novels or fantasies; she simply didn't have the mental space for it. Instead, her stack of books was a desperate stand-in for professional help: self-help guides, therapy workbooks, healing scriptures, woman empowerment manifestos, and deep dives into trauma, resilience, healing childhood wounds, and breaking generational cycles. Lord knew she desperately needed proper therapy, but without insurance and with every penny stretched so thin it practically snapped, professional help was an impossible luxury.

So, instead, she tried to be her own therapist.

Kay knew, undeniably, that Richard was the root of much of their chaos. However, her focus had shifted from his faults to her own survival. More importantly, she needed to confront a deeper, more painful question: Why did she allow it? What was fundamentally wrong with her that she accepted this pattern? Her mission became clear: she had to understand and heal herself so she could stand strong and move forward without crumbling under the weight of her past.

Late every night, the house finally quiet, she journaled, pouring out her anxieties onto the page. She performed breathing exercises painstakingly learned from a dog-eared library book. Her entire world became a canvas for healing: she underlined crucial passages in her texts and taped motivating scriptures—to the fridge, the bathroom mirror, and even the inside of her wallet—creating a constant, visual affirmation of her resolve.

"God is on the side of the oppressed and abused."

• **Psalm 56.**

"It is God who arms me with strength and keeps my way secure."

• **Samuel 22:33**

"I can do all this through him who gives me strength."

• **Philippians 4:13**

And sometimes, when everything felt too heavy to hold, and her hands trembled as she turned the pages, she would cry—quietly, so the boys wouldn't hear.

Running home to her parents was not an option. Her mother had offered more than once, gently nudging her over the phone: "Just come to Florida, sweetheart. Start fresh."

But Kay couldn't.

Part of her didn't want to uproot the boys again—not when Lucas had finally adjusted to his new school, not when Aiden had a team of doctors who understood him. But mostly, she knew Richard would fight her in court the moment she tried to leave the state. He'd accuse her of kidnapping. He'd try to make her look unstable.

He might win too, now that he had an attorney—and not just any attorney, but a good one. The kind who could twist words until they lost all meaning, who swallowed Richard's lies whole and preached them like gospel in court.

How he could afford someone like that, Kay would never understand. Previously, he was always late on rent, always "tight this month," blaming phantom overtime that never showed up in his pay. But suddenly, he had legal firepower.

Kay had a theory. It started the day she saw *her*—the girlfriend—when she first went to the police department about visitation. Probably the one footing the bills: rent, groceries, gas. Maybe even the lawyer. Maybe Richard funneled every dollar he could spare into this legal battle while his girlfriend kept the rest of his life afloat. Wouldn't that be something—paying to help him fight for custody of kids he never even cared to raise?

The thought made Kay sick. But it tracked.

Richard had always been a master manipulator, particularly adept at playing the victim and finding the exact audience needed to believe he was the wounded party. His skill became a dangerous advantage in court, where image often carried more weight than documented truth. He managed to appear just clean enough, just wounded enough, and just reasonable enough to successfully frame Kay as the difficult, unreasonable problem.

So no. Running wasn't an option.

She had to find a way to heal right here. Not for him. Not even for herself.

But for those two little boys in the next room who deserved a mother who could carry them through the storm and still manage to find the sun.

And God, it wasn't easy. Especially not with Richard.

Because even when he wasn't there, he found ways to haunt her—through dozens of court orders, emails, and the cold, calculated voice of his attorney. The man was a machine. The kind who didn't just play dirty, he specialized in scorched earth. Motions, filings, threats—endless waves of legal noise designed to wear her down.

One afternoon, Kay received a devastating call from her attorney—a decent man, but one who possessed a paper-thin tolerance for legal dramatics. His voice was bone-tired. "Kay, I can't continue. I have to withdraw," he admitted. "This case is too volatile, and frankly, it's becoming too time-consuming, requiring a level of attention I simply cannot sustain."

At first, Kay didn't understand why. She only thought about finding another attorney as she said, "Okay."

She couldn't afford to keep the guy anyway. But then it began to dawn on her. It wasn't just about money.

He dropped it because he was being swamped under a relentless barrage of motions, objections, procedural delays, and bad-faith filings. Richard's legal team was waging a war of attrition, flooding the docket with paperwork designed to drain time, energy, and resources. They weren't trying to win; they were trying to exhaust.

Kay must've called over fifty law firms after that. Each time, the same pattern repeated. There would be an intake, a flicker of hope, and then, "We're sorry, Ms. Jean. We've had prior contact with Mr. Richard. There's a conflict of interest."

It happened again and again.

Eventually, she understood the full scope of what was happening. Richard had weaponized the legal system itself, deploying litigation harassment with brutal precision. Death by a thousand paper cuts. And it worked.

She had then asked a paralegal, "How is that even legal?"

The paralegal on the other end sighed. "It's not illegal. It's just... tactical. And it's working."

It felt like he'd blacklisted her from the entire legal system. Kay was out of time, out of money, and nearly out of hope—until she finally found a small firm in Franklin, Tennessee.

The receptionist at the firm answered the phone with a calm warmth. "Yes? How can I help you?"

Kay explained everything. Again.

This time, the intake didn't end with an apology. Instead, an older man picked up the line.

"Mrs. Anderson," he said, "Sounds like you've been through hell. Let me help."

There was no fear or hesitation despite the looming threat of Richard's harassment.

She was silent for a beat. Then, softly said, "Are you sure? I don't have much."

"We'll figure it out," the lawyer on the other end said. "Right now, you need someone in your corner."

Desperate, Kay reached out to her mother for assistance. Her mother, knowing the urgency of the situation, scraped together the $5,000 retainer, drawing down every last available resource to provide the initial funding.

For the first time in months, she felt that maybe she wasn't entirely alone. But that wasn't the end of it.

Richard's harassment only intensified. He had escalated to stalking—parking his car down the road from her house, a looming, silent sentinel watching and waiting. Every time Kay left or returned home, she felt his presence lingering, a malevolent shadow that never quite vanished. She called the police repeatedly, but their response was always the same: there was nothing they could do. Because he was on a public street, Richard was technically breaking no laws, leaving Kay trapped in a constant state of unnerving, powerless surveillance.

Then, it got worse. Richard called 911 every night for over a month, claiming he was concerned for his children's safety. He insisted that officers come to Kay's home to "check on them, make sure they were okay."

Each time, the police were left feeling annoyed and frustrated. "The kids are fine, Richard," they would tell him, but he wouldn't stop. It was either 'Kay wasn't answering his calls' or 'Kay wasn't a good mother.' He made up new stories every night, all with one purpose, which was to torment her.

One night, an officer came inside. Kay had braced herself for the usual exchange, but this time, the officer seemed different. His patience had worn thin. "This has gone on long enough," he said, as though he were finally seeing the full extent of Richard's madness. "He's taking up department resources. Enough is enough."

Kay felt a flicker of hope. Finally, someone believed her. He asked for Richard's number, and Kay handed it over. The officer stepped outside to make the call. She didn't hear the conversation, but when he came back in, there was a change in his demeanor. "I think that's the end of it," he said. "I warned him—one more call, and we'll arrest him for filing false reports."

Kay's breath caught in her throat. It was the first time anyone had taken her seriously. She explained again—about the abuse, the divorce, the threats. The officer was kind, understanding. He even promised he would check in on her in a few days.

But she never saw him again.

A few days later, Kay learned that Richard had gone straight to the police chief. Somehow, the officer who'd helped her was fired from his job. The news hit her like a punch to the gut. Richard's influence reached farther than she ever could have imagined. And with it, Kay's fear grew.

Paranoia became her constant companion, suffocating her mind with the certainty that Richard was capable of anything. The threats—the gruesome specifics about her murder and the deliberate concealment of her body—replayed on a terrifying loop, preventing all peace. Every time she returned home, she performed a nervous inventory: a missing item, a drawer slightly ajar, a tiny detail out of place. She felt a sickening certainty that he was finding ways to breach the house when she was absent, a silent, invisible trespasser. The psychological torture was complete: she knew the intrusion was real, but without physical evidence, she could never prove the violation.

So, she resorted to desperate, secret measures: she started sprinkling baby powder in fine lines across the thresholds of the doors and windows, hoping for a footprint that would reveal his intrusion. It felt insane—she knew it was illogical—but the consuming fear demanded proof. The need to know was too great; she simply had to get out of that house, away from him. Yet, her financial reality was a cage: she had zero savings and no viable way to organize an escape.

Her paranoia intensified, no longer confined to the house. It became omnipresent. She began looking over her shoulder when she went shopping, peering around every corner, half-expecting Richard himself to be there, watching her, or, worse, having someone else execute his threats. The fear followed her like a suffocating, inescapable shadow. She couldn't shake the chilling feeling that he was always one step behind, planting the seeds of terror wherever she went.

The harassment wasn't confined to their neighborhood; it became a public spectacle. Richard started showing up at Lucas's baseball and football games—events he had never once bothered to attend before the divorce. Now, he would conspicuously appear, sitting in the stands with his new girlfriend, putting on a flawless performance as "Dad of the Year." He was openly playing the part of the caring, engaged father he had never genuinely been, making sure Kay and everyone else witnessed his calculated hypocrisy.

But Kay knew better.

Richard wasn't there to support their son. He was there to make her uncomfortable, to intimidate her. He'd find a way to pull her aside, away from the crowd, and whisper things in her ear like, *"This ain't over, Kay. You're never gonna win. You'll see."* Each time, the words felt like a knife twisting deeper into her chest.

Kay saw the truth plainly: Richard was engaging in psychological warfare. These cruel, calculated "games" were his way of ensuring she never forgot that he was relentlessly devoted to tormenting her and systematically wearing down her will to live in peace.

One night, exhausted after a long shift, she picked up Lucas from after-school care and headed home. (Aiden was safely with the nurse.) As she pulled into the driveway, chatting casually with Lucas about his day, a tiny pinprick of red light caught her eye in the driver's side mirror. In an instant, her heart slammed against her ribs, the casual moment shattering into pure, cold panic. Without thinking, she slammed the truck into reverse, the tires spitting gravel as her mind raced to identify the threat.

"Get down!" she screamed, her voice tearing. "Lucas, on the floor—now!"

He obeyed instantly, hiding into the footwell as she threw the car into reverse, tires screeching. Her hands trembled on the wheel, her thoughts spiraling into terror.

Richard must be trying to kill me. He must've hired someone. This is the end, she thought.

Fighting a wave of raw panic, she fumbled for her phone and frantically dialed 911. She managed to report the suspicious car parked down the street and the chilling sight of the red light pointed directly at her. Her hands shook uncontrollably as she sped away from the house, fleeing the lethal danger she knew was closing in. The police response was lightning fast, arriving to surround the suspect's car on the street in mere moments. Inside her truck, Kay was left breathless and completely terrified, the adrenaline seizing her lungs.

As the officers quickly searched the source of the red beam, they found not a gunman, but a private detective inside the car, calmly filming her. The terrifying red light was merely the recording indicator on his camera. It was just another of Richard's calculated pawns.

Once again, the police were powerless to act. Since he was parked on a public street, Richard had found another perfectly legal way to relentlessly torment her. Kay was left with endless, suffocating questions: What was he hoping to find? What did he want? What could he possibly gain from this cycle of harassment? The answers remained elusive, but one terrifying truth was certain: Richard would not stop.

The sheer onslaught of incidents—each one more invasive, chilling, and psychologically disturbing than the last—made it impossible for Kay to maintain a clear record in her head. Her thoughts were a frayed, chaotic blur, and the mounting events began to feel like a single, terrifying nightmare. Desperate to claw back some control, she started a journal—a plain, simple notebook that quickly became her sanity's anchor. With meticulous, almost obsessive focus, she diligently recorded every single detail: the precise dates, times, locations, and chilling specifics of each event. This relentless documentation was her only way to impose structure on the madness, to make sense of the emotional fog, and to build a cold, undeniable record of Richard's escalating, malicious campaign against her.

26

A Scar That Wouldn't Close

There was a new queen in Richard's crumbling castle.

Her name was Samantha. Kay had seen her once before the official introduction—a figure with a loud voice echoing across the school parking lot, wearing a skin-tight top that clung like a deliberate threat, and a cheap, cloying perfume that wafted in the wind like a toxic warning. Samantha laughed too loudly, invaded personal space, and wore an unwavering, arrogant expression that announced she had life completely figured out and was utterly uninterested in anyone else's input. She didn't just think she was superior; she knew it in that delusional, absolute way that made people quietly shrink back whenever she turned their way.

Conversations wilted in her vicinity; even silence seemed to recoil. She monopolized every room, talking incessantly about herself—her sacrifices, her stress, her accomplishments, her importance—until no one else could mentally breathe. And despite all the aggressive bravado, she was profoundly plain. Not just in her physical appearance, which was ordinary, but in her spirit. There was no warmth, no genuine depth, just a surface aggressively polished to reflect back only her own self-serving delusion.

Richard, of course, had found his match. Two snakes in one pit, hissing into each other's egos.

Kay had heard bits and pieces, but it was Lucas who told her the rest—innocently, with that small, unsure voice children use when they aren't quite sure they're allowed to be upset.

"She wants me to call her *Mom* now," he'd said one night, fiddling with his shoelaces, not looking up.

Kay's stomach flipped. Something inside her went ice cold. The word *Mom* belonged to her. She'd earned it through countless tears, sleepless nights, and whispered lullabies. And that word being twisted into something grotesque by *that* woman. It made Kay sick.

"Listen, you don't ever have to call her 'Mom' if you don't want to. I am your mother." Her heart was pounding so hard against her ribs it felt like it might burst. It was more than a statement; it was a fierce, protective vow to her son.

Because it wasn't just Samantha, it was all of it. Every other weekend visitation was another chapter in a horror story that no one wanted to read.

The change in Lucas was immediate and deeply unsettling. He was coming home abrasive, mouthy, and aggressively rude, his once-sweet demeanor replaced by a sharp defiance. Kay watched, bewildered and heartbroken, realizing she had never witnessed such a distressing side of her son. Aiden frequently came back with filthy, sour-smelling clothes, diapers so saturated they hadn't been changed in hours, and rashes so red and raw it hurt Kay just to look at them. The evidence was undeniable and sickeningly clear: the boys were not being cared for, and Aiden was actively suffering neglect.

"They put us in a room with black blinds," Lucas had said once. "And then they lock the door from the outside. The knobs are reversed, so you can't get out."

Kay had to sit down when she heard that. Her mind refused to process it at first.

"What do you mean, they *lock* the door?"

"So we don't wake them up too early," Lucas said, like it was normal. Like it made sense. "We get in trouble if we're loud."

The room had no toys. Just a bed. Heavy blackout blinds that swallowed the sun. It wasn't a room—it was a cage.

And what haunted Kay most was that they often left Lucas in charge of Aiden. An eight-year-old. To feed, clean, protect, and entertain a special-needs five-year-old with feeding tubes and sensory sensitivities. They left white bread and a jar of peanut butter on the counter. That was "breakfast." That was "care."

They weren't just negligent. They were cruel.

The final straw hadn't come with a scream but with a whisper.

"They hit me sometimes," Lucas said, barely audible. "They say it's cause I talk too much. I try not to. But sometimes I can't help but."

He'd come home with a bruise on his arm and a scrape on his back. He said he'd fallen, but when Kay gently pressed, the truth spilled out.

"Samantha pulled me. To my room. I didn't move fast enough."

She wanted to scream. The rage in her veins burned so hot she could barely see straight. She imagined gripping the wheel, flooring the gas pedal, and crashing her car straight through their house—splintering wood, shattering glass, and crushing every smug secret hidden within those walls. She wanted to tear that place apart. To make them feel the wreckage they had left inside her.

It took a special kind of sickness—a rotting, twisted cruelty—to raise a hand against a special child already fighting battles the world could barely understand. A child whose innocence should have been shielded, not shattered, by the very monsters who preyed on weakness.

But all she could do was hold him. Rock him. Promise that she'd never let anyone hurt him again—even as the court still demanded she send him back every other weekend.

They were losing pieces of themselves every time they went over there. There was one time that Kay only found out about *later*—a story that slipped out of Lucas's mouth like a confession weeks after it had happened. By then, the bruises were gone, but the ache in Kay's chest would never heal the same.

It had started with Lucas doing *exactly* what he was supposed to do.

Aiden's feeding tube had come out again. It wasn't the first time, but this time was different—this time, there were no adults around. Richard and Samantha had left them home alone, with no way to call for help, no neighbors checking in, not even a working phone in the house.

Eight-year-old Lucas was left to handle it alone, a terrified child trying desperately to care for his four-year-old brother, whose body depended on that tube to survive.

Lucas didn't know how to fix it. He only knew Aiden needed it. His little hands fumbled, panic rising in his chest as he tried to remember anything he'd seen the adults do before. But the truth was, he was just a kid—too young to understand how dangerous it was, but old enough to know something was very wrong. So, Lucas did what any brave, terrified child would do. He went to get help.

He ran down the street, barefoot and shaking, to a neighbor's house he barely knew. Banged on the door until someone opened it. "My brother's feeding tube fell out," he said in a panic. "He needs help and my dad is not home."

The neighbor didn't hesitate. They called 911. An ambulance came, flashing lights cutting across the quiet suburban street, paramedics storming into the house. Lucas went with them, being the good older brother that he was.

However, being a firefighter, Richard heard the dispatch on the radio when he was out doing God-knows-what and turned the car around. By the time he got back, Aiden was being loaded into the ambulance, and Lucas was punished for leaving the house.

"*Severely,*" Lucas whispered from the backseat days later, eyes darting to make sure Aiden wasn't listening. "Because I left the house. And because the ambulance came. He said... he said we made them look bad."

Kay's heart stopped.

"What do you mean by *severely*, sweetheart?" she asked gently, trying to keep her voice even as every muscle in her body screamed.

But Lucas didn't answer. His silence gripped Kay's heart tighter than whatever answer he had. Kay gripped the steering wheel until her knuckles whitened. Her jaw locked. And all she could think was: *They didn't even call me. My son was taken to the hospital, and they didn't call me.*

She had to hear it from Lucas, a child who barely understood what he was saying.

And it didn't stop there.

One Sunday, Kay was out with friends, driving down the Natchez Trace Parkway. They had been on the road for three hours, enjoying the sunset through the windshield, when her phone rang. It was 9 p.m., the kind of hour when the world starts winding down, and the sound of a call felt out of place. Kay glanced at the screen, and it was a number she didn't recognize. A sudden chill crept over her as she answered.

"Hello?" she said, trying to steady her voice.

"Ms. Kay Anderson?" the woman on the other end asked, her voice formal and clipped. "This is Marie Miller, a social worker with the Department of Children and Families. I'm calling to inform you that your children are in the ER. We've received allegations of abuse, and I am calling to notify you that they will *not* be coming home with you."

Kay froze, the words hanging in the air like a thick fog. Her mind couldn't process what was happening. "What? What do you mean, they won't be coming home?"

"I'm sorry to have to inform you this way," the social worker continued. "But there are allegations from Richard and Samantha, stating that you've been abusing the children. I need you to come to the DCF office on Monday for an interview. The kids will remain under their care until the investigation is complete."

Hysterical crying overtook her as Kay's world shattered. "No. No, this can't be real! Richard is lying. I never hurt them! You have to believe me, I—"

The social worker's voice remained detached. "I understand this is difficult, but you will need to come in on Monday. We'll talk more then. But right now, I need to stress the importance of your cooperation in this process."

Kay's mind spun. Her friends had quietened when they heard her, and the only thing remaining was the car's hum. "But tomorrow is Sunday. and Lucas has a project due on Monday—" She was gasping for air, unable to process the crushing weight of what was happening. "Please... They're lying. My children are *not* in danger."

"I'm afraid there's nothing more I can do at the moment," the social worker said, her tone unchanging. "We'll see you Monday at the office. Goodbye."

Kay dropped the phone into her lap while her friends tried to comfort her. Kay's hands and her whole body trembled. Her breath was shallow and fast, every heartbeat a painful reminder of the injustice unfolding. She couldn't believe Richard could go so far as to take the kids away from her.

Tears streamed down her face as she dialed her mother's number, nearly dropping the phone in her desperation.

"Mom," Kay choked out, "They took the kids. They're in the ER. The social worker just called. They're saying I hurt them. Richard and Samantha—" She sobbed, the words impossible to push through her panic.

Her mother's voice was calm, a soothing presence in the midst of her daughter's hysteria. "Kay, slow down. You need to gather yourself. We'll handle this, okay? I'll call your father. You need to get home. Take pictures of every room in the house, time and date stamped. Gather the boys' school and medical records. Don't waste any time. Get it all together."

Kay's mind raced. "I can't believe this is happening," she whispered. "How could he do this to me?"

"Don't worry, honey. The truth will come out. Just take action, okay? Don't let them catch you off guard. We'll figure this out."

Kay hung up; her vision blurred with tears.

Kay raced home, Kay snapped pictures of every room—Lucas's room, Aiden's, the kitchen, the hallway—each photo timestamped to prove that nothing was out of place. She maintained an immaculate home, where every corner reflected her relentless pride and discipline. The house was exactly as it had been; every corner and shelf was untouched by the false accusations that were now weighing heavily on her. She had never raised a hand to her children. Never once had she been the source of their fear or pain. Where were they getting this from? Did they even talk to Lucas? He was old enough to tell them the truth. Why wasn't anyone listening to him?

Kay's thoughts spiraled, sharp and cold, but she slammed the mental door on doubt. There was no time. Her fingers flew, snatching the thick school binders and the meticulously organized nursing records. Each file was a shield—a stack of irrefutable evidence. Doctor visit summaries, school progress reports, emergency contact sheets, anything that could annihilate the lies Richard had spun.

The pile of papers and binders on the kitchen table grew, but Kay didn't stop. She had to be prepared for whatever was coming. The worst was always a step away and waiting.

It was 8:00 a.m., Sunday morning. The silence of the weekend was her enemy, every ticking second a lost advantage. She had to reach her attorney, but how could she bypass the layers of a weekend office closure? The clock was not just ticking—it was roaring. With a heart slamming against her ribs, she tried his office number, hoping for a miracle, an answering service, anything. No answer. She hit redial immediately. Once, twice, then a third time, but the line simply rang out, each empty chime mocking her growing desperation.

The wave of panic broke, replaced by a surge of cold, razor-sharp resolve. She would not let this day slip away. She seized the phone book, her mind already tracking the next step. Flipping to the 'S's, she found the section for Stafford. Hundreds of names. She didn't hesitate. Desperation was fueling her now, but it was a focused, determined fire. She began dialing, each number a step forward, a direct challenge to the silence. Twenty-two calls had already gone unanswered, but Kay was unmoved. She paused only long enough to draw a deep breath, and then, without a tremor, she punched in the next Stafford number. Failure was not an option she would entertain.

Please, someone help me, she thought as the phone rang.

"Hello?" A soft voice answered on the other end of the line.

Kay's voice cracked, barely able to get the words out. "Hi, I'm sorry to bother you, but I'm looking for Mr. Gary Stafford. He's an attorney... and it's an urgent matter.

The woman was quiet for a moment, then replied in a calm tone, "Yes, that's my husband. Please, hold on a moment."

Kay's breath caught in her throat as she waited. Her mind raced a mile a minute, a whirlwind of fear, guilt, and frustration. *What if they don't help me? What if nobody believes me?*

A moment later, the line clicked, and a new voice answered.

"This is Gary Stafford," the man said, "How can I help you?"

The moment Mr. Stafford answered, her last pretense of composure shattered. "I am so sorry, Mr. Stafford. I know it's Sunday, and I know this is a ridiculous time," she stammered, the words rushing out. "I'm invading your privacy, calling you at home, but I didn't know what else to do." The tears came, hot, sudden, and blinding. Choking on her sobs, Kay dumped the entire crisis into his ear—the call from the social worker, the monstrous allegations from Richard and Samantha, the raw, gnawing fear that had been tightening like a vise. The narrative was disjointed, a flood of fragmented horrors, but she forced every terrifying detail out.

Mr. Stafford was silent for a moment, then spoke with confidence. "Kay, I know this is overwhelming, but I need you to get a hold of yourself and trust me. Don't panic. We'll take care of this. I'll meet you at the Department of Children and Families office tomorrow at the scheduled time. You'll be there, I'll be there, and we'll make sure everything is addressed. You're not alone."

Kay finally allowed herself to breathe. It wasn't over, and it wasn't going to be easy. But she wasn't alone. She wasn't fighting this on her own.

The deadline for Lucas's school project was tomorrow. With her attorney's approval, the next morning, she arrived early with Lucas's backpack and completed project. Inside the school office, she kept her explanation brief and professional, confirming she was only there to drop off Lucas's belongings. Every muscle in her face was dedicated to maintaining the mask of normalcy. She offered the office staff her bright, familiar smile, concealing the storm raging inside. There was no hint of the drama with Richard; she was just a mother ensuring her son didn't miss a deadline, waiting quietly for Lucas to walk through the doors.

The moment Lucas entered, his face ignited with a huge, unrestrained smile. He shot forward, arms wide, his pure, relieved excitement palpable across the room. Kay's controlled facade finally softened as she opened her arms, clutching him in a tight, protective embrace. "Here you go, sweetheart," she murmured quickly, her voice thick with emotion, "your backpack and your project.

It was at that moment that Richard appeared, and without any warning, yanked Lucas from her arms, and snapped at him, "Get to class, Lucas."

Kay stood frozen, caught off guard by such a scene. This wasn't the version of Richard that had always been so careful to maintain the image of the "perfect dad." His behavior was so far from the facade he usually put on, and the office staff, who had witnessed it all, looked equally stunned.

Lucas, a flicker of confusion clouding his smile, gave his mother one last longing look before he reluctantly walked away. The office staff exchanged uneasy glances, and a few offered muted words of comfort. Kay barely registered them, offering only an absent nod. Her mind was already racing ahead, processing the immense risk she had just taken. She offered the staff a small, polite smile that didn't reach her eyes, gathered her purse, and quietly turned, slipping out the door without a single unnecessary word or glance—no scene for Richard, if he were watching, just a swift, silent departure.

That morning, after his long drive from Florida, Kay's father arrived and immediately accompanied her to the Department of Children and Families. She had dressed in a commanding blue pinstripe suit, a deliberate choice to project strength—it was her battle armor. The last couple of days hadn't been spent in panic, but in strategic preparation, meticulously organizing her thoughts, questions, and comments for this meeting. As she walked, her resolve was palpable; it was a physical echo in every step. Crossing the threshold, she felt an unmistakable surge of power: the deep conviction that she was no longer a victim, but a focused, unstoppable force.

They were ushered into a large, stark conference room, dominated by a single, imposing table that seemed to stretch the length of the space. Across the polished wood sat a silent, unreadable row of strangers—a formidable, judging panel. Conspicuously absent were Richard and Samantha, adding a layer of unnerving tension. Kay's hands were steady with resolve, though a tremor ran through them as she set down her massive stacks of evidence. Lucas's school and medical files, Aiden's entire complex medical history, nursing reports, abuse documentation, and her own detailed journal logs came down with a muted but assertive thud. She had brought an arsenal—every shred of proof, every document meticulously collected to demolish their lies.

She settled into her chair, and the powerful, unfamiliar sensation she'd felt earlier coalesced—a cold, steady force she had never known.

A silent shift took place inside her, an inner strength that did not merely fill the silence of the room, but commanded it. She was no longer Kay, the victim, but Kay, the determined survivor. There would be no meek submission today; she was impenetrable, and she would not allow them to tear her or her family apart.

Kay asked, "Do you have photos of the alleged abuse of my children?"

A woman slid a handful of photographs across the dark table. Kay's gaze flickered down, instantly registering the poor quality. The images were blurry, badly framed, and entirely unconvincing—clearly amateur attempts at evidence. She gave the pictures a single, dismissive glance, then raised her eyes immediately, meeting the woman's gaze with a steady, unwavering defiance. There was no flinch, no hesitation; only an implicit judgment of the weak case laid before her.

Kay leaned forward slightly, her voice cutting through the silence, cold and steady as steel. "I see nothing in these photos," she stated, making it a professional judgment, not an opinion. Then her questions struck like blows: "Why exactly am I here? Did you speak to my son, Lucas? What precisely did he tell you?"

The woman paused, looking down at her notes. She hesitated for a moment before replying, her tone clinical, but there was a subtle shift in the air as if she were sensing Kay's growing determination.

"Lucas reported in his interview that you do not spank them," the woman said, her eyes meeting Kay's.

Kay's patience was beginning to thin. "Okay, so why am I here then?" she pressed, leaning forward slightly.

The woman's demeanor shifted slightly as she moved to the next point in her report, "There's also the matter of a bruise on Aiden."

Kay didn't flinch. She had prepared for this. She'd been expecting this exact accusation, and she wasn't about to back down now.

Kay didn't wait; the words tore from her in a single, cold burst: "Are you talking about the minor bruise Aiden got on his shoulder from a physical therapy fall? His nurse reported it to me while I was at work, I drove home, and I immediately ensured an incident report was filed because I knew Richard would try something like this. I notified Richard myself that Friday during the visitation exchange—the nurse was there, she explained everything to him, and he received a copy of this very report." She didn't pause for emphasis, simply sliding the documented evidence across the table with a sharp flick of her wrist.

Without drawing a breath or breaking her verbal momentum, Kay immediately opened Aiden's Medical Binders, aggressively fanning the thick volumes across the table. She launched into a precise account of his complex medical diagnosis, detailing the ten hours of daily nursing care he required, then walked them through the incident step-by-step. The room did not just fall silent; it froze. Her attorney sat back, effectively sidelined, as Kay seized total command of the conversation. She was direct, strong, informative, clear, and undeniably firm. She was a force of nature on fire, commanding not just the table, but the very air in the room, refusing to allow them a single second to paint her as an abuser.

At the far end of the table, a man shot to his feet, his face a mask of hardening displeasure. "Wait here," he commanded, his voice a blunt instrument cutting across her relentless testimony. The sudden interruption finally forced Kay to stop. She immediately inhaled, sucking in the long, ragged breath her body had demanded for minutes, the adrenaline-fueled fire in her veins finally beginning to consume itself. Without another word or glance, the entire group of strangers rose and filed silently from the room.

Long, grueling minutes bled into the silence. Kay felt every one of them. When the door finally opened, the man who had commanded her to wait returned, but his authority was gone; his face was stripped of its earlier hostility. He approached the table slowly, his tone low and heavy with regret.

"We are truly sorry," he said, the words genuine. "We were operating under the false information that they were the custodial parents. Your evidence proves otherwise. Your children will be returned to your custody within the hour."

This is a powerful, final question from Kay, capturing her frustration with the system and the emotional toll of the experience. To enhance this section, we'll maintain the raw emotion while making the disbelief and demand for justice more pointed.

Kay stared at the man, the immense relief of victory immediately eclipsed by a searing disbelief. "So, they just walk away?" she asked, her voice tight with suppressed rage. "Richard and Samantha put me and my children through absolute hell, traumatized them with a false report, and there's zero recourse for that? How can a system allow someone to file blatant lies with such devastating consequences and face no accountability whatsoever?"

The man sighed, looking uncomfortable. "The state doesn't go after people who file false reports, but we regret the way this was handled."

The immediate wave of relief that they wouldn't take her children was swift, but fleeting. It was instantly drowned by a powerful surge of frustration that boiled in her chest. The anger wasn't just an emotion; it was a bitter, flooding tide that refused to recede, leaving her heart pounding with the injustice of what she had just endured.

Her attorney, who had remained utterly silent throughout Kay's performance, finally leaned forward, a genuine laugh breaking the tension. "Honestly," he admitted, shaking his head slightly, "I'm not entirely sure why I was here. You didn't need me at all. That was absolutely masterful. You did amazing."

Kay's eyes instantly welled, the hard-won composure shattering the moment the pressure lifted. She had been running on pure instinct; she had no idea where that seismic strength had come from, only that it had carried her across the finish line. The breakdown was complete and immediate, the release coming like a violent, unstoppable flood. Her children were her absolute north star, her entire, irreplaceable world. Nothing else mattered—she would tear down mountains to keep them safe, loved, and cared for.

That evening, her sons were finally returned, and the silence of anxiety was replaced by the chaotic joy that made the house feel whole again. But Kay didn't mistake this for peace; she knew the battle was far from over. Richard was not the type to back down. She now understood the chilling depth of his cruelty: his hunger for revenge was insatiable, and he would stop at nothing—no lie too vile, no attack too personal—to punish her.

And now, he had found a weapon that was most effective against Kay: the children.

He had started lying to them. Whispering poison into their ears. Twisting their love for their mother into doubt, fear, and anger.

Telling them that she is too stressed and sad to properly take care of you. She's not okay..

That she was trying to move far away to keep you from ever seeing me again.

She wants to keep you both, just for herself.

Lucas—her bright, cheerful Lucas—was slipping away.

The every-other-weekend visitation schedule with Richard continued, but it was less a schedule and more a flashpoint for conflict. When Lucas had games or scheduled school events, he routinely refused to go, and this always ignited Richard's immediate fury.

The predictable rage revealed a chilling pattern: Richard never took Aiden without Lucas. It was sickeningly clear that he only desired the simpler company of Lucas, treating Aiden's complex medical needs as a deliberate complication they were unwilling to shoulder. A profound, private wash of relief settled over Kay every time Lucas opted out. She preferred keeping her Aiden close because Lucas could defend himself or at least clearly communicate if something went wrong. Richard, predictably, would blame Kay for Lucas's absence, but she remained unyielding: she absolutely refused to force either boy into a situation they actively resisted.

The years that followed brought a rapid succession of shocking and deeply unsettling developments in Richard's new life: he and Samantha went on to have one child after the next, quickly building a large family. This relentless sequence of births was unthinkable to Kay for deeply personal reasons.

Kay remembered the decision vividly: after the heartbreaking loss of their daughter and the immense demands of caring for Aiden with his special needs, she and Richard had made the mutual decision to stop having children. It was an agonizing choice for Kay, who always envisioned having many children herself. The vasectomy, meticulously documented after Aiden's birth, was meant to be the final, painful seal on that chapter of loss and acceptance. The sudden arrival of Richard's new children was not just a violation of that shared history; it was a constant, deliberate shove in her face—a cruel reminder of the family she could not have with him.

Because of the vasectomy, Kay knew, with absolute, cold certainty, that none of these children were Richard's biological offspring. This revelation was not a personal betrayal; it was evidence of a monumental, continuous lie at the very heart of Richard and Samantha's fabricated family structure. This lie solidified Kay's view of Richard as fundamentally dishonest, manipulative, and capable of long-term public deception.

To exacerbate the situation, Richard and Samantha weaponized this fabrication, pressing the lie onto Lucas and Aiden. They were forced to accept each new baby as their "sister" and "brother," an insistence that made Kay physically sick. This act of psychological manipulation—forcing her sons to acknowledge a manufactured bloodline and participate in a lie—filled Kay with dread. She questioned constantly: What exactly was happening over there?

The bizarre circumstances of the rapidly expanding family, coupled with Richard's capacity for lies, gave rise to dark, sickening rumors that filtered back to Kay. Whispers suggested Richard and Samantha were involved in a "swinging" lifestyle and other unconventional, morally compromised sexual activities. While unverified, the sheer thought that her boys were being exposed to a chaotic, deceptive, and potentially unstable environment built on serial falsehoods and sexual complexity was a corrosive source of maternal fear. It fueled her determination to ensure the custody battle would never end until her children were truly safe.

And yet, Richard and Samantha insisted otherwise, parading the story to friends, family, even to Lucas and Aiden, telling them these children were their siblings.

"Don't listen to your mother," Richard had told Lucas once, as they sat in a fast-food restaurant, the sound of trays scraping across tables in the background. "Those kids are your family, too. You are siblings, you get that?"

Lucas wouldn't say anything and just quietly listen. Because how else was he supposed to respond?

It was like a violation every time Richard hijacked reality, molding everything she knew into a grotesque version that served only his own warped narrative.

It wasn't long before Lucas began to return from visitations with a nasty, corrosive attitude. He was snapping, talking back with a sudden venom, and being short and mean toward Kay. This was a painful contradiction to the boy he was: loving, caring, thoughtful, and genuinely funny. Kay felt a cold, deep dread settle in her stomach, urgently worried about the psychological toll the back-and-forth was exacting on her eleven-year-old son. Lucas was naturally reticent—a boy who kept his thoughts close—but she knew, with absolute certainty, that something far darker and bigger was taking root. The clearest signal of the severity was that his defiance wasn't reserved just for her; he was even talking back to Richard and Samantha.

Lucas would recount some of these moments to Kay, piecing together a terrifying pattern: Every time Richard or Samantha leveled an accusation or made a derogatory comment, Lucas would instinctively snap back. "Don't touch me!" he'd scream. "Leave me and Aiden alone!" "You're not my mother!" These were the desperate, reflexive protests of a scared child that should have warranted gentle redirection and comfort. But there was no mercy. Lucas paid a brutal price for every single word.

Richard and Samantha were not ones to let a chance for control slip away. They didn't see a boy struggling under immense pressure; they saw a challenge—a defiance that needed to be violently crushed. Lucas was physically punished every time he dared respond, ensuring that any utterance of self-defense or protest became a trigger for retribution. The violence was their cold, hard method of "putting him in his place."

There was one weekend story that never stopped replaying in Kay's mind.

It was just a few weeks after Lucas had broken his arm during a school football game. He had been sprinting toward the end zone, football tucked tight under his arm, when another player tackled him hard from the side. Lucas went down fast, and the break was clean but rough. They'd put him in a cast—bright blue, covered in signatures from his team and classmates—and Kay had been so relieved he'd handled it all with such strength.

But when he came back from Richard's that weekend, Kay noticed that the cast was dirtier, like they hadn't bothered helping him clean around it. Also, the way Lucas was holding his arm which was too close to his chest also seemed off.

And it wasn't long before Lucas filled in the blanks, his voice barely above a whisper.

"They dragged me," he said one night, curled up next to Kay on the couch. "Down the hall."

Kay's heart sank. "What do you mean they *dragged* you, Lucas?"

Lucas's voice was a tight knot of shame and anger. "I—I yelled at Samantha," he choked out. "She said something really bad about you. And... and I couldn't hold it in. I got so mad! I told her she should not talk about you like that. Then Dad came flying in, told me to shut my mouth. I just looked at him and said 'No!' and then..."

Kay's stomach turned.

"They got really mad," Lucas rushed on, his voice cracking. "They yelled at me to go to my room. I said 'No!' And that's when it started. Dad grabbed both my arms, and Samantha grabbed my legs. They ripped me right off the couch." Lucas's face was etched with the memory. "I screamed and kicked, begging them to stop, but they wouldn't. They just dragged and threw me into the room and locked the door.

Kay couldn't breathe.

"They didn't check your arm?" she asked, praying for a *yes*.

Lucas shook his head. "They said if it hurt, it was my fault."

They were *insane*.

Awful.

Mean.

Twisted.

And everything was always, *always* about Kay. Somehow, Samantha and Richard couldn't go five minutes without turning the kids' existence into a battle over her. She was the villain in every story they told. The reason the boys were "soft." The excuse they gave for why Aiden cried too much and Lucas "acted like a spoiled brat."

"She babies you," Samantha would sneer.

"She's filling your head with lies," Richard would bark.

It wasn't parenting. It was psychological warfare. On children.

Lucas had stood up for his mother, and they had hurt him for it.

Samantha and Richard systematically manufacturing elaborate narratives to poison the boys and the outside world against Kay. They would consistently craft and deploy disgusting, baseless lies, turning simple truths into grotesque accusations. This behavior sparked a burning, futile question in Kay's mind: Why couldn't they simply co-parent and act like normal, mature adults?

What was so impossibly hard about finding a basis for mutual respect? The marriage was over—a definitive, closed chapter. Kay found herself spiraling into the injustice of it: Why did the end of their relationship necessitate this endless, malicious war?

She saw the profound failure in their actions. This wasn't about divorce; it was about willful cruelty. It was about punishment masquerading as parenting. What was the ultimate, sick point of expending so much energy on destruction, when the only real casualty was the boys' fragile sense of peace? The lack of purpose behind the relentless malice was the most maddening part of all.

Sleep was a cruel impossibility. Kay spent the long, suffocating night hunched on the edge of her bed, a solitary, rigid sentinel. She stared blankly at the dark window, her hands trembling in her lap—physical anchors to the rage coiling in her gut. She knew the brutal truth: the court might still mandate those terrifying weekend visitations. But something fundamental had to shatter. Because if her boys kept returning to that house of poison and violence, Richard and Samantha would ensure there would be nothing left of their spirits or their light to bring home.

Every time the boys returned home harmed, Kay launched into her grim routine of meticulous documentation. Lucas's recounted stories, while heartbreaking, were merely hearsay—not the hard proof she desperately needed. She knew, with chilling certainty, that without irrefutable physical evidence of Richard and Samantha's actions, no one in the court system would ever believe her word.

Her camera became her only ally. Whenever Aiden came back with angry, deep rashes that screamed of prolonged neglect from being left in a soiled diaper, or with unexplained bruises patterning his legs and back, Kay snapped picture after picture. These photographs were undeniable, visual evidence, cataloging the systematic abuse inflicted upon her children.

Kay filed three separate, increasingly desperate reports with Children and Family Services. Each time, she poured her energy into filling out the tedious forms and enduring interviews, always met by a social worker whose eyes were dull with institutional exhaustion. The workers would nod vaguely, their rote promise to "look into it" sounding like a dismissal.

The social worker documented the undeniable, visual proof of ne-glect and abuse: snapping real-time photos of Aiden's skin—broken, black, blue, and raw with open sores. They always interviewed Lucas, since Aiden, due to his needs, could not speak for himself. Lucas would sit silently, a terrified, rigid figure, unable to articulate the hor-rors he'd endured. Kay was strictly barred from these sessions, while the damning visual evidence and the child's silence were utterly failed by the system.

And then nothing. There would be no follow-up or calls returned. She was *labeled*—not as a mother begging for someone to *see* her chil-dren, but as "the bitter ex-wife." It was as if grief over what was hap-pening to her sons was just leftover resentment. As if trying to *stop the cycle of violence* made her some unstable woman with an axe to grind.

People smiled politely. Nodded through her pleas but then took no action. Yet, the visitations continued and each time the boys came back home, they grew angrier.

Aiden, normally quiet, came home stormy. He couldn't even speak full sentences—his words came in fragments, frustrated and jum-bled—but he'd learned one thing with perfect clarity: *bitch.*

That was the word Richard and Samantha had taught him.

"Bitch!" he'd shout when he was frustrated. He'd hurl that word every time he became angry.

Kay didn't cry when he said it. She didn't scream or scold him.

Because she knew where he learned it. She knew what they were turning her boys into, and it terrified her.

She tried going back to court. Hired an attorney she couldn't af-ford. Tried to get a restraining order—just for the kids, just to buy time, to create space, anything.

But it was as if they didn't care. It was as if she were throwing rocks at a wall that would never crumble.

She even tried talking to Richard. Maybe he'd ease off, she had thought. But every conversation between them only spiraled. Every phone call became a war zone.

He would shout, and she would back down. He twisted her words, which she tried to explain, but he would shut her down, making her feel *small* again.

All of this made her so tired. The system had worn her down to the bone. The very people who were supposed to help her had turned away. And the man she had wanted to run from trapped her so tight that no oxygen could reach her. Richard thrived on her fear and silence.

Richard didn't just control through volume or fists—he manipulated Lucas through carefully curated lies. He wove a narrative that made Kay look unstable, irrational, and mentally unstable even. It was a slow erosion of her credibility until even those closest to her started to doubt their own memories.

Richard didn't just assign blame; he made Kay the singular, malignant source of all misfortune. To the boys, he would declare that every ounce of tension, fear, or chaos that fractured the peace—all of it was her fault. The divorce, the court battles, the lack of money, even their own sadness—it was all systematically traced back to their mother. He worked relentlessly to instill the belief that if she had simply behaved differently, none of this would be happening.

Even during the chaotic, sterile reality of Aiden's hospitalizations, Richard never missed a chance to tighten his manipulative grip. He would wait for the precise moment, then pull the exhausted floor nurses aside, speaking in hushed, conspiratorial tones amidst the constant beep of monitors. Wearing the impeccable mask of the burdened, long-suffering father, he'd lean in: "It was their mother. She's got issues," he'd sigh, his voice heavy with carefully manufactured concern. "She makes it worse for him—her instability complicates everything. I'm the only one here holding this family and his care together." He only appeared for the minimum time necessary to gain the medical staff's trust—just long enough to ensure Kay, who was living at the bedside, looked disorganized, frantic, and emotionally unstable in comparison.

To outsiders, she was the one unraveling. And the more she fought to prove otherwise, the more he spun her resistance as instability. Her tears, her exhaustion, her desperate attempts to be heard—he twisted them into confirmation of the lies he fed everyone else. He turned her humanity into ammunition.

Kay's life was a relentless, staggering marathon of commitment. She juggled a demanding, full-time career with going back to college to finish her degree, managing side projects to keep their finances stable, and dedicating herself as a football team mom—all while seamlessly supporting every single school project, extracurricular activity, and medical appointment her boys required. Anything Lucas or Aiden wanted or needed, Kay made it happen, often sacrificing sleep and personal time to maintain the illusion of a stable, functional home.

But even as Richard tightened his manipulative grip and his lies spread like an insidious, corrosive infection, Kay never stopped fighting for her children. Her battlefield was not just the courtroom or the tense, closed-door meetings; it was every ordinary, sacred moment of their day-to-day existence. She waged this war through meticulous routine, unwavering presence, and profound devotion. Every meal she cooked, every load of laundry, every minute spent helping with homework—these were her acts of resistance, establishing a bedrock of stability that Richard's cruelty could never entirely erode. Kay ensured that, despite the surrounding storm, her boys always felt seen, safe, and profoundly loved.

Kay started creating magic in the mess. She knew her children were being pulled into a storm they never asked to weather, so she built little pockets of peace—shelters they could return to. She poured everything she had into giving them a sense of normalcy, of joy, of childhood untouched by the chaos surrounding them.

Although she couldn't afford any outings that had a cost, she found ways to have fun at home without spending money. They enjoyed playing basketball on the street, throwing a football in the yard, and watching sports and movies on the living room floor.

Dinner was a sacred ritual of laughter. One spaghetti night, Kay declared the rule: no forks allowed, which instantly erupted into wild giggles and noodles flying across the plates. They were fearless co-chefs, cooking together even though it guaranteed flour dusting the ceiling fan and tomato sauce streaked across every available surface and shirt. That kitchen, once just a place to prepare food, was now a vibrant space of pure warmth, shielded entirely from the cold worries that lay just beyond the front door.

She'd turn up the radio, the lively music filling every room, and they'd dance through the house while they cleaned and cooked. Chores became an adventure—vacuuming to the beat, wiping down counters with rhythm, and making each task fun. She'd dance, teasing Lucas around the living room, laughing as Aiden clung to her leg, a giggling anchor. They cared for each other in small, ordinary ways, finding joy in the most unlikely places.

Outside, they planted flowers together, digging up worms for Lucas to fish with, coaxing life from the dirt like a quiet rebellion against everything trying to break them. On the best days, they found refuge at the lake. Lucas thrived on mastering the fishing line. Kay taught him to bait the wriggling worms, and his casts were long and clean, mimicking the best anglers at the water's edge; his excitement was a bright, contagious spark every time they went. It was never about the fish count. It was about the undiluted connection: about being validated, being cherished, and being loved without condition.

One beautiful Sunday afternoon, they had a picnic on a lake in Hermitage. Lucas had been fishing, and Kay and Aiden were finishing lunch at the picnic table. Lucas, however, had left a deadly souvenir: a cricket lure with far too many hooks still attached. Kay had constantly reminded him to put away his gear so nothing got lost or, worse, hurt someone.

As Kay reached across the table to wipe it down, her hand slammed right into the lure. A mass of razor-sharp hooks instantly burrowed deep into her palm. She cried out, "Lucas! You left a lure on the table, and it's stuck to me!"

The pain was blinding, but when she looked up at Lucas's wide-eyed, panicked face, all she could do was laugh, even as the tears streamed down. Lucas, unable to process the absurdity of the moment, erupted into hysterical laughter. Kay laughed too, the sound mixing with her cries of agony—because sometimes, facing a disaster this ridiculous, laughter is the only defense you have. The more they tried to gently loosen the lure, the deeper the hooks drove in, sending a sharp scream tearing from her throat. With the stupid, painful thing still embedded in her hand, she had to gather the rest of the picnic, clean up, and then drive herself to the ER.

By the time they arrived at the ER, Lucas and her, despite her pain, couldn't stop laughing either. The doctor, trying to remain professional, carefully removed the cricket and hooks from her hand, but even he cracked a smile at the absurdity of it. It was a story they would tell for years to come, one of those memories, full of chaos and love, that never really fades.

Kay was fully dedicated to immersing herself in their world, even if it meant embarrassing digital defeat. She played fierce video games with Lucas, often badly, but always enthusiastically. Lucas would roar with laughter, covering his face or dramatically rolling his eyes every time his mother inevitably ran headlong into a wall, wandered straight off a virtual cliff, or accidentally detonated a grenade. She didn't mind the teasing; in fact, she welcomed the affectionate mockery. She took the humiliation in stride, understanding that her ineptitude was the fuel for their shared fun.

Her true dedication became clear with one game in particular: Guitar Hero. Despite her initial struggle with the complex button patterns, Kay was determined. She practiced alone, eventually becoming a surprisingly masterful shredder—a silent, concentrated effort undertaken purely to meet him on his own level. The result was worth every clumsy note: seeing Lucas's face light up with pride as they flawlessly nailed a difficult song together was the purest form of victory.

She was there, a steady, protective figure who appeared relentlessly and without fail. This consistent presence was her ultimate act of resistance, silently telling her boys that no matter what storm came their way, her devotion was the one truth that would never shift or falter. She immersed herself completely in their world: from the roar of football games, to the speed of skating and track meets, the patience of baseball, the chaos of video games, and the joy of every birthday party. In everything they loved, she showed up. Always.

And with Aiden, who required unending patience, specialized care, and a devotion of both hands and heart, Kay discovered a wellspring of energy she previously had no idea she possessed. Between the blur of constant medical appointments, the grueling physical therapy sessions, and the restlessness, she still fiercely carved out moments of unadulterated joy for both her sons.

Her resolve was absolute: she refused to allow their childhood to be contaminated or defined by Richard's malice or the constant threat of manipulation. Even when her heart felt heavy with injustice and her body was raw with exhaustion, she donned her armor of joy. She smiled until her cheeks ached. She cracked absurd, silly jokes that brought light to the darkest corners. She initiated spontaneous dance parties in the kitchen and sang loudly in the car, turning routine moments into unforgettable theatrical performances.

Every single laugh, every whispered secret, and every shared adventure was a conscious, deliberate act of resistance. Kay made a sacred, fierce commitment to construct a childhood for her boys—one built on genuine love and stability, entirely untainted by the bitter drama and legal shadows that stalked their lives.

Two years later, still tangled in the throes of a divorce that felt more like a slow bleed than a clean break, Kay was exhausted—but still holding on. Every visitation with Richard came with its own set of dread. Incidents had stacked up like bricks around her, heavy and cold. She had called child services more than once now. She had pleaded, shown them bruises, and told them stories. Still, there had been no response. Richard and Samantha consistently slipped through every net, their actions seemingly invisible as the system remained either blind or willfully looking the other way. The truth was, Richard was a masterful manipulator, a chameleon of deceit who knew precisely how to leverage the bureaucracy. He had a chilling, insidious knack for evading accountability, ensuring that every report, every piece of evidence Kay compiled, disappeared without consequence.

But one time, all limits were crossed.

Lucas made a last-minute decision to stay home that Friday, skipping the dreaded visitation, and when Richard arrived, his face was a thundercloud of resentment. He took Aiden with palpable reluctance, the action clearly signaling his fury at being burdened with only the special needs child.

When Aiden returned, he was appallingly filthy. His clothes were stiff and abrasive with ground-in filth, his small hands were caked with gray grime that rimmed his fingernails, and his skin had a dull, that spoke not of playing, but of being ignored. Kay didn't need to ask questions; her panic instantly transformed into protective instinct. She scooped Aiden into her arms, feeling heavy and foreign with the grime, and carried him straight to the bathroom.

As she carefully peeled the stiff, soiled shirt over his head, she began her ritual of reassurance. She spoke softly, asking what "wild adventure" he'd been on to acquire such a spectacular amount of dirt, instantly turning the harsh cleanup into a game. Kay made bath time a fun, musical experience, using the familiar, loving routine as a powerful, cleansing shield to wash away the physical evidence of Richard's neglect and restore her son to his own sweet, clean self.

And then she saw it as she took off his shoes.

The burn.

It was raw, raging red, completely encircling both feet in an unmistakable ring of damage. It was not a simple bruise, not a friction rash—it was a massive, badly blistered, second-degree wound. While past injuries had been limited to marks or faint bruises, this was a stark, violent departure. This enormous burn mark wasn't accidental; it was a physical testament to a new, terrifying level of malice.

Panic surged up through her chest, tightening her throat. She called for Lucas.

He came quickly, sensing something was wrong. When he saw the burn, his eyes widened, and he went still—then angry. "If you don't do something, Mom," he said, voice shaking, "*I will.*"

Lucas was really furious. Although Kay had seen him like this before, she had never heard him say such words with such raw determination. His jaw tight, eyes burning with something deeper than just anger—it was protectiveness, fear, love. He was only eleven, but in that moment, he looked older. Wiser. As if the weight of everything they had been through had finally rooted itself in him.

Kay met his eyes, her voice soft and heavy with resignation. "I hear every word you're saying, sweetheart, but it's not worth it," she murmured. "Things have finally been quiet. If we report this, it's going to stir up a maelstrom of drama and chaos, and we both know no one is actually going to do anything about it." Her eyes pleaded with him: "It would be like waking a sleeping bear."

She didn't want to reach for the phone. The fights, the legal skirmishes, the pure, corrosive drama—they weren't just events; they were tidal waves, a relentless cycle of chaos that kept dragging her under. She was bone-deep, soul-weary of drowning in the undertow of Richard's making.

But Lucas wouldn't let it go this time, and, eventually, she gave in. With a shaky breath, she dialed his number.

Richard picked up on the third ring. "What now?" he muttered, already defensive.

"What happened to Aiden's feet?" Kay said, trying to keep her voice steady. "Aiden came home with huge burns."

"Jesus, Kay. Are you serious?" He let out a harsh laugh. "You always do this. Nothing happened."

"I'm not blowing anything—"

"You're always looking to start shit."

The words hit like a slap, but she said nothing. Just ended the call, her hands trembling as she lowered the phone.

She turned to Lucas, who had been listening from the doorway, arms crossed, face tight with anger.

"What did he say?" he asked.

Kay sighed. "He said... he said nothing happened."

Lucas's eyes narrowed. "That's it? You're just going to believe him?"

"No, I—"

"Call for help," he said, his voice cracking, "or I will."

Kay stared at him, stunned by the conviction in his words. In that moment, it was no longer about hesitation or fear—it was about doing what was right. For them.

Before the water touched him, Kay quickly documented the truth. She used her phone to capture multiple pictures of Aiden's raw, blistered feet. Only then did she gently finish Aiden's bath. She slathered the wounds with Silvadene cream and wrapped his feet in sterile gauze. She knew what came next. With a heavy sigh of pure exhaustion, she picked up the phone for one final, agonizing call to the Department of Children and Families to file the report she desperately wished she didn't have to make

But this time, the system couldn't afford to ignore her. The game had changed. Kay had done more than just file a report; she had assertively secured and paid the retainer for an attorney to represent the boys directly. This single action shattered the inertia. Suddenly, it wasn't the easily dismissed word of Kay against Richard's elaborate lies; it was now a full-scale legal confrontation: the traumatized children, armed with their own legal representation, against the abusers, Richard and Samantha.

Lawyers got involved quickly. Kay found herself sitting across conference tables with an attorney for her oldest son, going through paperwork she barely had time to read, but she signed what needed signing. She told her story again, as many times as it was needed. She brought the photos and documented dates of countless bruises and incidents.

The emergency court hearings began almost immediately. Lucas now had his own attorney, a professional appointed solely to advocate for the children, injecting instant credibility into Kay's claims. When the next crucial hearing arrived, it was Lucas who was called to take the stand. What should have been a protective, structured process devolved into something cruel and perverse the moment Richard announced he would represent himself.

Unwilling or unable to pay for counsel, Richard stood in court as his own attorney—utterly unprepared and radiating self-righteous arrogance. This disastrous decision meant that he had the legal right to question his own son directly. Kay's stomach twisted violently as Lucas was sworn in; the system designed to protect him had just handed his abuser a weapon.

Richard sounded cold as he began, "Isn't it true, Lucas, that you've been acting out? That you have trouble listening? That your grades are slipping?"

Lucas looked confused. Caught off guard. "No... my teachers say I'm doing really good. I got a math award last month."

Richard did not so much as blink. He leaned in, his voice taking on the sharp edge of a prosecutor cornering a liar. "You've been defiant, haven't you, Lucas? Specifically with your stepmother, Samantha. Isn't it a fact that you screamed at her, 'You're not my mother! I don't have to listen to a word you say!'?"

Lucas's eyes flicked nervously toward Kay. "I only said that when she yelled at me. I didn't mean—"

"You've been disobedient," Richard cut him off. "You don't follow rules, you talk back, and you've hit people, haven't you?"

As Richard launched his calculated attacks, every instinct Kay possessed screamed at her to stand and object. But she couldn't. She was not the plaintiff, not in the driver's seat; she was merely a witness to the weaponization of her son. Sitting silently was the most agonizing physical feat she had ever attempted. Her entire body was rigid, her jaw clenched, her mind a silent, internal scream of white-hot rage. She could only sit there, a vessel of controlled fury, pinning every last shred of her hope on the court—praying the judge would see through the thin, cruel veneer of Richard's manipulation.

But Kay couldn't look away, couldn't unsee the raw, devastating wound visible on Lucas's face—a torturous mixture of shocked betrayal, deep confusion, and utter, crushing heartbreak. His own father was standing just feet away, viciously dissecting his son's character, painting him like a vandalized delinquent in front of a cold, judging courtroom full of strangers. The humiliation was absolute, and Kay felt every ounce of her son's pain as if it were her own.

And the truth?

Lucas was undeniably a good boy—a child of good manners, inherent kindness, and boundless love. At home, he was a diligent helper and a protective, devoted big brother. He contributed eagerly with chores. His teachers adored him.

Outside of school, he was a natural leader. He excelled in multiple sports, where coaches universally praised his unshakeable discipline and quiet leadership. He was the kind of remarkable kid who instinctively stayed late to help clean the field and would patiently help younger players. Ask anyone in his life outside the toxic confines of that courtroom, and their assessment was singular: Lucas was kind, brilliant, genuinely passionate, and exceptionally well-behaved—a truly remarkable son.

But Richard did not see that version of his son. More accurately, he willfully refused to see it. Lucas's kindness, his brilliance, his leadership—all of it was irrelevant, discarded in favor of a single, malicious purpose: to aggressively paint Lucas as the intractable problem, a spoiled brat, thereby justifying his own abusive actions and undermining Kay's fitness.

In his closing remarks, Richard pulled out a wrinkled piece of paper. He squinted as he read the words Samantha had written for him.

"No one has the right to tell us how to discipline our own children," he read aloud. "We know what's best for them. And that includes consequences when they misbehave."

It landed in the courtroom like a threat.

But the judge had heard enough, and his ruling was clear. *A full order of protection for one year from Richard.* There was to be no contact between Richard and the children for one whole year.

And when that year passed and the case came up for renewal, the silence from the opposing side was deafening. Richard and Samantha did not even bother to show up for the hearing. There was no desperate call, no legal filing to request visitation with the children—not even a single, token protest. Their absence was the final, tacit admission of defeat, a chilling end to their campaign of abuse and manipulation.

So, the judge granted another year.

Although this was fortunate in Kay's eyes but she could not celebrate looking at the sadness in her son's eyes.

Even then, it wasn't over, not by a long shot. There were more hearings to come. More paperwork. More tension and backlash. But for the first time in a long time, Kay didn't feel powerless. She was fighting tooth and nail.

She stood straighter in those courtrooms.

She answered questions without flinching.

She pushed past the fear that had once paralyzed her—and she did it for her boys because they deserved peace. Because they deserved safety. Because they deserved *her* at her strongest, even if that strength was held together with nothing more than willpower and love.

Enough was enough.

Kay gathered the fractured pieces of herself—not because she was whole, but because she was willing to fight while still healing. She no longer shrank to survive the storm. She *became* the storm. And she would not stop, would not rest until her children were truly free.

Because Kay's greatest fear wasn't just losing custody or another courtroom battle—it was what the trauma might do to her boys. She feared that what they'd endured would change them, rob them of the light in their eyes, the laughter in their lungs, the childlike joy that every kid deserves to carry untouched. She was terrified that the weight of fear and confusion might harden them into something they were never meant to be.

But she also had a vision—a quiet, determined dream—for their future.

A life where Aiden had the care he needed, where every doctor's visit wasn't a crisis but a step toward progress. Where he grew stronger, his smile came easier, and his days were filled with learning and progress.

A life where Lucas could finally and simply be a kid. Where he was free to run wild, unrestrained on the football and track fields, to stay up late laughing loudly while playing video games with friends. A life where he could smile and laugh without the toxic shadow of fear or confusion lurking behind his eyes. Where the crushing burdens of an adult's cruel drama were lifted entirely from his small, healing shoulders.

She dreamed of stability—not just emotionally, but practically. No more fear of empty cupboards, overdue bills. No more holding her breath at the checkout line. She worked relentlessly.

During the day, she juggled jobs and held her boys together with tenderness and grit. And at night, while the world quieted and the boys finally slept, Kay cracked open textbooks and chipped away at her Bachelor's degree.

She didn't stop there.

She studied for her real estate license in Tennessee, driven by the thought that if someone else could unlock doors for families, so could she.

Soon, Kay began aggressively hustling in the real estate market. She started by covering open houses and showing properties for busy, out-of-town realtors, filling her weekends and evenings with unfamiliar neighborhoods. Her work quickly expanded to developing real estate marketing plans and providing virtual administrative support. It wasn't glamorous work—it was pure, grueling effort—but it helped. Every extra dollar she earned was a crucial brick in the foundation she was building, making every small step forward an absolute necessity.

Eventually, her efforts added up. She got them into a new home—better, safer, full of light. A fresh start, not just in structure but in spirit.

Every single day, Kay became a living testament to resilience. Her work was not just about income; it was a deeply personal process of self-healing, built through hard work, self-study, and unwavering prayer. Her fierce determination to provide for her boys, to give them a great life—one free of abuse, marital fights, and corrosive drama—was the engine that drove her forward. She wanted them to be happy, safe, loved, and to see a side of life defined by peace and possibility. She was a quiet storm of honesty, relentless effort, and unbreakable heart. Kay proved that even when the odds were mercilessly stacked against you and the nights stretched on without mercy, you could still rise. You could carve out a rich life worth fighting for. You could endure. You could triumph.

This was the unspoken curriculum of Kay's new life—the most vital lesson she taught her boys by her own example. She taught them that pain does not eclipse love, but that love is the fierce, protective force that allows you to outlast the pain. They learned that wounds can, and must, heal, not by ignoring them, but through the courageous process of self-study and honest emotional processing. Kay modeled the core tenets of trauma recovery. She showed them how to recognize and manage the intense emotions—the anger, the fear, the confusion—that were direct remnants of the abuse, establishing healthy coping mechanisms instead of letting those feelings control their behavior.

Furthermore, she helped them shift their perspective toward Post-Traumatic Growth (PTG). She didn't allow the painful experiences, as horrible as they were, to leave them permanently broken. Instead, these experiences would forge new inner strengths, deeper connections, and a profound appreciation for life's simple, peaceful moments. Above all, she taught them the power of Conscious Self-Authorship: that their history—the drama, the lies, the violence—was merely a chapter, not the entire story. No matter where they came from, they had the absolute power to create something beautiful. They learned to write their own narrative, consciously choosing resilience, safety, and joy as their future instead of inheriting the chaos of the past. Her boys would know that their past, and the malice inflicted upon them, did not define their future.

That was the future Kay fought for.

And she was just getting started.

This was the end of the beginning.

Kay's quiet revolution—her rise from victim to warrior, from survivor to sovereign—was a testament to deliberate, day-by-day effort. She had gathered the shattered pieces, the broken promises, and the raw, burning pain, and used them not as an anchor but as the bedrock of a new, unbreakable foundation. She had fought for safety, for peace, and for her sons' right to live free from the chaos of Richard and Samantha. That first brutal chapter was finally closed.

Yet every warrior knows that the end of one battle marks the beginning of another. The slow, demanding work of rebuilding a life—not only for herself but for the two young boys watching her every move—was entering its most crucial phase. Healing is not a destination; it is a pilgrimage. The chaos had passed, but the ghost of the storm lingered like a cold shadow. The road ahead was open, though the rearview mirror—and the lessons forged in fire—could not yet be ignored.

Kay and her boys now stood on the threshold of a new existence. They had won their freedom.

The future—their future—was finally ready to be written.

About the Author

Elizabeth Pierce poured her own life onto the pages of Stronger than the Storm, a book born from her fierce desire to spread resilience and optimism. It serves as evidence of the human spirit's power to face adversity and emerge victorious.

A survivor of domestic violence and a dedicated single mother of two, Elizabeth is defined by her journey. She not only grappled with crushing burdens but rebuilt her life brick by deliberate brick, demonstrating that a damaged path can lead to a stunning, potent destination. She is a fierce advocate for her son, who navigates complex special needs, a role that taught her that refusing to accept limits is the greatest act of love and power. Professionally, she secured a Master's degree and advanced certifications, a monumental feat achieved while simultaneously fighting for her career and family.

Elizabeth's mission is simple: to reach the person who feels invisible, comfort the one whose past threatens to define them, and remind every reader that they are not alone. Her message is clear: the strength to overcome has always been within you. This book is the blueprint to unlock it.

Visit www.elizabethpiercebooks.com to find out more about Elizabeth's work, get in touch with her, or keep up with her upcoming endeavors. Your story is eagerly anticipated by her.

Stronger than the Storm

www.ingramcontent.com/pod-product-compliance
Lightning Source LLC
Chambersburg PA
CBHW071630140626

46555CB00022B/2043

* 9 7 9 8 9 9 3 8 1 7 9 1 0 *